BEING THERE TOO

OTHER BOOKS BY JOHN DILLON

The Middle Platonists (1977/1996)
Salt and Olives:
Morality and Custom in Ancient Greece (2004)
The Heirs of Plato: A Study of the Old Academy (2005)
The Roots of Platonism (2018)
The Lockdown Papers (2021)
Being There: Travel Diaries, 1970s-1980s (2023)

AS EDITOR

The Greek Sophists (Penguin Classics, 2003)
The Enneads by Plotinus (Penguin Classics, 1991)
Tourism and Culture in Philosophical Perspective,
Marie-Elise Zovko & John Dillon *(Springer Verlag, 2023)*

FICTION

The Scent of Eucalyptus (2019)

BEING THERE TOO

TRAVEL DIARIES, 1990 – 2010

JEAN & JOHN DILLON

Being There: Travel Diaries 1990-2010
1st Edition
Published by Katounia Press,
Dublin, 2025

www.KatouniaPress.com

© Jean and John Dillon 2025

This book is sold subject to the condition that it shall not, by way of trade or otherwise, be lent, resold, hired out, copied, digitally reproduced or otherwise circulated without the author's prior consent in any form of binding, cover or digital format other than that in which it is published.

ISBN: 978-1-8383454-5-7

This book is set in "Aviano Royale", "Mrs Eaves" and Palatino fonts, sourced from Adobe Creative Cloud, 2024.

Photo credits:

Pages: 83, 84 (top), 85, 86, 183, 84, 185, 186 (bottom), 247 (top), 250 sourced from AdobeStock.com

Pages: 175, 176, 177, 178: sourced from AdobeStock.com

Pages: 245 (portraits), Dillon family private collection. P. 246, 247 and 248 sourced from AdobeStock.com

Cover photo: Dillon family private collection.

All text originates from original diary entries written as it happened by the authors.

Table of Contents:

INTRODUCTION	7
1. TRIP TO LIVERPOOL AND NICE: SEPT, 1990	11
2. VISIT TO MOSCOW: DECEMBER, 1990	25
3. TRIP TO GREECE (KATOUNIA): JUNE 1991	47
4. TRIP TO BRISTOL & SW ENGLAND: AUG, 1992	71
5. SECOND VISIT TO MOSCOW: OCT 1993	87
6. TRIP TO CORSICA: JUNE 18 – JULY 3, 1994	102
7. THE PHILO EXPEDITION: NOV 15-25, 1994	117
8. VISIT TO TRIER: JULY 18-25, 1999	135
9. TRIP TO WARSAW: MARCH 16-22, 2000	145
10. TO THE PELOPONNESE: AUG-SEPT, 2000	155
11. TRIP TO RIGA, LATVIA: MARCH-APRIL 2001	179
12. VISIT TO JAPAN: MAY 9 – 18, 2001	192
13. VISIT TO KATOUNIA: SEPT, 2001	208
14. AUSTRALIAN TRIP: JULY – AUGUST, 2002	218
15. VISIT TO ATHENS: APRIL, 2003	249
16. EXPEDITION TO MÜNSTER: SEPT, 2003	257
17. EXPEDITION TO PRAGUE: OCT 2003	267
18. TRIP TO SOUTHERN ITALY: MAY, 2006	273
19. RETURN TO KATOUNIA: SEPT-OCT 2008	293
20. THE ADDIS ABABA EXPEDITION: NOV 2008	303

Biographical Note

Jean Dillon (née Montgomery) was trained as an artist and graphic designer, studying in Rome (1961-3), and later in Dun Laoghaire, and is one of the founding members of the Leinster Print Studio. Her works are in a number of private collections. She originally painted in oils, but turned to print-making after her return to Ireland from Berkeley in 1980. After her marriage in 1965, however, she devoted herself primarily, both in Berkeley from 1966 to 1980, and back in Dublin after that, to running a household.

John Dillon is Regius Professor of Greek (Emeritus) at Trinity College, Dublin. Born in 1939, in Madison Wisc., U.S.A, but returned to Ireland in 1946. Educated at Oxford (B.A., M.A.), and University of California at Berkeley (Ph. D.). On faculty of Dept. of Classics, UC Berkeley,1969-80 (Chair of Dept. 1977-80); Regius Professor of Greek, Trinity College, Dublin, 1980-2006. His main focus of research has been Greek philosophy, and in particular Plato and the Platonic Tradition.

INTRODUCTION

Can there be any justification for adding a sequel to our previous volume of travel diaries (*Being There*, 2023)? Possibly not, but, since that was an act of self-indulgence, let this be accounted a further such act. A possible excuse, however, as was put forth for the former volume, might be that these adventures are a record of an age which, if not already bygone, then surely soon will be – at least if the present manifestations of hyper-tourism are allowed to proceed unchecked.

Not that we generally headed for venues favoured by mass tourism. Katounia, on the north of the Greek island of Evia, continues to be a favourite, but we also took a tour, in late August and early September 2000, through the Peloponnese, which is a not much frequented part of the country. In addition, we visited Corsica (June-July 1994), and Southern Italy (Puglia) – which is a good deal more popular now, I believe, than it was then – and even South-West England (August 1992), in connection with a conference I was attending in Bristol.

Indeed, conference travel, once again, forms an embarrassingly large part of the subject matter, with Jean (and sometimes Ruth) only able to come along occasionally – but notably to Japan, in 2001, and Australia, in 2002. Otherwise, I am off on my own, rather guiltily, to such venues as Moscow (twice), Poland, Latvia, Prague, and even a rather wild excursion (1994) to the United States, taking in Notre Dame, Chicago, and Berkeley, which it exhausts me even to read over now!

One class of travel, though, on which Jean occasionally accompanied me, during these years, is not included here, and that is the Westminster Classic Tours, which took us on various delightful excursions up and down the coast of Turkey, and into the (Greek) islands adjoining – and even, on one occasion, inland, to the rock-churches of Cappadocia, before coming back, via the holy city of Konya, to the coast at Antalya. There we were able, since we were cruising in smallish boats called *gulets*, to largely sidestep the gross over-development that was in full swing even then on many parts of the Turkish coast, and which will be that much worse now, I fear.

All in all, I find myself deeply grateful, and not a little guilty, to have been able to travel in conditions which are very much more difficult to avail of these days. We did indeed continue to travel in the decade following 2010, up to the great Covid lockdown, but those excursions will have to remain uncelebrated. The reading public can only take so much!

As to the title of this second collection, I regret to say that it involves a pun, but it serves to celebrate the fact that a number of new venues were visited, as well as old favourites.

Being There Too

1. TRIP TO LIVERPOOL AND NICE:

SEPTEMBER 23 – 30, 1990

This involved attendance at two conferences, one after another, both in the area of late ancient philosophy, and both involving many old friends, one at the University of Liverpool, organised by Henry Blumenthal, on the philosopher Iamblichus, who is a particular favourite of mine, the second on the topic 'Platonisme et Néoplatonisme: Antiquité et Temps Modernes', organised by a Greek scholar, Evanghelos Moutsopoulos. Even reading over my progress from one to the other of these events now leaves me exhausted!

DAY 1, SUNDAY, SEPTEMBER 23RD

I am now established in my modest room in Roscoe and Gladstone Hall, at 10.30 pm, reading some of the texts I should have read earlier, and still trying to unblock my ears after the plane journey. An uneventful flight from Dublin to Liverpool, in a little Manx Airlines Short SD 360, which was full, and landed on time in Liverpool, which is still a modest little airport, at 6.25pm or so. I came straight to the student residence in a taxi (£5 – not bad), with a most voluble driver, who discussed the old airport, now taken over by the National Trust as a museum (!), and the foolishness of the university in not selling off their student residences on prime suburban building land, and moving into town beside the university itself.

    I arrived just in time for dinner, which was not bad (Chicken Kiev), and found myself beside Werner Beierwaltes[1] and the

---

1 Werner Beierwaltes (1931 – 2019) was a German academic best known as a historian of philosophy. His most important areas of specialisation

redoubtable Francesco Romano[2] accompanied by two women colleagues, Lorenza Cardullo and Daniela Taormina, and chatted to them both, though mainly to Beierwaltes. I greeted Henry[3] and Gillian Clark on the way in, but they went home when they had got us settled. The rest of us, after settling in, adjourned to the bar, where I talked mainly to John Finamore and Greg Shaw – and Mark Edwards – but also greeted Dominic O'Meara, Annick Charles-Saget, John Rist, Tony Lloyd, and Pamela Huby. A great gathering, really, in honour of our great man. It is presumably the first Iamblichus conference in the history of the world.

It is good to be on the road again, though I hate the process of travelling. Just at the point when I am fed up with the absurdities of Trinity College (e.g. scheduling me to teach at 6.00 on a Friday), and with myself, as a feeble figure, I needed to get away, to be greeted by people to whom I mean something.

---

were Neoplatonism and German Idealism. He was an Emeritus Professor of Philosophy at the University of Munich. His many books include *Proklos: Grundzuge seiner Metaphysik*, *Denken des Einen: Studien zur neuplatonischen Philosophie und ihrer Wirkungsgeschichte*, *Eriugena: Grundzuge seines Denkens*, *Platonismus im Christentum*, and *Platonismus und Idealismus*. He was among the original Editorial Advisors of the scholarly journal Dionysius, in which English-language examples of his writings may be found. He was a Member of the Bavarian Academy of Sciences from 1986 and a Member of the Royal Irish Academy – anappointment that I had something to do with! He wa a most amiable and generous old boy, as well as being a great scholar.

2 Francesco was Professor of Ancient Philosophy at the University of Catania, and a most hospitable and jolly man, as well as being a respectable scholar. Both of his above-mentioned colleagues are now considerable scholars in their own right.

3 That is, Henry Blumenthal, who organised the conference, and was Professor of Ancient Philosophy at Liverpool. Gillian Clark, married to the philosopher Stephen Clark, was also on the faculty, and a very respectable scholar. The proceedings were later published as *The Divine Iamblichus: Philosopher and Man of Gods*, edd. H. J. Blumenthal & E.G. Clark, by the Bristol Classical Press, in 1993.

It is mainly, perhaps, the effect of sitting around in Ireland all summer, but I needed to get out for a bit and hear nothing about Ireland for a while. Then perhaps I can face the term – though of late this has become harder and harder to do. Perhaps I should make a bolt for it?[4]

Anyhow, this looks like a hard-working session – 14 papers in two and a half days, no breaks. Carlos Steel, Fr Saffrey,[5] Richard Sorabji,[6] Anne Sheppard[7] have not appeared yet.

DAY 2, MONDAY, SEPTEMBER 24TH

Woke up fairly early, ears still rather blocked, and read a bit. Then up for breakfast at 8.00 am or so. The weather is sunny, but with hard showers. The surroundings of the student hostels is very pleasant parkland, with a family of ducks quacking under my window. I found Carlos, Richard S., Anne Sheppard, and Saffrey at breakfast. All had arrived later in the evening, and had come up to the bar after I had retired.

---

4 This tirade surprises and embarrasses me somewhat now. I survived sixteen more years before retiring, and no longer recall the stresses that brought this on.

5 Henri-Dominique Saffrey (1921-2021) was a French Dominican friar, and a distinguished scholar of Greek philosophy, particularly Neoplatonism. He had actually done a doctoral thesis with E.R.Dodds in Oxford, on the Platonic Theology of Proclus, and was a senior member of the équipe of the CNRS of which I was also a corresponding member, so I had the pleasure of meeting him there.

6 Richard (now Sir Richard!) Sorabji (b. 1934) is a distinguished authority on Ancient Philosophy, of Parsee Indian descent, but born in Oxford, and British to his fingertips. He was at that time Professor of Philosophy in King's College, London. He is author of many books, and initiator of the great project, the Ancient Commentators on Aristotle series, to which I have contributed a number of volumes.

7 Anne Sheppard was professor of ancient philosophy at Royal Holloway, University of London, a considerable authority on later Greek philosophy and its literary connections, and an old friend.

We had a hard day of papers, six in all, in one-and-a-half hour sessions – all good, in fact: Carlos Steel, Annick Charles-Saget, Fr Saffrey, Anne Sheppard, Andrew Smith, and Dominic O'Meara – mainly on the *De Mysteriis,* but Carlos gave a good study of a passage in the *In Parm.* There was really no break, even to get out of the building for a breather. I chatted to all concerned – except, I'm sorry to say, to Romano's lady colleagues, since my Italian isn't up to it, but I didn't want to appear stand-offish. He is set to give a quite pointless paper tomorrow, on all the compounds of *phu-*[8] in the *De Mysteriis,* without any discernible theme to it.

I phoned home after dinner, and all seems well. We had a good session in the bar after dinner, till about 11.00 pm. I gossiped with John Rist, Henry, Richard S., Andrew, Mark Edwards, and Greg Shaw. Shaw is an interesting lad, rather like John Bussanich.[9] He had a lot of experience with Eastern gurus, it seems, which led him to developing an interest in theurgy. Mark Edwards is a funny, old-world fellow, but learned.

DAY 3, TUESDAY, SEPTEMBER 25TH

Slept reasonably well, though up a few times during the night because of the beer. Got a little reading done before breakfast (very little free time at this conference, as I have noted previously!). I read Mark Edwards' paper – the same extraordinary fustian style as manifests in his conversation, but not at all bad as to subject-matter – and finished Gillian Clark's translation of the *Vita Pythagorica*; also read more of Dominic O'Meara's book, which is most fascinating.[10]

---

8 That is, the verbal root signifying 'generation' or 'growth'.

9 Gregory Shaw, I may say, is now a distinguished authority on Neoplatonism and the religions of Late Antiquity, and Professor of Religious Studies and Theology at Stonehill College, Massachusetts. John Bussanich, also now a distinguished authority in the same area of scholarship, and Professor of Philosophy in the University of New Mexico, had been a graduate student of mine in Berkeley in the late 1970s.

10 I think that this must have been Pythagoras Revived: Mathematics and

It was a pretty rough morning of Italian papers. Romano is a bit of a fraud, really – he delivered a formless paper listing all the uses of *phuo, phusis*, etc.,[11] in the *De Mysteriis*, without any real attempt to sort them out or draw any conclusions. Then we had one of his lady colleagues, Daniela Taormina, do the same with *dunamis* – very tedious. His other colleague, though, Loredana Cardullo, after lunch, was actually much better, with a study of *Iamblichus in Syrianus*.

I broke out during coffee to walk round the lake in the park opposite, which was pleasant. I just hadn't been out at all, and today is a lovely day. I walked again, round the block, with John Finamore, during tea – he is an attractive man, bright, and rather like Paul Simon in appearance.[12]

Pamela Huby delivered a most interesting 'report' on Iamblichus in Priscian's *Metaphrasis* of Theophrastus. Lots of interesting stuff in that for Iamblichus' *De Anima*.[13] She is doing a translation of it for Richard's series.[14] After this, there was a double bill of Mark Edwards and myself, on the *Vita Pythagorica*. I was being deliberately provocative by presenting it as a 'gospel', and provoked, in fact, a 'lively discussion'. I now feel I should have done something more serious, like a return to the question of the doctrine of henads, and might suggest to Henry that I substitute such a paper for the 'gospel' one, if publication ever threatens.[15]

After the papers, there was a reception in the bar, and then a jolly dinner, which was not at all bad. I sat beside Werner

---

Philosophy in Late Antiquity (Oxford, 1989).

11 That is to say, words to do with 'nature' (phusis).

12 This must have been my first personal encounter with John, who later became a valued colleague and friend.

13 And indeed John Finamore and I made good use of this in our edition of that work some time later, in 2002.

14 That is to say, the Ancient Commentators on Aristotle, edited by Richard Sorabji.

15 This I duly did, and it appears as 'Iamblichus and Henads Again', in *The Divine Iamblichus*; but the paper survives as a section of the introduction to my edition, with Jackson Hershbell, of Iamblichus On the Pythagorean Way of Life (Atlanta, 1991). What henads are you do not want to know!

Beierwaltes (who was interesting on the prospects academically in East Germany), Mark Edwards, Greg Shaw, Anne Sheppard, and John Rist. Richard Sorabji got us all playing a silly game with forks! I discovered that Mme Saget is going to the Kerylos conference (though Saffrey had heard nothing of it). She will arrive later than I, since she has to go to Manchester and then Paris.

DAY 4, WEDNESDAY, SEPTEMBER 26TH

2.30 pm: On the plane from Heathrow to Nice, having had a pleasant cold lunch. A lovely day, with very little cloud. We are now over the centre of France. I woke up with a start at 8.00 this morning, and rose hastily, but in fact I had time to grab some breakfast and say goodbye to most people before calling a taxi and heading for the airport about 8.40. I found that my copy of George Kerferd's *Festschrift* was defective, and got Henry to change it.

The plane to Heathrow was slightly delayed, but made up good time. I was able to send a postcard to the Mouse from Heathrow, and buy a rotten little Berlitz French dictionary – an extraordinary lack of French dictionaries in the bookstores – perhaps everyone *knows* French! I checked my bags through, so they'll probably lose them. I wonder will there be anyone there to meet me?

6.00 pm: Now sitting in a little café in Beaulieu, down the street from the Hotel Victoria, having a *bière* (*pression*), and reading Dominic's book. There was in fact *no one* there to meet me, so I phoned up, and got a surprised and apologetic lady at the other end (*not* Mme Michel, presumably), who didn't know I was to be met, but urged me to take a taxi. I suggested a bus, but she dismissed that as too complicated. So I did, and it cost me 280 fr (incl. tip), since Beaulieu is actually 20 km from the airport, which is to the west of Nice. She said they would reimburse me, however, so we'll see. It was a lovely drive, though, and the approach from the air was spectacular too. A few yachts in the bay, and towering cliffs behind the shore, at intervals.

I took a shower and rested, reading about the Villa, which is an extraordinary enterprise, it seems, built on the orders of Théodore Reinach, and then donated to the Institut de France, which maintains it. Reinach must have been more than just a Classical archaeologist![16] I look forward to seeing it. I have still no inkling of the order of papers, though there is an impressive sequence of receptions and excursions. The municipality seems to be doing us proud – even organising a Greek Week around us!

Denis O'B[17] and Monique Dixsaut arrived around 5.30 pm, but wanted to have a bit of a siesta, having driven down from Paris, so I agreed to wait till 6.45 for them, before walking down to the Villa for the Réunion, which is to begin at 6.00, followed by a *Reception* somewhere else at 8.00. I am uncertain as to whether to phone Elizabeth,[18] since I'm not sure what free time I'll have (there's a free evening tomorrow, but that's

---

16 Théodore Reinach (1860 – 1928) was a French archaeologist, mathematician, lawyer, papyrologist, philologist, epigrapher, historian, numismatist, musicologist, professor and politician. He had a brilliant career as a scholar, and was called to the Parisian bar, where he practised from 1881 to 1886, but eventually devoted himself to the study of numismatics. He became Chair in ancient numismatics at the Collège de France, and was a director of various journals. In 1916, he was awarded the medal of the Royal Numismatic Society, and in 1917, during World War I, he worked on assignment in the United States. In 1886, Reinach married Charlotte Marie Evelyne Hirsch. They had two daughters, but she died at age twenty-six in 1889. Reinach married a second time in 1891 to Fanny Kann, a daughter of Maximilien Kann and Betty Ephrussi. The Reinachs spent time on the Riviera, and in 1902 hired the architect Emmanuel Pontremoli to design a villa at Beaulieu-sur-Mer. Completed in 1908, the Greek-style property was named Villa Kerylos. Fanny Reinach died in 1917 and Theodore in 1928. He was a member of the Institut de France, and on his death he bequeathed the villa to the Institut. None of this, of course, did I know at the time!

17 My old friend Denis O'Brien, distinguished authority on Greek philosophy in general and Neoplatonism in particular, who had made his career in France, in the CNRS, to which he had introduced me some years previously.

18 That is to say, my cousin Elizabeth Pillet-Will (née Mathew), who had a villa nearby. For the background on her, see Being There I, Ch. 15.

all). Everything is laid for *two*, though, so Jean would have been provided for. Rather boring for her during the day, though.

Much later. Back to the hotel, collected Denis, and we walked down to the Villa. He left me at the gate, however, and went back to wait for Monique, who was resting. I wandered into a scene which became more and more like a Fellini movie. There is this splendid, crazy villa, out on a promontory sticking out from the town, with these weird people wandering about in it. A preposterous old Greek gentleman is holding forth to a rapt audience, mainly of ladies, in the bathroom of the house, about the glories of Greece. Then we all wander up to a bedroom, and he holds forth again. I am preoccupied because I can't identify Moutsopoulos. I have a vision of him as a squat, elderly person, and eventually approached a squat, elderly person who looked familiar, but turned out to be Maurice de Gandillac,[19] which was *most embarrassing*. He expects to be recognised *as such* – but I only met him once, after all, at my lecture back in April. Anyhow, he pointed out Moutsopoulos, who turned out to be a much younger, black-bearded gentleman whom I had *not* met before (I think), and who turned out to be most friendly. He begged me to chair the first session tomorrow.

Denis and Monique arrived finally, and we all strolled over to the Rotonde, a municipal centre of some sort (very magnificent) for the Reception, which consisted of a long session of Provençal folk-dancing, followed by a speech by the (very young) Maire, and then some champagne and titbits. It was good of them, but not entirely satisfactory, so four of us, Denis, Monique, self and Nestor-Luis Cordero (a very pleasant fellow,

---

19 Maurice de Gandillac (1906 – 2006) was a French philosopher. He was born in Koléa, French Algeria and died in Neuilly-sur-Seine, France. He wrote his thesis under Étienne Gilson on the Renaissance philosopher Nicolas of Cusa. In 1946 he was appointed professor in the history of Medieval and Renaissance philosophy at the Sorbonne. He supervised the doctoral dissertations of numerous students, including Louis Althusser, Jean-François Lyotard, Gilles Deleuze, Michel Foucault, and Jacques Derrida.

Argentinian, but at Rennes), repaired to a café for something to eat. I had a pizza, and we sat gossiping outside till after 11.00 pm. Then we strolled back to bed.

This is in a way a prestigious gathering, under the auspices of the Institut de France, but in another way it is quite preposterous. We will see how it develops.

DAY 5, THURSDAY, SEPTEMBER 27TH

I got a look at a paper yesterday, by the way. Still no war, but pretty plainly headed that way.[20] A tragic thing to happen just as the European world was getting itself together. The U.S. is facing a huge deficit and recession, while the poor old U.S.S.R is in complete chaos. Gorby has had to assume total powers for the moment.

7.30 I am in the same little café we were in last night, feeling a bit foolish, as I have just ordered the (Greek) menu, having intended to eat only a little, and having declined to eat dinner in the hotel with Professor Laura Westra on grounds of being stuffed. Anyhow, I must make the best of it.

We had a fairly full day of discourses, over the first sessions of which I had to preside, punctuated by a splendid lunch at the Hotel Eiffel next door (where we looked longingly at the swimming-pool). The weather was clouded over till the afternoon, though still very warm, but then the sun came out, and temperatures went well into the 70s. The papers were on the whole interesting, but on small points – as was the case with Monique, Cordero and Denis, only Denis being sound as to subject-matter, I'm afraid! There were a few rather preposterous ones as well. A jolly old boy called Jerphagnon from Caen talked well on Narcissus, though. A number of very ancient warhorses of the Institut, including the permanent secretary, were in attendance, encrusted with dignity.

Annick Charles-Saget only appeared this morning, having

---

20 I think I must have been referring to the crisis in the Persian Gulf occasioned by Iraq's invasion of Kuwait, which did indeed eventually lead to war.

missed her connection in Paris, and a rather frantic lady called Laura Westra,[21] who is connected with the ISNS, blew in from Canada during the afternoon. I have to go back and collect her now, to accompany her to a Greek dance evening at the Villa.

Later. I survived the Greek dance till the interval – it wasn't bad, but the atrium was very crowded. I found Denis and Monique going in search of a salad and joined them for a pastis – where we stayed till midnight. It is Monique's birthday! She kindly re-corrected my text, so it must now be perfect idiomatically, whatever about the content – and pronunciation![22]

I phoned home, I should say, at about 7.00 pm, and got Mouse, who told me she had just rescued a butterfly and was now proposing to imprison it. Joe Hickey is down the garden, doing the rockery. More expense!

DAY 6, FRIDAY, SEPTEMBER 28TH

Up somewhat more promptly, as we are under orders to be down at the Villa by 9.00, in a desperate effort to finish our business in time to go on an excursion. In fact, everything ran a little late progressively through the morning, and we were left at lunch-time with three papers still to go, including *mine*. In the middle of the morning I had slipped out and up to a clothes shop to buy the Mouse an outfit that I had seen in the window. In fact, I bought a different one, a sort of jodhpur-like thing for a ten-year-old, and a jersey, which will probably be too big – but better than too small! I got back just in time to hear old De Gandillac deliver a rather *thin* paper on Ficino.

A copious lunch up at the hotel, courtesy of the old

---

21 Laura Westra, about whom I am here being rather uncharitable, was at this stage quite a junior scholar, but went on to be a distinguished authority on Greek philosophy, as well as a great champion of ecological awareness.

22 It was ultimately published, in the proceedings of the conference, as 'Notre perception du monde extérieur selon Plotin et Berkeley', in *Colloque Platonisme et Néoplatonisme: Antiquité et Temps Modernes, Actes*, ed. E. Moutsopoulos. (Cahiers de la Villa Kerylos, No. l), Athens, pp. 100-108.

Ministre Bernard Chenot,[23] who I gather really *was* a minister, in De Gaulle's 1958 government, and a distinguished old boy. After lunch, back down to the Villa, to find that we had to go to the basement, since we were not expected to be still continuing. I delivered my paper adequately, but was surprised to notice that neither Monique nor Denis nor Annick were there. We learned the reason for this just after the paper. As they were all coming down, Monique tripped and fell against a wall, knocked herself out, and may have broken her nose, and was then taken back to the hotel in an ambulance.

We had to forgo our trip to the Fondation Ephrussi de Rothschild, but went off at 5.30 or so to a very pleasant reception at the Prefecture in Nice, which had been a palace of the Dukes of Savoy and is a splendid building. We were greeted by champagne, caviar, and speeches from the Prefect, the Ministre, and Moutsopoulos. Then back to the hotel – a lovely drive along the Corniche both ways, viewing Villefranche and Cap Ferrat – and, after a pause, Denis, Nestor, Laura Westra and I went down to the bistro for a snack. I am getting a little tired of Westra, I'm afraid; she complains a bit too much, and is slightly absurd. She lost her ticket on arrival at Nice, and is now ballyragging the poor Mme Michel to get her another one, or reimburse her in some way. I talked to Monique on the phone, and she sounds much restored. Her husband Jean is flying down to take her home tomorrow.

---

23 Bernard Chenot (1909 - 1995) was a French politician and senior official. Son of a Parisian barrister, he became a member of the Conseil d'État during the Third Republic, and worked in several government departments. He remained in his position under the Vichy government after 1940. Under the Fourth Republic he was director of the coal-fields of northern France for a while, and an official adviser to successive governments on economic matters. He served under Charles de Gaulle as Minister of Health, and then, until 1962, as Minister of Justice. When George Pompidou became prime minister, Chenot replaced him on the Constitutional Council for two years. He then went into business for some time, returning to public service in 1971 as the vice-president of the Conseil d'État, retiring in 1978. He also lectured at the Institut d'Études Politiques, and wrote a number of books about politics; his publications included *Etre ministre* (1967), *L'Hopital en question* (1970) and *Reflexions sur la cité* (1981).

DAY 7, SATURDAY, SEPTEMBER 29TH

Up during the night, in consequence of the wine, and read quite a lot of Thomas Keneally's *Towards Asmara,* which is a curious but entertaining book, introducing themes of some sentimental interest[24] The day got off to a bad start when I woke suddenly at 9.30 am! They had forgotten to wake me at 8.00 with breakfast. I threw on my clothes, however, and charged down the town to the Rotonde, where the bus was just warming up, with everyone on board. I sat down beside Nestor Cordero, and we were off for our day of pleasure.

We began with a drive round Cap Ferrat, past the Fondation Ephrussi which we were scheduled to visit yesterday afternoon. It is certainly a fabulous part of the world. Our first destination after that was the Maison de Renoir, 'Les Collettes', at Cagnes-sur-Mer. It is a delightful spot, and a good Renoir museum, with a fair selection of his works (they have to insure themselves for 6 billion francs, I believe!) – his atelier preserved just as it was – quite a lot of sculpture, which he took up in his later years (mainly of his children and his wife). The poor man, latterly, had terrible arthritis in his hands (and all over), and had to be helped. A reception was given for us then at the Maison (on the terrace), by the Mayor of Cagnes – and I attracted his attention when Denis revealed to him that I knew *Alain* Renoir.[25] I got some mileage out of that, and I must send Alain a postcard.

Then on to lunch (already slightly tiddly and stuffed), but first we were entertained to *another* aperitif by M l'Ambassadeur in his delightful home (actually three small mediaeval houses knocked together) in Tourottes-sur-Loup, a lovely little mediaeval town perched above the gorge of the river Loup, very

---

24 I had spent two enjoyable years, from 1961 to 1963, teaching English in Addis Ababa, in more or less the same part of the world – though I never got to Asmara!

25 Alain, who was the son of Jean Renoir, the film director, was a colleague in Berkeley, where he was Professor of Comparative Literature. He was a most lively character. We were closely associated for a while in an enterprise called the Division of Interdisciplinary and General Studies, of which I succeeded him as a Director.

like many little Italian towns we visited last year.[26] Lunch then took place at a little restaurant opposite, still in the old town, which served an excellent *couscous*.

Thoroughly stuffed and boozy by now, we proceeded to the Fondation Maeght at St Paul de Vence, where there was a major Miró exhibition. It is a fine private gallery-cum-sculpture garden endowed by the Maeght family, whoever they were.[27] Miró I get impatient with after a while, like Picasso, but he is undeniably lively. By 5.00 pm, though, I just needed to find a bathroom and then lie down, so mercifully we got back in time to do this, at about 6.00. I had a shower and rested, but at 7.30 we had to rise again and head for the Villa to undergo a *soirée de clôture*. I was feeling by this time distinctly queasy, and this did not get better during the (excellent) harp recital which began the proceedings.

After the recital, we were faced, first, with an aperitif of champagne and kir (which Denis named 'kir royale', but I think he made that up),[28] and then a sumptuous spread in buffet form. At first, I thought I could eat none of this, and sat and crumbled bread and sipped water, but then I revived and, under urging from all sides, went and got a sample of what there was, which was excellent. Denis had invited friends of Monique's who have a house in Menton, Umberto and Jacqueline Risset, to come along to the party, and they proved to be users and admirers of *A Classical Lexicon to Finnegans Wake*,[29] so we got along fine. Umberto is a professor of Latin in Salerno, and was urging me to come and visit them.

---

26 See *Being There I*, ch. 15.

27 The Maeght Foundation or Fondation Maeght is a museum of modern art on the Colline des Gardettes, a hill overlooking Saint Paul de Vence, about 25 km from Nice. It was established by Marguerite and Aimé Maeght in 1964 and houses paintings, sculptures, collages, ceramics and all forms of modern art. Aimé Maeght (1906 – 1981) was a French art dealer, collector, lithographer, and publisher.

28 Not so; that is indeed its name.

29 A work that I had produced, along with Brendan O'Hehir, back in Berkeley in 1977.

At the end of the party, I eventually got an undertaking from Mme Michel to provide for my transport to the airport tomorrow. This matter had been postponed all day, for the good reason that she really had *no* plans for this. But now I am to be conveyed to Nice by her (with Moutsopoulos, who is going to church) and put on an airport bus – which will be fine, if it works out. Otherwise, I must rush for the train.

The clocks go back an hour tonight, which I just happened to learn! I don't know if that co-ordinates with Ireland.

DAY 8, SUNDAY, SEPTEMBER 30TH

Mme Michel duly collected me, bless her, and drove me into Nice, where she put me at the bus stop for the airport bus, since she was going on to collect Moutsopoulos and other Greeks from their church service. The bus duly came, and I got safely to the airport, just as rain began to come down. No trouble at London getting from Terminal 3 to 1, and arrived home at about 4.30, slightly exhausted, but relieved and invigorated.

2. VISIT TO MOSCOW:

DEC. 7–16, 1990

This expedition was the result of an invitation from a young Russian scholar, Yuri Schichalin, who had written to me for a copy of my book, The Middle Platonists, to review in Russian, and had now devised, in the immediate aftermath of the collapse of the Soviet Union, a conference on the remarkable theme, 'The Classical Origins of Mediaeval Rationality'. It was a mind-blowing, most enjoyable adventure.

DAY 1, FRIDAY, DECEMBER 7TH

The expedition could be considered to have begun when I was picked up by J[ean] and R[uth] outside the Pearse St Gate of the College at 3.20 pm. J had the previous day put together an impressive food parcel, based on the best advice I could gather from colleagues in Russia, and I had armed myself with such essentials as jax paper and bath plugs and water purifiers. It is almost like heading for the moon, and perhaps wildly inappropriate. I had tidied away as much as I could manage of departmental business, but am still leaving a monumental mess on my desk. All the department is most excited about the visit to Moscow – no doubt simply a reflection of my own state of mind.

We began by driving out of town in the wrong direction – towards Galway – and only got onto the Naas road with some difficulty. Bad traffic, and a *snowstorm*, till Port Laois, where we stopped for a coffee, but it then slackened off, and we made good time to Limerick after that. Before going out to Paddy and Ann's,[30] we actually did a sentimental tour up O'Connell Street,

---

30 Old friends from Limerick days (1964-6), Patrick and Ann Reidy. Ann,

and up to Pery Square,[31] much to the impatience of the Mouse.[32] Found Paddy and Ann in excellent form. Fine feed of turkey, ham, and excellent desserts. Good company too – Eamon and Ann O'Riordan, their mother-in-law Patsy O'Sullivan, and Dessie O'Malley, among others, dropped in, straight from Brussels. He was, surprisingly, in quite lively form, after the fearful ordeal of standing up to the Americans in GATT Talks, and very entertaining about CJ and Lenihan.[33] He improves on acquaintance.

Paddy and Ann the same as ever, Paddy full of politics, chiding me about voting for the Robinson woman, scornful of Michael Noonan (which surprises and saddens me), and not very pleased with John Bruton either. Ann served an excellent dinner, but I think I consumed too much white wine.

DAY 2, SATURDAY, DECEMBER 8TH

Day dawned bright, but very cold – though snowstorms are predicted later. I woke up rather ill, in fact, in consequence of the feasting of the night before. Paddy fed me an Alka-selzer, and I managed to eat a bit of breakfast. Then off to the airport, which took only twenty minutes or so. I had forgotten how pleasant P & A's situation in Corbally is, just beside the Shannon.

Am now sitting, at 10.45, in the departure lounge, having stocked up on smoked salmon, whiskey, and Marlboroughs (as recommended by Sylvia Simms), surrounded by Cubans, some of them *very* Indian-looking, who are going off to the freezing temperatures of Moscow for God knows what reason – to learn about *glasnost* and *perestroika*? Should be boarding soon, when the adventure will really begin.

---

then Ann Clune, had been my essential back-up in various enterprises in which I had engaged when in Limerick, such as Tuairim and the Fine Gael Youth Group.

31 We had lived in a flat in 2 Pery Square from January 1965 to July 1966, before leaving for California.

32 Nickname for our daughter Ruth.

33 O'Malley was Minister of Industry and Commerce at the time, in the government of C.J. Haughey.

Duly boarded the plane, and flew to Luxembourg. Found myself beside a young fellow who did not look Indian, so assumed he must be Russian, and asked him: *"Vui gavaratiye pa-Angliski?"*, but he turned out to be German, and spoke English perfectly. He had been in Peru for eleven weeks, because the plane comes from Lima, and most of these people are Peruvians, and pure Incas! So the mystery deepens – what on *earth* could they want in Moscow? In fact, half of them got off in Luxembourg, as did the young German. He considers the reunification of his country a very bad idea.

While waiting in Luxembourg, I was approached by a young Irish woman, Ms Kearney, who was the friend of Ludmila, who was driving her down to Shannon. She proved to be most friendly – a young architect, she had gone on an exchange to some architects in Tver, near Moscow, and they had come to Ireland, and now she is returning just for a weekend, to greet them and bring gifts. We joined up for the rest of the journey, and compared notes.

No problem in the event about my visa being a day late, or about the parcel or the luggage – though the luggage took a little while – and I was met by Yuri Schichalin, clutching the cover of *The Middle Platonists*, accompanied by his wife, and a lady friend who speaks English (he and his wife prefer French, but only his wife speaks it fluently). They actually have a car, a rather battered Moskvich, which tends to cut out when idling, and did a couple of times on the way into town, but gets along.

They drove me first to my 'hotel', near the centre of town, but in a most dilapidated neighbourhood. The whole place has a nightmarish aspect, though inside is pleasant enough. It is in fact, they revealed to me with great giggling, *The Higher School of the Communist Party*, the former training college for Communist Party activists, now fallen on hard times, and renting itself out as a 'conference centre' for the Academy of Sciences. It is really very like a tatty old diocesan college in Ireland which, through a lack of vocations, has to take in boarders from the general public.

Anyhow, it was sufficiently grim that I rose willingly to their invitation to come round to have a bite to eat. I had presented them with the food parcel, which I hope will not cause offence! I also gave them some smoked salmon and Marlboroughs. We drove through the centre of town, viewing the Kremlin and Red Square, and many other wonders, including the Lubyanka, until we came to their apartment block, which is quite near the Novodevichy Convent.

Again, squalid exterior and hall, but much old-world charm inside. I met Mrs Schichalin's mother and father, who had plainly been preparing the dinner. Her mother spoke excellent French, so I chatted to her. A sense of old aristocracy. Schichalin showed me his antique books, including an Aldine of *Juvenal and Persius*, inherited from his grandfather-in-law, a distinguished translator of the Classics called Shyeninsky – translator of Ovid's *Metamorphoses*. Yuri was visiting East Germany with his wife this summer, and says that the people who led the revolution now feel betrayed by the takeover on the part of West Germany. I can well imagine. He tells me also that they are both quite involved in re-introducing Latin and Greek into the schools!

We gossiped till 1.00am over an excellent dinner, and Georgian white wine, and then they brought me back to the hotel. I am embarrassed already by the generosity.

DAY THREE: SUNDAY, DEC. 9TH

9.35 am: I am feeling quite proud of myself. I have found my way to the refectory, and am having breakfast – of black bread, tea and cottage cheese, which is actually quite pleasant. There were other preparations which were *not* so attractive – in appearance, anyhow. I had to ask my way, in Russian, and was directed, in Russian, and it was quite complicated. The breakfast, which I paid for (Yuri had given me some pocket money last night – 69 roubles, with apologies!) – cost *9 kopecks*. This is the unreal aspect of the economy.

I woke up, rather late – naturally (we are 3 hours out) – at 9.00, had a shower (plug came in *very* useful), and walked over to the refectory. The place is vast and cavernous, and there are plainly still students here – earnest, polite young Communists, still being trained, no doubt, to run a world that is crumbling around them. Perhaps, though, they are being instructed now that all is not lost, and they will be needed! The atmosphere is very like what must have been the atmosphere in a provincial seminary in Ireland in the 1950s – except that this is co-educational!

What is the most striking impression so far? I think it is of the *emptiness* of the city at night. Not just virtually no cars, but virtually no people, even at about 10 pm. It was almost like a city hit by poison gas or something. And the pervasive drabness of the ordinary buildings. I ventured to ask, unkindly perhaps, what people did with themselves on a Saturday night, and there was some embarrassment in answering – concerts, theatre, but restaurants close at 11.00 On Sundays, we visit friends!

At 10.45, Yuri came to collect me, and drive me to the Museum of Fine Arts (*Pushkin* Museum – named so for no reason, he indignantly pointed out; it was actually created by the father of Marina Tsvetayeva, the poet, who was a scholarly art-lover). There we were met by Mlle Zhenya, his assistant in the Department, and she showed me round (he had other business). We examined first the magnificent collection of casts of classical statuary, and then the Impressionists – very good Monets, Cézannes, Renoirs – then Post-Impressionists – fine Picassos, from the Blue Period and later – lovely *Girl on a Ball* – Rousseau – forget who else. Gauguin – lots of him!

Then, after an attempt to find a restaurant on the Arbat – where, in fact, a ferocious doorman was turning would-be diners away (very Russian scene, I imagine!) – we came back on the Metro to the 'hotel', and I found a copious lunch in the canteen for 34 kopecks! Salami, cabbage soup, meat balls and potato, lemonade. I wouldn't want to speculate as to what the meatballs were made of, but they tasted all right. I am beginning to see the bind they are in, contemplating this lunch. The fact is that the basic necessities are for *nothing*. You can have three meals a day in this place for about 50p, at unreal rates of exchange. You can travel on the Metro all over the city for only 5 kopecks

– about ½p. Medical service is *free;* education is *free;* rents are derisory. *But* – so are salaries! 200R a month would be an excellent salary; most make less than that. A kilo of meat in the free market costs 30R. So nothing can now be provided in a non-compulsory environment at a price which the government is prepared to pay, and which people can afford. There has *never*, it seems, been a realistic calculation of cost.

After lunch, I phoned Conor O'Clery[34] and got him. Arranged to phone again tomorrow morning, when he knows his schedule. I hope we can get together, as I have long been a fan of his reports. Then I rested for a while, and read my book for review – *The Duel* – seems good – the confrontation between Hitler and Churchill.[35] Then, about 4 pm, I decided to go for an experimental ride on the Metro. It went very well. We are only about five minutes' walk from Novoslobovskaya Street, on the Circle Line. One goes to Komsomolskaya, and changes to the Grey Line, then down to Lenin Library/Arbat. I did that, walked around a bit, and then back. The architecture of the metros is certainly magnificent, but they are an *absurdity*.[36] The Schichalins despise them as Stalinist. Actually, Mr Krushchev was the overseer of the Metro, back in the 1930s.

At 6.00 a knock on the door, and Yuri appeared, with Michel Tardieu,[37] who had arrived this afternoon by plane. Good to see

---

34 The Irish Times correspondent in Moscow, to whom I had an introduction. He worked for the paper for over 30 years, including as News Editor and Foreign Correspondent in London, Moscow, Washington DC, Beijing, and New York City, receiving various awards throughout his career, including one in 1987 for his reporting from the Soviet Union. He later wrote a most interesting book, The Shoemaker's Daughter, recounting the story of the family of his Russian-born Armenian wife, Zhanna, from World War II through to the fall of the Soviet Union.

35 I was at this time reviewing books, mainly on political subjects, for the Sunday Independent.

36 That is to say, the Metro stations.

37 Distinguished French scholar of Late Antiquity, particularly of Manichaeism and Gnosticism, working in the École pratique des hautes études, and later in the Collège de France.

him again. Went over to the Schichalin apartment, but via Red Square, where we got out and strolled about, despite biting cold, Michel grooving on everything. Then a very pleasant evening at the Schichalins, getting to know more about his parents-in-law, a very pleasant pair – among other things, his father-in-law is a cellist, teacher and composer, Fyodor Druzhinin,[38] and has made a number of recordings, which I must try to get hold of. *Her* father (Shenyinsky) is a great translator, from both Greek and French. She speaks French fluently, and is a very civilised old girl. They all regard the Communists as a sort of meaningless pestilence, but are very worried by the present chaos and lack of discipline. We consumed most of a bottle of vodka, drinking numerous toasts, feasted on the smoked salmon, and then had two other courses as well.

Helena Schichalin was saying that she had been trying to book a call to Dublin, but was not having much luck. She proposes to keep trying.

DAY 4: MONDAY, DEC. 10TH

Woke up this morning at around 8.00, feeling *slightly* crapulous after the vodka of last night, but not too bad, considering. Read a little of the Gary Snyder book that Kristen lent me, and found it very readable. Then up and showered (with the help of my plug), called Michel, who was already up, and phoned Conor O'Clery. He had been hoping to meet me for lunch, but we are going out to our monastery today. Evenings no good for him, as he has to file his reports. I am to call again tomorrow evening, and see how I am fixed for Wednesday.

I was conscious, after speaking to him of the Schichalins and their views, that I am speaking on the phone, in a Communist Party school, in a country which was until recently a total police state, and I was really *most indiscreet*. I very much hope that all that is in the past, but I will try to restrain myself in future. I notice, by the way, all round the ceiling in the room, little *fixtures* like

---

38 (1932-2007), distinguished cellist and composer – also referred to by his wife as Felix.

smoke alarms. They seem to serve no purpose, and I now think they must be listening devices. Are they still in use?

I led Michel over to the canteen, which we found closed (just after 9.30), but the buffet was open, and that was all we wanted – coffee, and a bit of sausage and bread. Yelena had also provided a whole breakfast, in case we were stuck. We came back and had one of her spice cakes, and I had some more coffee. We chatted about the economic system and its problems – that was before I noticed the little devices in the ceiling!

3.00 pm: Just back from a most stimulating tour to Kolomenskoye, a magnificent park full of churches and examples of traditional architecture, to the south of the city, on a bend of the Moskva. We travelled with Zhenya by metro, meeting Katerina Sergeyevna (Yelena's mother), at the Kolomenskaya Station. Then we walked up to the park. There are two particularly fine old churches, one with blue and gold onion domes, the other, the Cathedral of the Ascension (1532 AD), all white, erected by Ivan the Terrible. The only problem, as it emerged, was that I was not sufficiently well clothed – I had stupidly left off my jersey – and I did get pretty cold about the middle, but head and feet were fine. Anyhow, I survived, and now we are back in our rooms, waiting for a call from Yuri. I wish now he wouldn't feel he has to look after us *all* the time, but admittedly Moscow is not the *easiest* place to entertain oneself in – especially when one is starting from the Higher School of the Communist Party! It reminds Michel of army camp, me (as I remarked earlier) of a provincial Irish seminary.

At about 4.30, got a call from Yelena to say that Yuri would call for us at 6.00 pm, and take us to the Ballet – not the Bolshoi, which is booked out, but a new ballet company, an offshoot of the Bolshoi, based in the Palace of Congresses in the Kremlin. When she phoned, I was engaged in entertaining Mme Maria Suutala from Finland,[39] who had come to call on me. She

---

39 She went on, in fact, to become one of Finland's most distinguished ecologists. Her thesis, developed into a book, *Tier und Mensch im Denken der*

arrived this morning, while we were at Kolomenskoye, by train from Helsinki and Leningrad, which she says was really most uncomfortable – far too hot and noisy to sleep. She is a young scholar, now teaching in the north of Finland, at Oulu, and was primarily interested in Ecology, though she is by training a mediaevalist and Renaissance specialist. She has just published her doctorate, done in Germany, on the image of animals in ancient, mediaeval and Renaissance art. This is her first time also to the USSR, despite being so near, and she speaks no Russian. I feel quite like a veteran.

I went and got Michel, and we all had a cup of coffee and a chat for almost an hour. I am not getting much reading done! Then Yuri arrived and drove us to the ba ck of the Kremlin, with Katerina Sergeyevna, who took us to the ballet. We entered the Kremlin over a moat and through a gate. It is really a town within a town – it was, after all, the origin of Moscow.

The ballet I thought was excellent – *Macbeth* – music by K. Molchanov (whom Felix, I gathered later, regards as rather *mediocre*), choreography by V Vasiliev, who was apparently himself a superb dancer, now turned director. Macbeth was danced by N Schilnikov, Lady Macbeth by I Timofeevna, both excellent. The Three Witches were also very good.

Then back once again to Schichalin's for a supper, which only ended at about 11.00. They are endlessly hospitable.

DAY 5: TUESDAY, DEC. 11TH

Had to be roused at 9.00 by Michel, as I had woken at 5.00, and then gone to sleep again. Got up quickly, and staggered over with Michel and Maria to breakfast. Found a sort of porridge which is not bad – sort of maize meal, I think. Maria also had some meatballs, which we all sampled, but were not so salubrious.

At last the conference is due to begin.[40] We were collected

---

deutschen Revolution, was published in Helsinki in 2001.

40 The conference, we may recall, was on the (rather exotic) theme 'The Classical Origins of Mediaeval Rationality'.

at 10.30 by a young colleague of Yuri's, Vitali Zadvornyi (who has a rather better car, in fact), and driven to the Institute of Philosophy in Volkhonka Street. Usual dilapidated entrance, but the hall in which we meet has fine plasterwork on the ceiling – someone said Pushkin danced in the room when it was a ballroom! Michel started things off with a good discussion of 'Anti-biblism in Manicheism, Gnosticism and Porphyry', but it went on till nearly 1.00, since every phrase had to be translated by Zhenya, and then there many questions and comments. There are about 30 or more in attendance, mostly young, all interested. I thought I had made a blunder when making a comment: I ended by comparing the rational attitudes to sacred texts in antiquity to those being taken now in relation to Marx and Lenin. There was a sort of gasp and a giggle, but it turned out that it struck a profound chord.

After a competent talk by a lady, Dr Gaidenko, apparently the head of the particular section of the Institute which is sponsoring this conference, on 'Mediaeval Commentaries on the Hexaemeron', we went off to lunch. There I was ambushed on all sides by people who remarked what an apposite analogy I had made, except that now we are in a phase of total rejection of Marx and Lenin – the destructive phase of rationality. I talked mainly to an excellent lady (who looked rather like Barbara Wright[41]), speaking very good English, who expressed very well all the attitudes Conor O'Clery has been reporting on for so long. She feels total alienation to the whole history of the last seventy years, but is full of fears for the immediate future. "We intellectuals have our consolations – we can read what we like, and write and say what we like – but the ordinary people are not consoled by these things. They are concerned with basic living, with bread." The sense of unfairness over the privileges of the Party functionaries rankles particularly. It is interesting to find no support for Marxism in the halls of the Institute of Philosophy. She says a few of the older members would still

---

41 The Professor of French in Trinity.

cling to the old faith. I wonder where Mshveniradze[42] is now. I hardly dare to ask, but I am curious.

After lunch, I moved that I wanted to go downtown and shop, and an excellent young man, a philosophy Kandidat from Novosibirsk, Dimitri Nikulin,[43] was deputed to guide us. We walked, talking animatedly, from the Institute all the way to the Arbat, then strolled up it, and down Kalinin Street. The Arbat is now indeed pretty tatty and vulgar, but I was tempted by a Gorbachev doll – a variant of the matryoshka, which is amusing; it has all the previous rulers of the Soviet Union inside Gorby, going back to a tiny Lenin. The lads selling it demanded 300 roubles – almost two months' salary for a Russian worker – so I said I had only dollars. At first they wouldn't consider dollars, which I thought odd, but when I moved away, they clamoured after me, asking how many dollars. I consulted Dimitri, and he said 15-20 dollars, so I offered 20, which was promptly, but furtively, accepted. The official rate is 5-7 roubles to the dollar, but the real rate is about 10 (or more). So they did alright, but then so did I. $20 is little enough for one of these dolls, really.

We then went into an official antique store, where the prices were astronomical by Russian standards (3000R for an old balalaika, down to 950 for a rather battered icon, but not actually too bad in dollars – $95 for an icon is certainly as good as one would get, I think – though I wasn't really tempted. Next, in Kalinin St, we saw some nice old streets, and went to a record store. Melodya, where the prices of records were quite absurd – I was trying for a record of Druzhinin (Yelena's father), but no luck, so I settled for some others; but three records, one a double, cost 9R 50! Then on to a large bookstore, where I

---

[42] A visiting Georgian Marxist philosopher whom I got involved with entertaining back in Berkeley in the 1970s, when no one in the Philosophy Department wanted to do so. I had found him very jolly, and he had urged me to pay him a return visit some time.

[43] Now a Professor of Philosophy in the New School of Social Research in New York, I am glad to say.

bought some poems of Gumilev,[44] just issued, for 2 roubles. So I thought I did rather well.

After that, it was time to head for the Metro and make our way out to the Novodevichy Convent, where Katerina Sergeyevna was going to show us around. We reached there, as arranged, just before 6 pm. The convent is a delight. We viewed it first from outside, across a small lake, and then went in. All the buildings were closed at this hour, except one, the Cathedral of the Dormition, where a mass was going on – sparsely attended, but not bad for a Tuesday evening – which we listened to for a while. Dimitri is a devout Orthodox Christian, so he took particular pleasure in it. It seems that many young people are turning back to the Church – from one absurdity to another, one might say, but who can blame them? The main church is the Smolensk Cathedral (1524-5), built to commemorate the recapture of Smolensk from the Lithuanians. It apparently is marvellous inside, but we couldn't get in. The Convent (which means 'the new convent of the maidens') was originally for storing away young, or not-so-young, ladies of the aristocracy who might be dangerous for one reason or another (e.g. if someone married them), so it was really a 'gilded prison'. It was also fortified, and guarded two river crossings, being at a bend of the Moskva.

We walked back to the flat, I in somewhat of a fuss, because of the promised phone call home. On the way, we passed a beryoshka shop (hard currency only!), just outside their apartment block, and the others went in to look, while Katerina Sergeyevna and I hurried on. I was parked in a chair of honour to wait for my phone call, while the others came in then, after ten minutes or so, declaring that the beryoshka was an astonishing sight – goods piled high in all directions, but all for foreign currency or credit cards. It is a gross affront to ordinary Russians, and they certainly feel it. Michel said there were a lot of beautiful, be-furred Russian chicks in there, though. We wonder who they were.

The phone call came through about 7.30, and all seems

---

44 Nikolai Gumilev (1886-1921), distinguished Russian poet, husband of Anna Akhmatova, executed by the Soviet secret police in 1921, but now back in favour.

well. One never learns much on these occasions. The main thing is to make contact. It was a heroic effort on the part of Yelena, and I hope it didn't cost too much. They wouldn't hear of my paying.

An excellent dinner was served once again. The Jameson was broached and much appreciated, especially by Felix [Druzhinin]. I hope he doesn't have a problem in that regard. Some illness forced him to stop playing. It may have been a mild stroke. He points to his head and his hand when he talks of the illness. He still teaches and composes, though. I got interesting information from Katerina Sergeyevna about his father. He is now 98, but knew many of the great literary figures of earlier times, Gumilev and Anna Akhmatova, Mandelstam (who sat in the very armchair I was sitting in to read his poetry), and Pasternak. And then through Felix she knew Shostakovich and others, most of the top musicians as well. A remarkable family! She said that her father kept out of trouble by sticking closely to his work (of translating and writing on French literature and Classics), but he was able to help Anna Akhmatova, when times were difficult.

We were driven home by Yuri at around 1.00 am or so.

DAY 6, WEDNESDAY, DEC. 12TH

Today we went to Zagorsk. The day began with a light snowfall, which we hoped would not disturb the expedition, and didn't. I phoned Conor O'Clery in the morning, once again having to say that I couldn't meet him. He is actually very pressed at the moment, because things are at a crisis, and news is breaking fast.[45] We are in a sort of time-warp here in the Higher Party School, as no news reaches us, and Yuri and Yelena are too polite to fuss.

We were collected at 9.15 by Yuri and Yelena in the old banger. I thought there was to be a bus, but if so, that fell

---

[45] Mikhail Gorbachev's popularity was plummeting, and the danger of some sort of coup seemed to be increasing. In fact, he survived for another year, though progressively being supplanted by Boris Yeltsin.

through, and we were all packed into the back, Maria sandwiched between us. Michel gets a great rise out of her. She is a feisty little chipmunk-like person.

We drove through the suburbs and out onto a very respectable freeway, going north-east. Very foul conditions, cars spitting up mud, and Yuri's windscreen washer doesn't work, so we had to pull over every few miles to clean the windscreen, which rapidly became impenetrable. Still, we eventually reached Zagorsk unscathed. The countryside was flat and unremarkable, though interesting to see the individual houses (all wooden) in the villages – one had begun to think all Russians lived in vast apartment blocks (Yelena *did* point out some, though, of a wretched sort, built under Krushchev, and called *kruschoba's* – a pun on *truschoba,* 'slum'.

Zagorsk itself is dull as a town, but the monastery complex is quite spectacular. We visited just three of the churches, all splendid in their own way (attending a service in one), and drank holy water in a sort of baptistry, and then visited the fine collection of icons in the museum. By then, it was time to go home, so we went back to the car and had coffee and sandwiches.

Zagorsk, I should say, is more or less the Vatican of Russia, being the major seminary and church administrative centre. Founded in 1340 by St Sergius of Radonezh, whose tomb we saluted.

Another rather hair-raising ride back – the car, as I have noted before, tends to cut out when ticking over, and one never knows if it will start again, but we did get back to the 'hotel' about 4.00 pm, in time for a bit of a rest, and then some dinner, at 6.00 (meatballs again, the only alternative being *porridge*), before being taken off to a concert.

The concert was Mozart's *Requiem,* superbly performed by the Symphony Orchestra of the Moscow Conservatory, with three choirs, of men, women and boys, under the direction of Boris Kulikov – of whom the Druzhinins are old friends, so we went round to the dressing-room and greeted him afterwards. The choirs sang with tremendous power, but also great control, and the soloists were superb also. The bass had a long priestly beard, and may indeed have been a priest – Anatoly Safyulin.

Our night at the hotel was enlivened by a party of totally pissed Laotians, who were going home the next day, and were celebrating with a fearful racket (of pop music), just beside Michel and Maria. We all assembled at their door, and persuaded them to cool it *a bit*. They were perfectly friendly, but blind to the world. No doubt they were trusted Party functionaries! I also met Judith Devlin,[46] who is staying on the same floor.

DAY 7, THURSDAY, DEC. 13TH

Today, at last, I get to deliver my 'report'.[47] We were collected as usual at 10.30 am, after our 'porridge' – on which Michel waxes ever more lyrical – and arrived at the Institute to find that there was an unexpected lady on the programme, who was determined to speak on 'Flavius Josephus', and had to be accommodated first. Why she had to be fitted into the programme was not revealed to us, and why she only arose at this stage, but presumably some

---

46 At this time working in the Department of Foreign Affairs, later a professor of Modern History in U.C.D. It seems strange that she was staying in our 'hotel'. Her UCD biographical note states the following: "After a decade in Ireland's Department of Foreign Affairs, including a stint in the Moscow embassy in the mid- to late 1980s and eighteen months in Paris at the Ecole Nationale d'Administration, I took up a post-doctoral fellowship in the School of History, UCD, following which I moved back to academic life. My D.Phil and first book dealt with 19th century French popular culture and psychiatry. Since returning to research, my work has focused on Soviet and post-Soviet Russia, and especially on the culture and politics of the Stalin era. I published two books on post-Soviet Russia and my current research project concerns the Stalin cult. I have wider interests in Russian and Eastern European history of the 19th and 20th centuries, which are reflected in my edited volumes." I am sorry not to have kept in touch with her.

47 The paper was entitled 'The Roots of Reason in John Scottus Eriugena', and was ultimately published, in English, in Philosophical Studies 33 (1992), pp. 25-38. It is reproduced in my second collection of essays, *The Great Tradition* (Ashgate: Aldershot, 1997).

result of internal office politics! Anyhow, I only got started about 12.15, and it became rapidly obvious that, if my charming interpreter, Larisa, was to translate every line of my discourse after I uttered it we would be there all day. So I first proposed that she should just read it in Russian, and I would sit there and beam benevolently, but that wouldn't do – I had to *read* it. So I ended by cutting out the middle of it, and we ended by about 1.30, and had a lively discussion. There was one young man, indeed, speaking excellent English, who knew rather more about Eriugena than I did, and many who knew more about the Greek Fathers. There is a great upsurge of interest in these subjects, I gather, as hitherto it has been totally banned. (My translator Larisa, incidentally, learned her perfect English here in Moscow – she was only foxed by such items as 'Iamblichus' and 'henads'!)

After me, Dimitri Nikulin had to speak, on 'Time and Eternity in Aquinas' Commentary on the *Physics*' – a very competent address, but one was beginning to think about lunch, which finally took place around 2.30. Then another paper, by a pleasant fellow called Dobrokhotov, on the figure of Mathilda in Dante. I must re-read Dante with these things in mind!

There *was* to have been a discussion afterwards, on our current work and so on, but everyone was by this time exhausted – it was about 4.30 – so Dimitri and Michel and I returned to the office to have a cup of tea and some biscuits, while Yuri took Maria back to the 'hotel'. She had declined an invitation to the Circus tonight, because she wanted to work on her paper.

So Michel and I were accompanied by the long-suffering Dimitri out by Metro to the University station, opposite which is a fine building housing the circus. There we were met by Yelena and Katerina Sergeyevna, and went to the circus. I must say that the Moscow Circus is a marvellous institution – great for kids of all ages! The jugglers were superb, as were the performing bears, the man with the lions and tigers (his lions were old pets, especially, and supplicated him very like Thomas Catte[48]); also

---

48 Our cat of the time.

the trapeze artists, and the clowns, and the strong man. There was an interval, during which we had a (very frozen) ice-cream. Not even that could I persuade them to let us stand them!

After the show, we went home on the Metro, accompanied by the faithful Dimitri – *but no dinner!* We longed to invite Dimitri to stop off and have a little something with us in the centre of town, but there is just no question of that, it seems. So Michel and I shared some chocolate and Breton biscuits, and went slightly dissatisfied to bed.

Once again, no chance to get together with Conor O'Clery. However, on going out to the jax about midnight, I found a note from Judith Devlin, saying that he had come back with her around 11.30, and had *wanted* to call, but felt it was rather too late. Curses! It has been good to talk to him on the telephone, but it would be much better to get together for a beer or something.

DAY 8, FRIDAY, DEC. 14TH

Again up before 9.00 am, and went over to the canteen for 'porridge'. This morning we tried also the cottage cheese again, and even the *piroshka,* or little cake, which had appeared suddenly in large numbers, and wasn't too bad (we saw one enormous old cleaning lady putting away about fifteen of them – perhaps they only appear once a month!).

Before leaving for the conference, I called both Conor O'Clery (finally working out that I *won't* be able to see him, because he's leaving town tomorrow for the weekend), and Conor O'Riordan at the Embassy, to consult him about a fact I have noticed, that my visa expires a day early (even as it commenced a day *late,* which fact turned out to be insignificant). O'Riordan was encouraging – said it could hardly be fixed now, and if the worst came to the worst, an extension could be purchased at the airport for $25.

The Conference went rather more smoothly today. First, a young man called Lupandin (?), talking about Aristotelian cosmology in the Middle Ages, then Maria on her theme of Antique and Mediaeval rationalising of men's domination of women and animals (which I thought was not bad, if needing much more annotation, though Michel has been teasing her about it incessantly), and then finally Yuri gave an editorial discussion on the type of rationality we are dealing with, namely one based on the exegesis of 'sacred' texts, which is common to both Late Antiquity and the Middle Ages.

Then lunch, which began after 2.00, and went on till well after 3.00, after which it was resolved to have a session in the office, where Michel and I would be grilled on what we are working on now. Michel got me to go first, and I told them this and that, and then he told them of his work on the last Platonic philosophers of the Academy, and their adventures with King Chosroes (he thinks that they never did go further than Harran, in fact, and the journey to the King is a fable by Agathias).[49] But then Mme Gaydenko asked coyly what did we think of *their present situation*, but Michel pretended (I think) not to understand that, and went on talking about his views on the Platonic philosophers, so they had to be content with that. This desire of theirs both to analyse themselves and to have you analyse them is rather touching, but a sign of how worried they are.

But then we had to hurry off at 4.00 pm to be in time to get into the Kremlin at 4.30, and on the way out of the Institute, I *turned my ankle*. It had been snowing, and the path was uneven, and over it went. A fairly regular occurrence, on my recent excursions! Fortunately I was able to continue walking, but it was painful, and going round the Kremlin Museum (for that is what we did) was not pleasant.

The Museum itself is full of extraordinary treasures: all the exuberant wealth of the Tsars, from the Crown Jewels and the thrones on down, as well as the ceremonial plate of the Orthodox

---

[49] This all involves a remarkable tale, by the Byzantine historian Agathias, of an expedition to Persia undertaken by a group of Platonists. Following the closing of the Platonic Academy in Athens in 529 A.D. by the Emperor Justinian, the invitation came from the (remarkably intellectual and open-minded) Persian King Chosroes I, the result of which is a curious volume edited by one of them, Priscian, *Questions and Answers to King Chosroes*. Tardieu is being excessively sceptical, in my view.

Patriarchs, who inhabited the Kremlin as well. Marvellous things by Fabergé – not just eggs! But I would really have preferred to see the cathedrals. We were shown around charmingly by a former student of Yelena's, who now works in the Museum.

After our visit, we were picked up by Yuri and driven (a *long* drive through the Friday evening traffic) off to dinner with Michel's colleague in Gnosticism, Mme Trofimova. She is a dear old lady, who, in spite of having been ill, entertained us to a fine spread in the best Russian manner, laced with much vodka (with both lemon rind and orange rind in it – makes an excellent drink!). Her husband is still alive, but tied up on business in Leningrad – I almost said St Petersburg! She lives in a small but charming flat, in a large apartment building off Leningrad Avenue, on the way to the airport. What privations she must have gone through to serve this dinner God only knows, but all one could do was eat it with thanks: first, salads and a pie, then meat and *kasha,* then ice-cream and raspberry sauce, then cheese-cake and coffee and fruit. Michel and she were able to chat about Gnosticism, and she to reminisce about her trips to Paris.

She was solicitous about my ankle, and lent me her husband's slippers. When we were going, and it was observed that the ankle had swollen up like an egg, she insisted on getting a bandage and some salve, which Yelena rubbed on, then binding up the ankle.

And so home to the Higher School. Maria had been out with Mme Gaidenko, and arrived home at the same time.

DAY 9, SATURDAY, DEC. 15TH

This was a most extraordinary day, in various ways. Because of my ankle, I got out of a journey to a Museum of Oriental Art with Zhenya in the morning – it had more point for Michel, actually, since he knows a man there who has been excavating in Tashkent, and in fact that was the only point in going there. So I stayed home and read my books – both Grossman's *Forever Flowing,*[50] which is an excellent study of post-Stalinist Russia, and

---

50 Vasily Grossman, *Forever Flowing*, first published in English translation

my book for review, *The Duel*, which is also good – and studied Russian. Around 1.00 pm, I felt very suffocated, and went for a walk around the square – Mnisskoye Ploshchad – and watched the mummies and children playing in the playground, and wondered about things.

Michel and Zhenya got back shortly after I did, and we went and found some lunch in the canteen, which wasn't bad. Then I proposed our shopping expedition. Zhenya declared she had heard tell of an excellent *beryoshka* shop in the Rossiya Hotel, so we went there on the Metro – I limping along – but when we got there a militia-man told us that it was closed for re-modelling. The hotel itself had a grim atmosphere, with unauthorised persons being kept out by rather thuggish young men. We got in – I by waving my passport – but the few things for sale in the lobby did not attract me, so we left.

Then Zhenya decided that Michel really must get back in time to pack before getting off at 6.00 pm for his train to Vilnius. I became incensed at this, as I could see the whole shopping expedition dissolving, so sulked all the way to Novoslobodskaya, since I had *said* I could have perfectly well have gone off on my own, but Zhenya would not have that. She was so distressed, though, that she resolved to set out with me again, down Gorky Street this time, to see if we could find another. I now felt bad, but felt I *must* buy some presents.

As it turned out, I wouldn't have got far by myself. The confusion and difficulties facing anyone who wants to buy anything in these shops is unbelievable. It took us a very long time to find one, and then the first one could only be used by people *registered in the hotel*, and two other small ones only sold perfumes and bikinis, and Benetton clothes, respectively – plainly for *Russians* with dollars, not foreigners. I finally gave up, and bought Zhenya a drink instead, to her *great* confusion, in the 'Spanish Bar', a hard-currency rip-off joint. At least we could sit down, though, and it was interesting to see the workings of the system. A beer and a sherry cost me $6.50, though.

---

in 1988, a story about a man returning to ordinary life in Russia after 30 years in the Gulag.

So we went back to the 'hotel'. I was never *angry* with the system until now. It really is infuriating in its illogicality and counter-productiveness. Poor Zhenya's whole Saturday was spent in this futility. At least I bought her a drink.

When Yuri came to collect me, I asked him to give her also one of the jars of coffee. I hope he does. He actually only arrived at 7.35 pm, so my last hope of getting to a beryoshka – the one near them – became faint. However, we did in fact get there a few minutes before it closed, and I grabbed a few things, before we learned that there were *shapkas* (a kind of Russian cap) upstairs. Too late, though—they were closing! So I bought some little wooden objects and left it at that. It certainly is an impressive place. Yuri declared that he had never set foot in it in his life.

We had a most delightful evening. Another excellent supper – with some *Russian* smoked salmon this time, just to show me! Katerina Sergeyevna had a few whiskeys, and began to tell Chuckchi jokes – the Russian equivalent of Kerryman jokes – which were very funny. They often have a political edge: 'Two Chuckchis fishing somewhere up near the Arctic Circle. One says to the other, "Do you want to hear a political joke?" The other says, "Be careful! We might be overheard and sent into exile."' Another one: 'A Chuckchi and his wife arrive in Moscow, and are overwhelmed by the crowds. In the station, the Chuckchi loses his wife. He asks a militiaman, "Have you seen my wife?" Militiaman: "What does she look like?" "Well, she has one blind eye, all her teeth are gone, and she has this mole on her skin." Militiaman: "I wouldn't bother finding her, if I were you."'

So I told a few Kerryman jokes, and the evening passed very pleasantly, until I declared I must get back, around 11.00 pm. I made my goodbyes, and we set out. Yuri had muttered something about being short of petrol, but round Revolution Square we actually *ran out of petrol*. We had to push the car to the kerb, and try to get a taxi, or someone who would lend us some petrol. No question of a petrol station being open, of course! Would a taxi stop? No way! I got so angry, I was dancing out in the middle of Revolution Square, waving a wad of dollars and shouting abuse at taxis, to Yuri's great embarrassment. One actually stopped, to see what this lunatic was on about. I roared at him, in English, "Are you a taxi, or are you some kind of ornament?" He shrugged, and drove off. Finally, a private car, out to make a buck, stopped, and drove us to the Hotel, and Yuri then set off again to seek his fortune.

I learned next morning that he in fact found another kind motorist who not only brought him back to his car, but lent him some petrol. With a little help from one's friends, one gets by!

DAY 10, SUNDAY, DEC. 14TH

The phone rang at 7.00 am, as promised, and Yelena announced that Yuri had both recovered the car safely and acquired petrol, and they would be along at 7.45. I got everything together, and they were as good as their word, so by 8.00 we were bowling along Leningrad Avenue on our way to Sheremetyevo.

We got to the airport in excellent time, but by the time we had worked our way through various queues, the time had largely run out. Yuri and Yelena stuck with me until I went through the gate, and we parted, I think, with mutual regret. They certainly seemed very pleased that I had come, and I hope that I can do them some further good.

I had fears of being questioned about my money, or about the fact that my visa ran out yesterday, but in the event there was no fuss at all. They didn't even check the baggage. I commented on the Cubans going home, and wondered what Fidel thought about all this *perestroika*. Yelena remarked, amusingly, that they feel that Cuba and Albania should perhaps be preserved as museums of Communism, as it would be a pity if it perished entirely from the earth.

The flight home was comfortable and uneventful, despite departing almost an hour late, and we arrived at Shannon about 12.30 pm, not too much after the scheduled time. The sun was shining, unlike Moscow, but about the same temperature. I phoned home, and I am expected.

A short hop to Dublin, where it was raining and dismal, but good to be back safely.

3. TRIP TO GREECE (KATOUNIA):

JUNE 15 – 30, 1991

This was simply a family holiday to what was to become one of our favourite destinations on earth, the valley of Katounia, outside Limni, in Northern Euboea, home of the Sherrard family. For background to this visit, one should consult Chapter 14 of the previous volume. On this occasion – and subsequent ones – we rented a car at the airport, which made us much more flexible. Jean's contributions, being in the minority, are presented in italics.

DAY 1, SATURDAY, JUNE 15TH

We got ourselves substantially packed in the morning. I have had a hectic two weeks, between hiring new faculty, correcting exams, and latterly examiners' meetings, with and without externs Last night I joined Roger and Brian to entertain three of their four graduating seniors in AHA (at Judge Roy Bean's), so I am virtually collapsed. J's back has been giving her trouble for a week now, so we are in a dangerous state. Only the Mouse is well, but she is complaining of a pain – probably brought on by the unbearable excitement. I am also afflicted by (a) a sore heel, (b) water on the left ear, and (c) general loss of taste and smell from the allergy – this for the last three weeks or so, ever since Christine and Harley's[51] visit and party. Just an overdose of booze and coffee, I suppose. It is infuriating, though, because it had been half-way all right. I *hate* not to taste, especially when headed for Greece!

We got dog food and medicines in the morning, and I then

---

51 Jean's cousin and her husband.

took the chance to drive into town to check the office again. It is just as well that I did – found various long-forgotten items! Got back around 5.00 pm, to find that Hab[52] and the boys had arrived for tennis. I played with them a little, and then gave up, to do some useful jobs, such as weed-killing the yard. Then Frank[53] and children arrived, and Frank largely ran the barbeque – we had spare ribs, with the first of our own spinach and potatoes.

I phoned Paul Kalligas, and we fixed up dinner on Saturday evening, June 29th, on our way back. We have decided *not* to stop in Athens on the way out, seeing how much we disliked it last time – and Janet[54] says it has got worse. Our friendly hotel has gone out of business, according to Budget Travel, when I phoned this morning.

Frank brought us to the plane in good time, and we boarded without incident. It also left more or less on time. Once again, like last time, we were surrounded by the younger set, lads and lasses setting off (mainly) for Ios – though some for Mykonos. I wasn't as indignant as I was last time, because I was sitting beside two of them, and they were most friendly, though consuming vast quantities of beer, and one at least was totally plastered by the time we got to Athens. I refused all food and everything liquid except a Ballygowan, being afraid for my ears, and it paid off. I managed to doze a bit, but not much.

DAY 2, SUNDAY, JUNE 16TH

We arrived at 1.15 am our time, 3.15 am local time – a godforsaken hour! Passed through customs without incident, and found a man waiting for us from Hellascars, very efficiently. I put the whole thing on Visa, so we won't learn till much later what it cost. Probably a nasty shock, though it doesn't *seem* too bad; but

---

52 My old friend Peter Harbison, who then lived in Malahide, not far away, and his young sons.

53 Jean's brother, Frank Montgomery.

54 Our friend, Janet Coggin, the novelist, who lived there. See Volume 1, p.252.

certainly a great convenience! He fetched it for us, a small Seat Marbella, with a *sun roof*, which delighted the Mouse. We had to put the sun-roof down, which fascinated the citizens, many of whom were still driving about (at enormous speeds) at 4.15 a.m., when we started out.

We drove (or J did; I navigated) straight into the centre of Athens – Syngrou Square, Syntagma Square, Omonia – and then out through endless suburbs (including Kefissia) towards the north – direction Lamia. Dawn only arrived about 6.00 am, when we were well on our way to Chalcis.

The drive over the mountains of Euboea was simply lovely. The smell of pine and thyme! We saw wild hollyhocks, capers – with a really beautiful flower – oleanders, geraniums, a low-growing neat little broom, and in the flatter areas surrounding the river, plane trees. It would be nice to have time to really study the wild flowers of this area, they are so numerous. The Mouse slept for about three hours as we drove.

Even with a short snooze at the turn-off to Limni, we still got there at about 9.00 am, hoping that *something* would be open. In fact we found a bread shop, where we bought a sort of brioche and two *tyropitas*; and then our favourite *kafeneion*, on the sea front, where we had *café au lait* and *tyropitas*. It is an interesting reflection that one *can* have dinner in Drumnigh and breakfast in Katounia – if one is prepared to travel all night!

Then we drove up to the villa. However, the door was locked, and someone was inside. We went up to Liadain, to see what the score was, and found her on her verandah. In fact, it was her sister who was spending the night there, as their house is being repaired – the drains are blocked, and the roof collapsing! Men are working on it, though.

Anyhow, she moved out and we moved in. Then down for an introductory swim (Mouse a bit sore at the salt water, though). It was somewhat colder than I expected. Liadain says they had a very tough winter here, which really only cleared up at the beginning of June – but still very pleasant. Then we went back up to the house, and flopped down for a sleep.

We are established this time in 'Rhonnda's', or 'The Studio', which is actually a beautiful bungalow, also sporting a verandah with an excellent view. It has one main room, delightfully bright and spacious (it seemed smaller in Rhonnda's time), with a bedroom off it, separated by a curtain, and then another bedroom, with the kitchen and bathroom down a short passage. It really only suits one family, though, or perhaps two *very* compatible couples!

We struggled up again about 4.30 pm, and decided to go into town to search for a few supplies, there being nothing in the house. We did find one shop open, where we got some beer, retsina, fruit, and an instant coffee pack (for the morning), but nothing else. Then back for another swim, at 6.00 or so. It is still very warm (and had been *very* hot in the middle of the day), but pleasant. We are taking things cautiously, though, so we didn't stay very long.

We played cards for a while on the verandah – whist and poker – with Mouse in charge. Then down to the taverna for dinner, taking a little stroll up the road first. We were recognised and greeted warmly, first by the proprietor's son, Michaelis, and then by the owner.[55] Yiota is coming home from Aberdeen tomorrow, and there is great excitement. She seems to be doing very well. Mouse, after some hesitation, took up with little Yiota and friends – great interpreting took place – and it looks like they may all get on. I am sitting here writing this at 11.00 pm, rather hoping to get home to bed. It is just beginning to get a little chilly under the trees. Liadain and her sister Selga came down to dinner. Their Greek is quite perfect. We wonder about the status of both of them. Her sister seems rather tougher – was she perhaps married, and now no longer? And no sign of Tavener.[56]

Dinner was excellent: pork and veal chops, fried zucchini slices, spaghetti for Mouse – total 3,145 dr, not too bad! Home to bed at 11.30 pm, the Mouse protesting at being taken away so early, and suggesting a last game of cards on the verandah!

---

55 That is to say, David Yoannou. Yiota is his college-age daughter. Little Yiota (see below), as I recall, was a niece.

56 This was the distinguished British composer John Kenneth Tavener, with whom Liadain had been in a relationship on our previous visit in 1988.

DAY 3, MONDAY, JUNE 17TH

Woke up early, just after 7.00 am, and am sitting out on the verandah, mumbling some dry biscuits, with orange juice and a banana, and listening to the song of sundry birds (I wish I knew which), the cicadas, and an occasional frog. There are also waves lapping on the shore – always waves in the morning, whatever goes on in the night, whereas it is calm by the afternoon, even when there is a breeze! The oleander leaning over the verandah is a magnificent specimen. It is good to gaze at the Aegean through its branches, and that of a neighbouring pine-tree. I wish I could *smell* more of all this. It is a real affliction to be deprived of that.

I certainly needed to *unwind*. I had a frantic dream last night, the details of which I forget, but which involved getting in marks and recommendations on time. It is hard to get my mind off the mess I left on my desk. One feature of the dream – however it arose – was that a *tape* broke because the different professors, each of whom was involved in contributing to a reference for someone (I think), played it *in opposite directions* when recording. I know that doesn't make sense, but that is what I remember, and it is certainly symbolic of the events of the last few weeks. One recurring nightmare, which I'm sure I will have while I'm here, is that of suddenly remembering that one has forgotten some absolutely basic thing, such as, e.g. writing to a candidate offering them a job!

I am sitting reading Jaan Puhvel's[57] *Comparative Mythology* (which J would count as 'work', but I regard as entertainment),

---

57 Jaan Puhvel (b. 1932) is an Estonian comparative linguist and comparative mythologist who specializes in Indo-European studies. Born in Estonia, Puhvel fled his country with his family in 1944 following the Soviet occupation of the Baltic states, and eventually ended up in Canada. Gaining his PhD in comparative linguistics at Harvard University, he became a professor of classical languages, Indo-European studies, and Hittite at the University of California, Los Angeles (UCLA), where he founded the Center for the Study of Comparative Folklore and Mythology and was Chairman of the Department of Classics. It was he, as I recall, who invited my father to come to UCLA as a visiting professor in the early 1960s.

interspersed with George Steiner's *In Bluebeard's Castle*,[58] a most stimulating work. An oleander flower has just fallen on the book, reminding me of the passage of time. It is 08.45 – time to see if anyone else is prepared to wake up.

It's now just 1.00 pm and I'm back on the verandah again, after a shopping expedition to Roussos' Supermarket, where we spent nearly 7000 dr on supplies. We need to have a few home-meals as a result of that! We got such luxuries as würst, olives and ouzo, but forgot bread and tomatoes – so another expedition is indicated in the late afternoon. Little Yiota came on the expedition, Mouse herself indulging in approximate communication in Greco-English, myself interpreting (with much help from the dictionary). Then down for a swim, still with Yiota, and spent about an hour. In the interval, Philip and Denise came to call, and left a note. They will return at 8.00 pm

We had a lunch of cheese, sausage, oranges, bread and coffee on the verandah, and then retired for a bit of a siesta – the Mouse less than others. She eventually got us up by sitting on us in turn, and we decided to go back into town, towards 5.00, to see if we could find any bread or tomatoes. We met young Michaelis (Laki) at the car (Yiota's older brother), who said that Yiota was not allowed to go into town again, but he would like a

---

58 *In Bluebeard's Castle: Some Notes Towards the Redefinition of Culture* is composed of four brief lectures by Steiner with interlocking themes, chiefly the fragmentation and dissolution of Western culture from the French Revolution onwards (particularly from the perspective of a perceived break with tradition, whether Jewish, Christian, Greek or Latin), with a meditation on what kind of future culture might develop over the course of time. It engages with one of Steiner's perennial concerns: that of the long-term ramifications of the Holocaust on our cultural values and cultural productions, and the questions that arise from it in terms of the growth and development of anti-semitism over time. In Steiner's view, the existence of the Holocaust meant that the long trajectory of Western culture with roots in numerous different valuable sources such as Periclean Athens was effectively finished – a similar line of argument to that navigated in the 1967 work Language and Silence.

lift to a football match he was playing in. He told us that Monday was a half-day in Limni, as is Wednesday and Saturday (they look after themselves!), so no shops would be open – but a little town 9 km. up the coast, Rovies, would be open. So we took him in to his match, clutching his ball, and drove on to Rovies, where we found a vegetable shop (*lakhanopôleion*) open, but no bread shop. I suspect they only open in the mornings at the best of times. We bought a sliced loaf (*gia tost*) in a *pantopoleion*,[59] and will make do with that. Rovies is quite a resort, as is another little settlement, Khronia, half-way between it and Limni – lots of development on that side of town; very little this side yet, thank God!

We got back only about 7.00 pm, too late for another swim (and we're not sure that we're not a bit burned, anyway), so we sat on the verandah and waited for Philip and Denise to arrive. They came around 8.30, and stayed till after 10.00, before going on to the taverna. They were in fine form, and it was very good to see them again. Philip told us the fascinating story of old Michaelis, the grandfather of the Ioannous. He is a tough old bird, who was a volunteer worker in Germany during the War, and was repatriated after the defeat of Germany without a penny to his name – and *persona non grata* in addition. He started by presenting himself to rich olive farmers north of Limni, offering to prune their olives if he could plant vegetables in between the trees. He built a little tin shack (which Philip remembers), and sold his produce. He formed a liaison with a local woman and had some children (he had been already married before the War, so he couldn't get married at the time). Then he petitioned the local authorities for a bit of barren land south of Limni, at the end of a mule track, at Katounia, where he offered coffee and snacks to the muleteers going into the hills for wood. He also ripped off the old mining property in the valley. When Philip came to buy the mining property, Michaelis was established in a little shack, offering refreshments and doing odd jobs (he worked for Philip and Jack,[60] and Philip helped

---

59 That is, a general store – *gia tost* means 'for toasting'.
60 Jack Rivas, Philip's partner in the original purchase of the valley; see end

him in various ways). His children grew up, and he started the taverna. Philip helped him to get a divorce, and he married his partner – they are both still alive and well, and his two sons run the business now.

All this was à *propos* big Yiota's going off to study in Scotland. Many years ago, Philip had financed her father, David's, study at an American Farm College in Thessaloniki, but old Michaelis went and brought him back after a year. However, even the year put a mark on David, and gave him a vision of the outside world, which made him willing to let Yiota try, but it is a great strain for him to do so.

We had a modest dinner of spaghetti and fried eggs, and then Mouse and I settled down to a game of backgammon (or 'black gamma', as Mouse calls it), which lasted till midnight, and was left unfinished.

DAY 4, TUESDAY, JUNE 15TH

Up pretty early (7.30 am or so), and sat out on the verandah in the cool of the morning, reading Steiner and Puhvel, and meditating on life. There is a very active little bird around, with a distinctive song. I can't see it, though. And sporadic frogs. The sea is absolutely calm this morning, unlike the waves of the last two days. I made coffee and toasted some bread. Then I managed to rouse the Mouse about 10.00 for a morning swim. It was beautifully calm and clear. Mouse went down to the taverna, met big Yiota and little Yiota, and persuaded little Yiota to come for a swim. Little Yiota brought along a beach ball and a frisbee, but Mouse couldn't handle the frisbee, and tended to hog the beach ball, so little Yiota went away after a while – I hope not for ever!

Mummy and Mouse went into town for some bread and stuff, and I stayed behind and read. Lunch consisted of bread and cheese and olives and *würst*. Then a siesta, broken up at about 4.30 by Mouse, who does not believe yet in siestas, and wanted to play cards. We had another swim, and set out to walk

---

of Chapter 8 of previous volume.

up the valley before going out to dinner. The expedition ran into difficulties in face of a leak in the water-pipe, which was sending out a waterfall right across the path, and then from briars, so we came back. On our return we met Philip, who had come down to show Mouse a tortoise – a big one – who was hiding in the grass.

Then back to await Philip and Denise, who came at 9.00 pm to take us out to dinner. They brought us down to a restaurant at the end of the promenade in Limni, where there is good seafood. We started with *mezedes* and white wine, and then main courses. I had *gopes* – a fairly small fish, served whole, grilled. Not bad.

We gossiped till midnight about this and that. Philip knew Eric Dodds,[61] and a fellow called Andrews who was a friend of his, and writes travel books (in the Penguin travel series). He reported that Garth Fowden[62] has turned Orthodox, being baptised in a monastery near Mount Athos, and is married to an American girl from Princeton. He advised us on places to

---

61 Eric Robertson Dodds (1893 – 1979) was an Irish classical scholar, Regius Professor of Greek at the University of Oxford from 1936 to 1960, and a most interesting figure, who had interests in both Neoplatonism and psychical research. In my last year at Oxford, just after his retirement, he was appealed to by my tutor, Peter Brunt, to have a talk with me, to persuade not to choose a special subject in Plotinus for Greats, as I had a mind to do. This he did most amiably and persuasively, while entertaining me to tea in his cottage at Old Marston. Much later, in 1978, after the publication of his Memoir, Missing Persons, I wrote to him from Berkeley, revealing that I had not taken his advice to avoid Plotinus in the long run, and he wrote back, again very amiably, saying how glad he was to hear that. The Andrews mentioned here is presumably the Kevin Andrews mentioned in that work. He was indeed a distinguished writer on various aspects of Greece.

62 For Garth Fowden, see previous volume, pp. 103-5. He had been married to the rather forceful scholar of late antiquity, Polymnia Athanassiadi, but the marriage had, sadly, dissolved. He later became Sultan Qaboos Professor of Abrahamic Faiths at the University of Cambridge (2013-2020).

visit around the area, specifically St David's Monastery, up from Rovies. We might try that tomorrow!

DAY 5, WEDNESDAY, JUNE 19TH

This morning we decided to take a small trip, up to Saint David's Monastery, and round through the hills, to the main road to Histiaea, to get a view of backwoods Euboea. We got Mouse out of bed with difficulty, and poured her into the car. It is once again a breathlessly calm morning, promising a very hot day.

We got away at about 8.15, and drove off towards Rovies; then turned up the mountain, on a broad, but unmetalled, road, to Osios David from Geronta, 12 km up the road. No traffic, very prosperous-looking farming land, some nice houses, beautiful vistas back to the coast and of inland valleys. Then we came upon the monastery, nestling in pines on the side of the mountain. A busload of pilgrims was there ahead of us, but they were just leaving. We sat down in the courtyard beside the church, uncertain whether to go in, but got talking to an old monk, who was very friendly, and knew Philip (*'einai orthodoxos!'*), and he urged us to go in. We admired the icon of Saint David and the other treasures, lit a candle (donating 500 dr), and took our leave. I petitioned Saint David to restore my sense of smell, but really the solution is probably in my own hands. The Abbot is said to be a very holy man, and might have cured me on the spot, but we saw no sign of him. The atmosphere of ancient piety, I may say, was somewhat compromised by a young monk swinging into the church clutching a walkie-talkie, into which he spoke from time to time. Perhaps he was exercising crowd control, and reporting back to a communications centre, manned by the Abbot.

We then drove on, again through beautiful countryside, to a little town which I *think* was called *Kokkinomêlia* – 'Red Apple Town'. From there we drove out on a road and met a countryman, and asked how we could get to Kerasia – 'Cherry-Town'. He said we were on the wrong road – this road went nowhere (*'kovetai'*[63])

---

63 Literally, 'it is cut off'.

– and sent us back to town, to turn up to the right. We met an old lady in town, and asked *her,* and she confirmed this – 'Go to a river (*potami*), and turn *left*'. So we did that, and after seemingly endless kilometers of dirt road, thankfully reached a fine metalled road leading into Cherry-Town. We were tempted to tarry there and have a coffee, but thought we should get on to *Akhladi* – 'Pear-Town' – and then to Aghia Anna.

On the way we came to a petrol station, spanking new on this spanking new road (not on the map as such), filled with Super (2900 dr), and stopped for a coffee – and Pepsi for Mouse. While we were having that, a *manavis*[64] drove up in his van for petrol, with his whole family, and also opened up for business, so Mouse and Mummy went over and bought some potatoes and lemons and a pepper.

Then we drove into Santa Anna, which is a pleasant little town, and stopped and walked about. As it happened, we stopped in front of the Town Museum, where an ancient resting on his porch adjacent naturally thought we wanted to visit it (which we didn't *greatly* – it was a *folk* museum), and directed us to a neighbouring house. We entered the garden tentatively, but no one was about, so we retired, and walked round the neighbourhood instead, sneaking back to the car, and bolting before he could get back to us.

We drove on down the road to the turn to Limni, and so home. We stopped in town, because Mouse wanted to buy some more flip-flops, but failed to find the right size. It was getting *very* hot. I stopped to examine the monument in the main square, which bears an inscription by Ritsos,[65] but I haven't worked out yet what it's in honour of. Then back for a swim before lunch.

The family in Jack's house interest us. They inhabit the

---

64 That is, a grocer.

65 Yiannis Ritsos (1909 – 1990) was a Greek poet and communist and an active member of the Greek Resistance during World War II. While he disliked being regarded as a political poet, he has been called «the great poet of the Greek left». Philip did not approve of him at all.

other half of the beach, and have a little baby. There is an Englishwoman, but a young Greek man also, who takes the baby for rides in a little inflatable boat, up and down to the taverna beach. The baby likes this one way, but *dislikes* it on the way back, so that it is always roaring by the time they row back past us. Still, I suppose it is something to do.

After the siesta, we went down again for a swim, and this time we met the Dutchman, Mr van Leuwen (?), looking for a glasses case he *might* have left on the beach (but his wife found it later in the luggage). They are actually just leaving for Istanbul tomorrow, and were there in the big house alone, not filling it at all, except with friends who had come to stay. It seems more like a *consortium* of Dutch who take the house during the summer. He is a perfectly pleasant fellow, bronzed and fit, in his mid-50s (I should say), with flawless English (as one expects from the Dutch). I didn't see the wife.

In the evening, after the inevitable card-games with the Mouse, we went down to the taverna for dinner. Big Yiota was there to greet us, looking fine, and obviously profiting from Aberdeen. Little Yiota wouldn't even *talk* to Mouse, initially, which depressed us all, but then half-way through dinner she appeared, very cheerful, and joined Mouse in weaving.

David put us on the spot by announcing that he had just caught a John Dory that afternoon – in 120 metres of water, however he worked that out! – and it was available for eating. So, with much apprehension, we volunteered. It was certainly a splendid fish, and the bill only came to 5900 dr – large, certainly, but the price of *one* dinner back home, at £21. I wasn't feeling very sprightly by the end of it, since we also had a large flagon of wine *ap' to vareli*,[66] so I went home a bit early. Liadain and Selga were down for dinner as well.

DAY 6, THURSDAY, JUNE 20TH

We rose reasonably late, read, and then went for a swim. Then into town to shop. Mouse and Yiota had got together for

---

66 Viz. 'from the barrel'.

some weaving in the morning, and card-playing. We shopped at Roussos', getting frankfurters for this evening. I got a sandal fixed whose strap had come loose (100 dr). Also changed £100 stg at the bank, getting a little over 30,000 dr. I hope that will do us for a while. We've got through the best part of £200 since arrival, which is not too good.

We took the usual siesta after lunch, and then, acting on some suggestions from Liadain, we decided on an *evening* drive to the other side of the island, to see if we could find the site of ancient Cerinthos. We headed down from new Cerinthos, in the direction of *Krya Vrysi*,[67] which took us through prosperous fertile fields, down beside a fine river, and a marvellous herd of mountain goats, with splendid horns, like oryx. We reached the coast, to find a rather grotty beach, covered with drift-wood and bits of plastic, but just facing us, to the south, there rose up the acropolis of Old Cerinthos, unfortunately just the other side of the river, which, though narrow there, was deep and fast-flowing, so we couldn't cross. It was fascinating, though. I wonder if it has been excavated. Only the fortifications are visible, and a nice little harbour, though now silted up.

We drove back up to the main road, and down the next road to the coast, to *Kymasi*. This was not a good idea, since we ran into the territory of a vast cement factory, *Fimisco*. There was no way back to Old Cerinthos, just a grotty little port.

So home, slightly baffled, to a modest dinner of franks, fried potatoes, eggplant and peppers. Not bad, in fact. We had more of Philip and Denise's wine.

I wonder how our mileage is going. We're paying no attention to that!

DAY 7, FRIDAY, JUNE 21ST

Started the day with a discussion as to whether this was Thursday or Friday. I was convinced that it was Thursday, until we consulted the diary. We are beginning to lose count of time. Had a morning swim, and then Mouse and I went into town to

---

67 That is to say, 'Cold Spring'.

see if we could make a phone call. We couldn't find the other alleged telegraph office, and the one public phone was out of order, so we bought *miso kilo ntomates*,[68] and came back to lunch.

After a siesta, I walked up to Philip and Denise to ask some questions – about phoning, about Cerinthos, etc. They were out, as it happened (in Chalcis, getting tiles for the roof of their extension), but I met Liadain, who told me (a) that one could make calls at the taverna, and (b) that one could get across to Cerinthos by walking upstream a ways to a suspension bridge – so we might try that some time.

Then down to the taverna, where I called up Drumnigh (1700 dr), and got Frank – no problems, except that the toaster won't work, and the weather is not good. We had a beer/ouzo in the taverna, and then went for a walk and explore up towards the monastery. There is quite a lot of activity up in that direction, in fact, including a *Camping*, and an Oceanographic Museum (!), open from 10-12 in the mornings, which we must explore. We had a lovely walk on the shore below the monastery, and then back to dinner at home – omelette and chips.

A game or two of whist, and so to bed.

DAY 8, SATURDAY, JUNE 22ND

We decided on a trip this morning, first to Cape Artemision, then to Haghios Georgios on the north-western peninsula. Everything conspired against the smooth running of this, however. First, we felt we must lay in some milk and other supplies for the weekend, and that meant a visit into Roussos' and out, which took half an hour. We only drove out of Limni at five to nine. Then, I suggested a short-cut to Haghia Anna *via* Kerameis, which ended in a very bad road, and we had to retreat. Then, just short of Agriobotano, the nearest town to the Cape, we decided to give a lift to an old lady. She turned out to be quite deaf, very voluble, and quite interesting, but she screwed up the expedition. She wanted to go to Hestiaea, to visit a doctor. We tried to explain what *we* wanted to do, but this made

---

68   A half kilo of tomatoes.

no impression. She revealed that she had been in the partisans, against 'the Fascists'. She had recently been to East Germany (seven years ago) to have an operation on her back (I think!). She spoke of Erich Honecker[69] as a lovely man (*kalos* – I think even ôraios!). I would assume she was a staunch Communist. A great old girl, but we ended up by driving her to Hestiaiea, and lost all chance of finding the temple of Artemis at Artemision, which was my goal. The wretched guidebook spoke of it as being near the village of Artemision, but we asked at a gas station there, and the proprietor maintained that there was no longer any temple at all. Certainly there was no sign or directions – so what was one to do?

One really needs a friendly local antiquarian. No sign, either, indicating Cape Artemision, which Liadain had recommended. We drove back disconsolately through Pevki – the beach – and Oreoi, viewing the Bull, but finding no *Mouseion* this time, open or closed. Then to Aidepsos, and on to the peninsula on which Haghios Georgios is situated. We drove round a beautiful bay from Haghios Nikolaos to Yialtra, stopping in an olive grove by the water to have a swim, and things began to look up. It was a long, but beautiful, drive to Haghios Georgios, where we found a pleasant little restaurant on the seafront, and had *kalamari* (chips for Mouse), with beer. HG is quite a sophisticated resort, in fact, though when the guide-book was written there was only a mule-track out of Loutra Aidepsou – otherwise one had to go by boat.

After a leisurely lunch – and coffee in a *very* raunchy but friendly café – we drove back to Limni along the coast, by the new road – very spectacular, but *bare*. We got petrol at the station outside the town, The little car is doing very good mileage, but one of the clasps to the sun-roof has snapped, which may prove to be awkward.

For the evening, we went down to the taverna, and had excellent pork, with fried peppers – 3500 dr, including yesterday's drinks, and tip.

---

69 The leader of East Germany (DDR).

DAY 9, SUNDAY, JUNE 23RD

Decided to get up and go up to the monastery, to see if we could take in a bit of the service. Fortunately we got there as some other people were arriving – late, about 8.30 – and got in, since the gate was closed and had to be knocked on. However, the cranky old janitress took a dislike to J's very modest and baggy culottes, and made her put on a dress that they had handy, and this annoyed J extremely. Philip and Denise were there somewhere, since the jeep was outside, but we couldn't see them in the church. We left about half an hour later, since without a prayer-book things seem interminable. I wouldn't be surprised if God himself switches channels after three or four hours of this stuff. All I could grasp was when the priest emerged from the sanctuary and said *Agapômen allêlous!*[70] and then an old nun chanted the *Pater hêmôn*.[71] The old birds are all ancient – I saw no nun under about 70 – so what is to be their future?

Back then to a bit of breakfast, followed by a swim. The tide was very low this morning, and the water strangely *cold*, though I can't see why there should be a connection. We continued to clear our path[72], and Mouse began to build a ring-fort. Then a strange man arrived with his son, and we retired.

At around 12.30, Mouse went down to the taverna to play with Yiota, and stayed there for lunch, and then on into the afternoon. When I finally went down to root her out about 4.00 pm, she had been in the sun for *hours*, and was a brightish shade of purple. We have the direst fear of what she has done to herself, but time will tell. Mummy anointed her with Sudocreme, and we wait.

At 8.00, we went up to Philip and Denise for a drink, which involved sampling a *new* barrel of their white wine – a sort of *pithoigia*[73] – which went down very well, and by 9.30 all were quite tiddly. Very pleasant *mezedes* as well, so we hardly

---

70 'Let us love one another!'

71 The 'Our Father'.

72 This will have been a path into the water, made by clearing stones.

73 'Barrel-opening ceremony'.

needed the plate of spaghetti and eggs we had prepared for ourselves. We learned much from Philip about antiquities – particularly Cerinthos and Limni. We have agreed to go back to Cerinthos on Thursday for dinner – and *Kryo Vrysi* – and look at the site before that. It *hasn't* ever been excavated, apparently, but P and D once found fellows with metal detectors pacing over it. Limni also needs excavating. The acropolis seems to be where I thought it must be.

DAY 10, MONDAY, JUNE 24TH

Up rather late. J feels there has been a mass in the little church of St. John on the seashore, and indeed it is somewhere near St. John's Day, as far as I can remember.[74] We went into town to shop, around 11.00 (Mouse has to be kept out of the sun, but this is better than the beach), and then went to the end of the promenade to see if there was anything promising. We found the *skete*[75] of St. Christodoulos of Patmos, which Philip had mentioned – a cave in the rock, now made into a little shrine. We walked along the beach, but there was no way up the cliff. Then we found a little man in a street off the main street who actually mended the clip of the sun-roof, and refused to take any money. Perhaps we will leave him the bottle of whiskey when we go.

Back for a spot of lunch, and then cards with Mouse. Followed by a rest. I am still in the middle of Puhvel's Comparative Mythology, which I find fascinating, but heavy going on the Indian and Iranian levels. It is full of interesting parallels to Greek motifs, however. I haven't broached either of the books I brought to review, though.

In the evening, we waited till 7.00 before going down for a swim. Before that, we made another assault on the acropolis of Elymnion, but got bogged down in olive groves. The ancient town is in fact probably under the present old town, up the hill at the back of the church. I might take a stroll there later.

---

74 St. John's Day is indeed June 24th.
75 This is the residence of a solitary monk, or small group of monks.

We had an excellent dinner of roast chicken flavoured with wild thyme picked by J on the side of a path. We went to bed relatively early, in view of our expedition planned for tomorrow, but first had an amusing diversion planned by Mouse, in the form of the Nine O'Clock News, which she performed through the back of a chair, very cleverly.

DAY 11, TUESDAY, JUNE 25TH

I dreamed this morning of arriving home. Bim[76] was in the house, which was in perfect order, except that all the light-bulbs had gone, and she was wandering around with a light-bulb in her hand, trying to fit it into a socket. We woke quite early (J had in fact hardly slept), rousted out the Mouse, and managed to get out of the house shortly after 7.00, packed and all, which was quite an achievement.[77]

In fact, we got all the way to Eretria, uneventfully, by 9.15. We had a bit of trouble finding the ancient town (having driven right past it, in fact, but it was very badly signposted), and I cursed the Greeks for hiding their antiquities when they can't charge for them. However, we did find the ancient city – fenced off and locked, but we got in through the fence, where it had been broken down, and tramped about among the old houses and streets (finding an interesting bath in one of the houses), and then went over to the Museum, where there is much of interest. In fact, Lefkandi is just up the road, towards Chalcis. I had climbed earlier onto the acropolis, and one could look across the Lelantine Plain (the occasion of all the feuding) towards Chalcis.[78] When we looked back from the Museum to the town, we saw the theatre, but we couldn't be bothered to walk up and view it. I called in to the Temple of Apollo, though,

---

76 My sister Elizabeth.

77 We had decided on a tour of the whole island of Euboea, right down to its southern tip at Karystos, viewing various antiquities on the way, and over-nighting in Karystos.

78 One of the features of earlier Greek history was a series of battles between Chalcis and Eretria over control of this plain.

of which parts of the pediment are in the Museum of Chalcis, which we may see tomorrow. The visit was worth it, just to fix it in one's mind. Eretria was one of the great cities of Greece in its time, after all!

It was already getting hot when we left, at about 11.00, to strike south to Karystos. We stopped for a coffee frappé on the seafront at Amarynthos, which must again be an ancient foundation (with that suffix![79]), but no sign of that was visible. Then on down the southern peninsula – with a diversion to Dystos, but no luck in finding an ancient town. We are now (2.35) sitting in a little café on the seafront in Nea Styra, having had a rather rough ride down the coast from Polypotamos, and hoping for a better one back. We have had an excellent piece of chicken and a plain pizza, but we haven't seen the bill yet.

The bill was actually very reasonable – 1750 dr – so we don't complain at all. We set off again, in searing heat, and reached Karystos, after an exhausting drive, about an hour later. It is actually quite an imposing town, with a central square, facing onto a Cathedral (!), and a fine esplanade, with another square. We lighted on a nice new hotel on the seafront, called the Karystion, and agreed that if it was not too expensive, we'd take it. We were quoted 7200 dr, with breakfast, so we decided to go for it, and indeed it proved very pleasant – a clean, simple room, with a balcony looking onto the sea.

We tried to have a bit of a siesta, largely broken up by the Mouse, who was too excited. Finally, we drove out the Mouse, who struck up a friendship with the proprietress, and brought down her weaving to show her (they discovered a common interest in weaving). At about 6.00, I moved for a swim on the hotel's beach, which was sandy, and pleasantly shaded by a fig-tree, but I ran into, not one, but a series of sea-urchins, just below the water-line, and ended up with a number of quills in my right hand and foot, which are rather nasty, and resisting all attempts to get them

---

79 That is to say, *–ynthos, which would normally indicate Mycenaean provenance.*

out. This rather put everyone else off, so we decided to go up and find the marble quarries (*I Myli*) before it got dark.

I got instructions, as I thought, from the lady in the hotel, and we set off towards the west. This led to a round-about trip, which ran through attractive suburbs, and appeared to end at some quarries, where we certainly found marble. J took many photos, and I collected a fine specimen of marble to bring back to Roger.[80] There were fine views on the way back down to the town and the bay. After coming down from there, however, I asked two girls who were passing if this was *I Myli*,[81] and they said no, it was farther on! Actually, though, what I think they meant was the suburb of *Myli*, which is a beautiful area, obviously rather rich and fashionable, stretching up a ravine into the mountains, just opposite the hill on which sits a Venetian *kastro*, which is the site of the old acropolis. The area is adorned with little parks, and bridges across the stream that comes down from the mountain, and beautifully appointed homes (perhaps summer homes?). We admired it for a while, driving up as far as we dared, and then came back down to town.

We found ourselves in the main square, in front of the Cathedral, where there is a playground (presented by Carystians in America, it seems!), and the Mouse had a good time on the swings and slides and roundabouts. After a drink of beer back at the hotel, we went down the seafront to find a modest restaurant. We found a delightful one, in fact, just up a side-street (which is the place to find them), where all the dishes were laid out up front, and you choose – really the best kind of place! J had a beef stew, and I had a liver stew (which wasn't such a good idea), stuffed tomatoes, and flagon of wine – Mouse had spaghetti! – all for 1900 dr. There were some slightly weird American girls with California accents (one Chinese-American) at the next table, who seemed to be staying for a while in Karystos. At one point, some other Americans passed by half-way through the meal, and greeted them. One wonders what they would be up to.

---

80 That is, my colleague in the department, Roger Wilson, our Professor of Classical Archaeology.

81 'The Mills'.

After that, we found coffee and *loukoumades* on the sea-front, and so home to bed, leaving orders to be wakened at 6.15 am.

DAY 12, WEDNESDAY, JUNE 26TH

We were duly wakened (not having slept too well, from the heat), rose, packed, had a very pleasant breakfast, and so off, just after 7.00 am. It is a long haul up the peninsula, but we made good progress. I drove the first half, up to the turn to Kyme, and reached Chalcis at about 10.00. I was allowed to visit the Museum in the centre of town, in Venizelou Street, but as soon as I got in there, my back went, so I had to be propped up, and J rushed back to the car for water and pills. A strange thing – we had been expecting *her* back to collapse, but it hasn't at all. We cautiously viewed the Museum – which is quite small, and hardly as good as the one in Eretria. The curator said that the frieze of Apollo Daphnephoros has been returned to Eretria, but I can't recall seeing it. Afterwards, we drove out of town, and stopped eventually for coffee up in the mountains at an *exokhiko kentro*,[82] which we had viewed on our original way up, but had been too early for. Now we had a good iced coffee, and then a fried cheese pie (*têganita tyropita*), which we saw other people having. So excellent was it, indeed, that we decided this would constitute lunch.

We stopped at Prokopi, where we had heard there were *crafts*, and indeed this proved to be so, as regards basket-work and pottery, in the main square. We bought a few little things. We left for home about 2.30, getting a car wash on the way, in the gas station just out of town. The man did a great job (800 dr), but unfortunately the leaking petrol has made a corroding mark on the side of the car. One villain had filled it too full, and it bubbled over in the heat.

Mouse and Mummy had a swim later, but I rested the back. We had a pleasant dinner at home, of chicken risotto (spaghetti for Mouse), and then decided to go down to town and join in

---

82 A rural tourist centre – as was our local taverna, in fact.

the *peripatos*,[83] followed by a coffee. This was most entertaining. We sat in our usual café, *To Neon*, and had frappés and ice-creams. All human life passed by, doing their various things. We really should have done this more often. We looked into the cinema, which was open, but not for business, and found Selga in there, with a young man. She said it would only open on Friday, so we'll hardly get to it.

DAY 13, THURSDAY, JUNE 27TH

Local election day at home. I wonder how they got on without me! We have really had *no* news of the outside world for two weeks, except that I bought an evening paper a few days ago, which described a split in the Communist Party here, and a visit by James Baker[84] to Yugoslavia and Albania (where he got a hero's welcome). Yugoslavia is still moving towards disintegration – unless the army makes a move!

Into town at 10.30 to change another £100 – perhaps too much – and finally post some cards. I hobbled about on a stick. J bought some presents. Then back to entertain Philip and a young man from the town, Yannis Livadias, who wants to come to Dublin to study Business Administration (his father owns a builder's providers business here, just this side of town). He has just graduated from university, and seems pleasant and bright. He has a friend who has been at UCD for some months, and who has met Chrysanthi.[85] I tried to advise him about Trinity, but it really *is* a bit late in the year – and he hopes to find a job in Dublin!

J had bought a pizza for lunch, so we had that and some beer, and then a rest. In fact, we had no time for an evening swim, before setting off in convoy with Philip and Denise to revisit the site of Old Cerinthos, and to have dinner in Kryo Vrysi, at a taverna known to them. The acropolis of Cerinthos

---

83 The Greek name for the evening perambulation, so common in Mediterranean lands.

84 Baker was the U.S. Secretary of State at the time.

85 I regret to say I have forgotten who she was.

is remarkable – quite untouched, it seems, except by villains with metal detectors! One gets to it by taking the *Fimisco* road, and then taking the first left onto a dirt road. We would never have found it. Only when on the mound did it occur to me to get J to open up the camera and find out whether it had in fact ever been threaded. We opened it, and found that it had *not* – a repeat of our Mexican experience![86] So *no* Eretria, *no* Carystos, and almost no Cerinthos, as the sun was going down. I threaded it in a fury, and took snaps all round me, so I hope that works. We will see. It is preposterous that there should not be some warning on these instruments. Opposite the mound we were on is another mound, equally possibly inhabited – perhaps Helladic or Neolithic, as opposed to Classical.

As the sun went down, we drove back to dinner. Denise and Mouse got out (Mouse travelled all the way with P and D! God knows what she was saying to them), to cross a suspension bridge over the river, and met us on the other side. Dinner was excellent, in what I had not recognised as a taverna when we drove over there the first time. It is run by a young fellow called Yannis, who has a university degree and is something of an antiquarian. We had *mezedes* and swordfish (*xiphias*) – J had a nice pork chop; Mouse *chips*. There was also loads of wine, and even some ice-creams, so it all came to 5200 dr. We stayed talking till 12.30 or so. A young English couple were there, helping at the taverna and in the fields, and surviving in a tent. An amusing pair. They plan to go off to South America next.

Denise, after a few flagons of plonk, began to speculate on the end of civilisation, and this so depressed the Mouse that she questioned us about the end of the world all the way home, and had to sleep with Mummy in the big bed.

DAY 14, FRIDAY, JUNE 28TH

We rose rather late, especially Mouse, who was exhausted from the previous night. Down to the taverna to make a few phone calls. I got on to Paul Kalligas, and confirmed dinner tomorrow night.

---

86 See the Trip to Yucatan in the previous volume, p. 47ff.

Then got onto Donald Nicol[87] at the Gennadion and arranged lunch, and onto the American School, where I said we'd be by about 11.30 am tomorrow. That done, it was time for a last swim, and then into town for lunch. While we were down on the beach, Philip and Denise called in, but missed us, and then went off to Athens, so we didn't have a chance to say goodbye to them.

We had a good lunch at the *Platanos* on the sea-front, where we had not been before. We managed to fit in a siesta, followed by packing and cleaning, and finally, down to the taverna in the evening for a last meal.

DAY 15, SATURDAY, JUNE 29TH

We started off for Athens early (7.00 am), to escape as much heat as we could, but stopped off briefly in the little town of Prokopi to pay homage to St. John the Russian, whose shrine is in the Cathedral.[88] We arrived during Mass, and were glad that we went. He is mummified in his coffin, looking rather small and brown. We bought a little icon of him to bring home.

When we got to Chalcis, we met great traffic coming *out of* Athens. At least we are going in the right direction! We stopped for some breakfast in a sort of trucker's café, where a young Indian was serving. Very pleasant, in fact.

We got to Athens without a hitch around 11.00, and parked in the American School.

And here the diary unfortunately peters out. We must assume that our last few engagements were successfully kept, and that a smooth return to Dublin followed the next day!

---

87 Donald MacGillivray Nicol, FBA, MRIA (1923 – 2003) was an English Byzantinist. He was Director of the Gennadeion Library in Athens from 1989-1992. He was a great lover of Greece, and had strong connections with Ireland, having taught Classics at UCD from 1952 to 1964. He subsequently taught in King's College, London.
88 He is the patron saint of Prokopi, whose inhabitants are largely refugees from Greek cities on the Black Sea coast.

4. Trip to Bristol and SW England:

AUGUST 23–30, 1992

This was a family trip, partly academic and partly touristical, to attend a conference of the International Plato Society in Bristol, devoted to the topic of Plato's Statesman. We had also planned to visit my old school, Downside, and an old school friend, Auberon Waugh, in his lair in Combe Florey, Somerset, and generally to see a bit of south-west England. Jean's contributions are in italics.

DAY 1, SUNDAY, AUGUST 23TH

We made a leisurely start, since Rosslare is only about three-and-a-half hours away. This holiday is taken under the shadow of the sad circumstances of the sale of the house and the search for another, so it is something of an escape.[89] I hope that the combination of holiday and conference does not prove too much of a strain. I bought the *Sunday Indo*, but Aengus did not put me in[90] – crowded out by Woody Allen, Fergie, unemployment, George Bush, and the Supreme Court decision on cabinet confidentiality. Quite a lot for a week in August! I mowed the last few lawns, and was going to weed-kill a bit, but Clare and

---

89 We had in fact just sold our house in Portmarnock, Drumnigh, the previous month, and were in search of another, smaller, residence, preferably in Howth, which we duly found, in the shape of our present home, which we called Katounia.

90 I was at this time writing occasional pieces for the Sunday Independent, but they were liable to be crowded out by last-minute sensational developments. 'Aengus' refers to Aengus Fanning, the editor.

Paul[91] arrived to greet us, so that was postponed. Then Caroline[92] arrived to get her orders – she is looking after the house for us for the week.

We set off at 2.15 pm, to call in on Tom and Mo[93] on the way down, and stopped there for a pleasant tea. The weather is slightly uncertain – a bit windy, but sunny. We left there about 5.00 (Tom was going fishing in Brittas), and set off for Kilrane, stopping at Ferrycarraig on the Slaney, just short of Wexford, to check out the Heritage Park, which seems most interesting. We also called into a nice guest-house, Slaney House, overlooking the Slaney, where we *might* return some time. We got to Kilrane House about 8.00, and are now sitting in the Ivory House in Tagoat, a pleasant little restaurant, waiting for our dinner.

The dinner was good, though my rainbow trout had to be sent back for more grilling. It came to just over £20 for all three of us. And so to bed. There is a little noise from the street and the lounge upstairs, but no great problem.

DAY 2, MONDAY, AUGUST 24TH.

We awoke quite early – the alarm clock provided by Mr Whitehead being fixed for 6.50 am – and had (a very good) breakfast at 7.30. Then down to the boat. There was no great crowd, so we got on without trouble. A large Swedish liner – the Stena *Felicity* – was on service. It is very comfortable, and the crossing was smooth. Mouse and I went to the movies, to see *Hook*. It was actually very good, and enormously clever – Robin Williams, Julia Roberts, Dustin Hoffman (as Hook), etc. This left only half-an-hour or less to appreciate the boat.

We arrived on time, at 12.30, and were off and running by 1.00. The weather clouded up as we drove through Wales, and then began to drizzle. We were attracted by a strange sign saying 'Chocolate Farm', and went to investigate, through very

---

91 Sister and brother-in-law of Jean.
92 My niece, Caroline Gore-Grimes.
93 Jean's brother, Tom Montgomery, and his wife, who lived in Delgany.

pleasant Welsh countryside. It turned out to be the home base of *Chocolates,* and very popular – though not a soul seemed to be stirring throughout the rest of the countryside. We had a pleasant hot chocolate and cake, but then found the shop so crowded that we didn't stop to buy anything – though there were excellent chocolates and *fudges* to be seen.

The rain got worse as we headed for the M4, and we drove across the Severn and into Bristol in dismal drizzle. We followed Exit 17 from the M5 down A4018 into Clifton, and found the Rodney Hotel without too much trouble. It is a pleasant old Georgian mansion, but it has no lift, and we were put in the attic, because the room up there was more commodious for the third bed. It was too much, especially with J's back, and we got ourselves moved to a slightly smaller room on the first floor. They are putting up all three of us for £50 a night, which I suppose is not too bad, though it will mount up!

We had a reasonably good dinner in the restaurant (except for some very soggy tagliatelle that we had to send back!), and then went for a pleasant stroll around Clifton, noticing fine old Georgian and Victorian houses, but also a remarkable amount of *For Sale* and *To Let* signs on the High Street.

DAY 3, TUESDAY, AUGUST 25TH

Up at 7.30 am or so, had a good (continental) breakfast, then headed up to Wills Hall,[94] to check it out (Clifton Downs is a pleasant piece of parkland, and the Hall is very splendid), and then set off to drive to Downside for the mid-morning, hoping that the Guest-Master had got my letter. We took the A37 towards Wells, and then got slightly lost, but reached, first, Chilcompton, then Stratton-on-the-Fosse, and then the Abbey – just on 11.00.

Our reception, I regret to say, was somewhat disappointing. A pleasant, but brisk, secretary type brought us up to the Bursar in the monastery, and he simply greeted us, and then went about

---

94 Wills Hall is one of the halls of residence of the University of Bristol, where our conference was based.

his business. First we went round the church, which is very splendid (I only dimly remember it from my time), and then back into the school (also dimly remembered), where a pleasant man met us and guided us to the Old House, where we met the Caverel House Master, who was pleasant, and who guided us over to the Barlow House Master,[95] who was also pleasant, and took me through some old school photographs. But no one so much as offered us a cup of coffee, never mind welcoming me back as the Prodigal Son. So I left feeling rather deflated, and vowing never to return.

We went on from there, through very uninteresting and forgettable Somerset countryside, to Bath for lunch. We parked in a parking structure and walked into the centre of town, mainly pedestrianised. I must have been in Bath before, but nothing was familiar. We found our way to the Pump Room, and the Roman Baths, and, after a snack in a café, went for a tour. They have laid it out very well, I must say, and it was most interesting, even for Mouse, but slightly spoiled for me by the fact that I suddenly became faint. At 3.30 we left, driving out *via* the Royal Crescent, a very fine piece of architecture, and got back to Wills Hall just on 4.30, in time for the welcoming ceremony and opening talk (the De Vogel Lecture) by Charles Kahn.[96] This was good, though Charles had omitted to distribute copies, which made things difficult for non-English speakers.

Hayden Ausland[97] found me at reception, so I had dinner with him (and Dmitri Nikulin[98]). He seems in excellent form,

---

95 My former House.

96 Charles H. Kahn (1928-2023) was a classicist and professor of philosophy at the University of Pennsylvania. His work focused on early Greek philosophy, up to the time of Plato. He had been helpful to me, back in the mid-1970s, by inviting me to complete a translation of Proclus' Commentary on the Parmenides begun by his colleague Glenn Morrow, and left unfinished at his death, which was duly published in 1987.

97 A former student of mine from Berkeley, and a man of some eccentricity. He subsequently gained tenure at Montana, and spent the rest of his career there.

98 Dimitri is a most interesting man, originally from Novosibirsk in Russia

and has a temporary position at the University of Montana at Missoula. The talk after dinner by David Robinson, on the new Oxford text of Plato's *Politicus,* turned out well.

Ruth and I came back to the hotel and found a pizza house in a street across the road, called 'The Cul de Sac'. I had a veal and mushroom dish, which was very mediocre, and Ruth had a good (she said) pizza. We returned to collect John, who was still at a meeting, so we strolled over to watch a game of squash, played by a very good girl and two opponents.

Also: around 9.00, Teresa Waugh phoned to say that Bron[99] had been taken to hospital in London, so our visit to Combe Florey is regrettably off. I hope it is not too serious.

DAY 4, WEDNESDAY, AUGUST 26TH

We drove to drop John at Wills College, and Ruth and I went to the zoo at 9.00 a.m. Bristol Zoo is really lovely. It's on a small scale, but beautifully laid out, with specialised flower beds – herbaceous, dahlias, Acer herb, etc. It is a small zoo, and they have been gradually moving some of the larger animals out to safari parks, in line with current thinking. No polar bears, They had a pair, but one died and the other was so miserable that they had to put it to sleep.

At 11.00 am we set off for Deirdre's[100] house. She lives about one hour's drive east of here, in a lovely old farm-house in a tiny village called Great Bedwin. Christine and Harley came along. The boys (very pleasant) and Ruth and I had a walk in the rain down by the river behind them (where there are lots of barges). Very pretty countryside, but we got soaked, as it lashed rain. Deirdre is in very good form. As we left, she was still trying to get Christine out, watched by a very patient Harley.

(he had helped to show me round during my visit to Moscow – see Ch. 1, above), but now working at the New School of Social Research in New York

99 That is to say, Auberon. It cannot have been too serious, though his health was far from perfect. He died in 2001.

100 That is, Jean's cousin, Deirdre Montgomery. Christine Downes, married to Harley Patrick, was another cousin.

The conference arranged a bus tour of Bristol in the evening (after we had all dined at the College). It was very enjoyable. Some very attractive buildings, especially a little street with its old cobbles down by the docks, where its timber-frame houses remain.

My talk went off OK, I think.[101] Luc Brisson couldn't be found for a quarter of an hour, so we started only at 9.15, which left us a bit short. Luc sort of summarised his thesis, which is pretty weird, so it left enough time for me to give most of mine. Question-time was a farce, unfortunately, taken up chiefly by Despotopoulos and Julius Tomin, the Conference Bores. Julius engaged me in lively conversation afterwards, on the evils of stylometry (in defence of his pet belief that the *Phaedrus* is Plato's earliest dialogue), and I then got from him a long and mad missive about his having been excluded from the conference because he was unemployed. He pretty well blackmailed Christopher into letting him in free. He is getting madder and madder, I'm afraid.[102]

The talks after coffee were OK, but a bit perverse, especially those of Tom Robinson and Eric Ostenfeld.[103] I had lunch with various people, Matthias Baltes,[104] Rosemary Sprague, etc. The rain came down heavily, making it unavoidable that I attended the discourse of Despotopoulos on 'Praxiologie'. In fact, very few turned up, only those like me who had nowhere else to sit. Incomprehensible nonsense ensued. A loyal Greek asked a question. He is an unbelievable character. I found him just before the talk explaining to an unfortunate lady behind the

---

101 I talked on 'The Neoplatonic Exegesis of the *Statesman*'.

102 Tomin was a rather dotty Czech scholar, who had represented himself as being persecuted in his home country, and was in consequence adopted by a number of Western Classical philosophers; but it turned out that the Czechs were quite right in their assessment of him, and he was generally dropped.

103 Eric Ostenfeld was Professor of Philosophy in the University of Aarhus, Denmark, and an authority on ancient psychology.

104 Professor of Ancient Philosophy in the University of Münster, and an old friend.

desk that he was the Vice-President and President-Elect of the Academy of Athens, and that this should be duly noted. She promised faithfully to do this.

More talks after tea, and then Mouse and Mummy joined us for dinner, and we went on an excellent tour of Bristol, by bus, as mentioned above.

DAY 5, THURSDAY, AUGUST 27TH

I only went up to the conference for the 11.00 meeting – or rather, for coffee beforehand, since there were only some Italian talks.

I made phone calls home to Celia, to find out about negotiations for the house in Offington Ave. [105] *The owners had a fit when they heard we had cancelled Cathal's surveying, and said they would* consider *the £148,000 offer we made, provided that we went ahead with the survey. This was duly done, and was, according to Celia, very devastating. All sorts of things are wrong. Now we have to think again.*

Mouse and I went shopping in downtown Bristol – first stop John Lewis, to try and buy some saucepans.

I also phoned the office, where I heard that Roger[106] had stormed in and out, leaving a trail of havoc. I will doubtless hear more of that next week. I went up to hear a series of workshop papers, which were not as interesting as I had hoped. What is actually happening is that a great deal of repetition and hot air is being uttered – characters from Caracas or Seoul coming in and re-inventing the wheel – young Italians reading rapidly in low monotones. But I suppose it all serves a purpose. For me, I'm afraid, the gossip is the only thing.

---

105 Celia Scott (née Gore-Grimes) is the sister of my brother-in-law, Anthony. We were in the process of trying to find a house in the Howth-Sutton area. Offington is a very attractive location, but we subsequently found a better deal on Howth Head. Cathal Crimmins was a cousin of Jean's, who was an architect. He subsequently helped to re-design the house that we bought (Katounia).
106 That is to say, our Professor of Classical Archaeology, Roger Wilson.

Had lunch with Livio Rossetti.[107] I agreed to send the Society a mailing list from the ISNS, since all members of the latter should logically be prepared to join the former.[108] Then I collected Hayden and Barry O'Donnell, and we went on a drive to the Cheddar Gorge. The weather was pretty foul, but the rain stopped long enough for us to walk from the car to the main cave, Gough's Cave, and do a tour of it. The Gorge is fine, but very touristical, as is the cave, but it is interesting nonetheless. I'm sure I came here from school, but I remember nothing. They have found more in recent years about human habitation, up to 7000 B.C. or more, and even traces of cannibalism! We bought a few cheddar cheeses as gifts, and then stopped off at the Butcher's Arms for a pint of cider, it being the drink of the place. The barman was actually rather rude about Mouse, but this only referred to the *front* of the bar, so we sat out at the back on a verandah, and it wasn't bad, despite the rain.

We drove past Wells (which looked lovely, but we had no time) into Bath for dinner and theatre. After we left Hayden and Barry at the train station, we parked, and went to find the theatre and somewhere to eat. We found a pizza place just beside it, and had good pizzas (for myself a pizza capricciosa, for the first time since Rome in 1960!). Then to the theatre, to *The Voysey Inheritance,* by Harley Granville-Barker, fresh from the Edinburgh Festival, and soon to hit London (it had been recommended by Christine). It was actually excellent – remarkably 'modern' (G-B was an admirer of Ibsen, it seems, as well as a great supporter of Shaw). It was billed as resembling the recent Maxwell scandal, but it is really more about a perennial problem of solicitors and clients' money. We had a box, and felt very posh!

And so back to Bristol, without difficulty.

---

107 Professor of Ancient Philosophy in the University of Perugia, and an authority, in particular, on Presocratic philosophy. I came to respect him greatly over the years, and have just contributed to a Festschrift in his honour

108 This refers to the International Plato Society, of which Livio was the upcoming President, and the International Society for Neoplatonic Studies.

DAY 6, FRIDAY, AUGUST 28TH

I went up to some talks in the morning, including Hayden's, which wasn't bad, and well delivered, but he was foolish not to have distributed texts in advance. We had been going to stay for lunch, but then decided, if we were going to go to Longleat, that we had better get going. So we slipped away at 12.30 or so. We had already checked out of the hotel (which was actually not too expensive in the end – £277 all in, including some expensive phone calls), and have booked into a farmhouse near the M4, where we need to check in around 6.30pm.

The usual sort of day, sun and thunderstorms, as we set off for Longleat, past Bath, between Warminster and Frome. It took us something over an hour. We feared it would be very crowded, on the beginning of a bank holiday, but not so. We started in to the animal park, rejecting a comprehensive ticket in favour of the basic £5 a head, and started our journey.

First we met the camels and the zebras. We were just getting out to consort with a camel, when a thunderstorm arrived. We fled to the car, and the camels all went and huddled under a tree. The zebras didn't seem to mind the rain much, though. Then on to the tigers (one beautiful white Siberian tiger 'sunning' himself on a bench), and a large pride of lions. Also a rhino, who wouldn't leave a certain tree alone, and had to be faced down by a keeper in a van. And then the *monkeys*. It was announced that the monkeys would want to climb on your car, but it wasn't noted that they liked *rubber*. One climbed up on us and set to work demolishing the left-hand windscreen wiper, before we drove on rather hastily.

All in all, it is very pleasantly laid out. We then drove up to the main part of the estate, to see what we might find. The first thing, unfortunately, was a very *bad* snack bar, where things were expensive, re-heated, and soggy (there was a restaurant in the castle, but we only saw that later). Afterwards, however, we visited a parrot show, which was great fun, and Mouse and I went on the Simulator, which gave us a hair-raising introduction to downhill ski racing at the Val d'Isère.

Then we toured the Castle itself, which is magnificent, with many treasures on display. Much of the magnificent décor, though, seems to date from the Victorian era, attesting to the continued prosperity of the Thynns, or Marquesses of Bath. It was built in 1580, though, about the same time as Trinity was founded. The Great Hall is more or less as it was when Queen Elizabeth I visited.

After that, it became time to find our farmhouse, Olivemead Farm, in Dauntsey, which we did without difficulty, the instructions being good. In general, there is not as much traffic on the roads as one might have expected for a holiday weekend. The farmhouse is most pleasant, though rather near the M4. Lots of room in the bedroom, anyhow, unlike the hotel. At the recommendation of our hostess, we drove over to dinner at The Three Crowns, in the neighbouring village of Brinkworth, which proved to be excellent – the best dinner of our tour! I had a steak with shrimps and stilton sauce, J had king prawns. Even Mouse got some nice pasta. And there were good desserts. They also served Murphy's stout, which I drank instead of wine.

DAY 7, SATURDAY, AUGUST 29TH

We spent a good night, except that we were rather hot under a duvet. Our landlady had fixed up a riding lesson for Mouse this morning at 9.30 – *possibly* a hack – so we drove over to a nearby stables, and left the Mouse to her devices, deciding to drive into Malmesbury (just five miles away) for an hour, to look around.

It is indeed a delightful old town, on the edge of the Cotswolds. We parked opposite the Abbey, and walked about a bit, mainly exploring the church itself, which is the remains of a monastery, once housing William of Malmesbury, and goes back to Saxon times. There are a number of nice old manuscripts in an upper room.

When we went back to collect Mouse, she was not entirely pleased, because she had not been let go out on a hack (too young), but had just been given a lesson in the arena. Still, better than nothing! We drove back into the Cotswolds, this time to Tetbury, a lovely old market town beyond Malmesbury, where we patronised a nice old hotel for a cup of coffee (but really to visit the loo), and then once again strolled about. This was an old wool-marketing town, and was rather overlooked by the Industrial Revolution. In general, one comes to realise, that in the English countryside, the last serious disturbance was the Norman Invasion (or in some cases, I suppose, the Civil War in the 1640 or so).

After Tetbury, we drove off to visit the Westonbirt Arboretum, one of the biggest in Europe, and certainly a magnificent collection of trees, though this wasn't the best time of year to see it. Acres and acres of walks. Mouse was suddenly unwell, so first I went for a walk, and then J did, while the Mouse rested in the car. But then she perked up after a bit, and we had quite a nice snack for lunch in the snack bar, and viewed the Visitor Centre, which had interesting data on rainfall. English rainfall in the first part of this year equalled the driest on record (1912, I think), but it has been making up for that since!

After the arboretum, we found a lovely little church at the village of Didmanton, and walked round there for a while, once again absorbing an interesting slice of English rural history, but then drove back to Bristol to catch a session of talks before dinner, since the weather wasn't very good (we had been lucky earlier). Back at Wills Hall, we got together with various friends for one last go round, notably Matthias, David Runia,[109] and Hayden, dined well enough, and left to go back to our farmhouse, which we found again without too much difficulty. We have fixed on an early start for tomorrow, being apprehensive about the roads.

---

109 David Theunis Runia (b. 1951) is a Dutch-Australian classical scholar and educational administrator who has worked in both Australia and the Netherlands. He is a major authority on the philosophy of Philo of Alexandria, and as such we have cooperated on various projects. He has served most recently as the Master of Queen's College at the University of Melbourne, but at this time he was still Professor of Ancient Philosophy in Utrecht.

DAY 8, SUNDAY, AUGUST 30TH

There was a storm during the night, and the day dawned pretty foul. We got going in good time, after a pleasant breakfast. It is a nice place, and she is a nice lady. We must remember it.

Once on the road, though, we encountered no trouble – the economy of Britain must really be in a bad way – and made excellent time into Wales, the weather cheering up all the while, so much so that we decided to divert ourselves, when we reached west Wales, by going to visit the Graham Sutherland Museum at Picton Castle, which proved fascinating. There was a good video to introduce one, and then an excellent collection of his works. I never knew much about him, thinking of him primarily as a portrait painter, but that is not so at all.[110]

And so on to the boat, which we boarded without trouble – it was actually rather empty – and had a fairly smooth crossing home. We reached the house about 10.00 All well.

---

110 Graham Vivian Sutherland OM (1903 – 1980) was a prolific English artist. Notable for his paintings of abstract landscapes and for his portraits of public figures, Sutherland also worked in other media, including printmaking, tapestry and glass design.

Vozdvizhenka Street Moscow

Seafront, Nice, France

St David's monastery, Euboea

John and Jean Dillon, South-West England, 1998

One of the churches at Kolomenskoye Park

St Basil's Cathedral, Moscow

La Canonica, near the ancient city of Mariana, Corsica

The "Touchdown Jesus', Notre Dame, Chicago

5. Second Visit to Moscow:

OCTOBER 16-22, 1993

My return to Moscow was occasioned by an invitation from my friend, Yuri Schichalin – my host from the previous visit (see above, Ch. 2) – to take part in a conference on the life and work of the Russian philosopher Alexei Losev, about whom I knew very little, but who was actually a most interesting figure.

DAY 1, SATURDAY, OCTOBER 16TH

I am now, at 1.30, seated in the aeroplane, an Aeroflot Tupolev 123 (a bit smaller than a 737), waiting to lift off. The day dawned cold and clear. Mummy and Mouse set off for Tigín[111] around 9.00, leaving me to lock up, and Katharine kindly came to collect me at 11.30 to take me to the airport.

    I am feeling rather guilty, but also rather defiant, as regards the College. Roger only really got back *yesterday* from Sicily,[112] and will start in on Monday (after hopping back to Oxford for the weekend), and Brian[113] only got back on October 1. I have been holding the fort all summer, and I need to goof off! I am also, however, feeling foolish, as going into a situation I know nothing of. As usual with things Russian, I know nothing of where I'm staying, where the conference is, when I'm speaking,

---

111 Our country cottage in North Cork, some way south-west of Mallow, in the hills.

112 My colleague Roger Wilson, the Professor of Classical Archaeology, who had an excavation in Sicily. He contrived to live in Oxford, while teaching for us!

113 My colleague Brian McGing.

or what section I'm chairing. At least, though, it is possible to phone Moscow these days, and I talked to Yuri this morning (apprising him that the plane will be stopping in Petersburg, and so will not arrive till 9.45). If he and Yelena can collect me, then presumably all will be well. I am provided with little nibbles to eat and so on, and various gifts.

I met Bill Coffey's friend Yuri, who is going back to teach, after yet another stint in Trinity. He is actually quite a cheerful bloke, and his English is now quite good.

3.53: Perfectly good lunch. Interesting flying over Sweden – a land of lakes! Weather clouding up, though. I am stuck with a watch that I don't know how to alter the time of – the new Casio – so I foresee interesting situations arising. The plane, I should say, is half-empty, which is not surprising. There seems to be quite a group of Irish students, though, heading, presumably, for a year or a term in Moscow, but rather late. Yuri said universities went back early in September.

5.48 Irish Time: Now *en route* for Moscow, after 45 minutes in Petersburg. We didn't even get off the plane, though, so I can hardly claim to have been there. It is dark, so I can only see lights.

I arrived duly in Moscow, but at 20.45, not 21.45. The girl in Aeroflot had wrongly calculated the true time difference! Fortunately, it took some time to get the bags – though customs was no problem – so I was only waiting about half an hour for Yuri and Yelena to arrive, which they duly did, right on time. I was approached by a number of sleazy taxi-men, but otherwise unmolested, though the airport is a rather miserable place to wait in, being rather run down.

Yuri still has the old banger of a Moskvich, but it seems to be running slightly better, if anything, so we made it back to the flat without incident. I (and Philippe Hoffman,[114] who is

---

114 Distinguished French ancient philosopher, then a member of the CNRS (as was I), but subsequently Directeur d'Études at the EPHE.

also here) have to stay with them for the first night, since our hotel place at the University only becomes available tomorrow. So, after some chat and a snack for me (too much, as usual), I bedded down in the study, and Philippe in the sitting-room – perfectly comfortably.

DAY 2, SUNDAY, OCTOBER 17TH

Up around 9.00 am, to find the day overcast but dry. Apparently it had been raining rather foully all yesterday, until I arrived in the evening. After a copious breakfast (omelette, bread and jam), Philippe and I went for a walk with Katerina Sergeyevna, who is in fine form (as is Fyodor, though he is a *bit* shaky), round the Novodevichy Convent, down to the Moskva River, and back through the Park to the Convent, which I am glad to view again.[115] It tries to rain a bit (and I have brought *no* rain gear – just my heavy overcoat), but then the sun actually comes out. Philippe and I called in on a Mass briefly, but KS stays outside, since she is wearing *trousers*. She talks animatedly about the *Putsch*,[116] characterising Rutskoy and his gang as horrible persons,

---

115 We are, I should mention, in the Luzhniki district, which means 'marsh', because it is low-lying, near the river, and was once marshy.

116 (From Wikipedia): "On 21 September 1993, Yeltsin, in breach of the constitution, announced in a televised address his decision to disband the Supreme Soviet and Congress of People's Deputies by decree. In his address, Yeltsin declared his intent to rule by decree until the election of the new parliament and a referendum on a new constitution, triggering the constitutional crisis of October 1993. On the night after Yeltsin's televised address, the Supreme Soviet declared Yeltsin removed from the presidency for breaching the constitution, and Vice-President Alexander Rutskoy was sworn in as acting president.

Between 21 and 24 September, Yeltsin was confronted by popular unrest. Demonstrators protested the terrible living conditions under Yeltsin. Since 1989, GDP had declined by half. Corruption was rampant, violent crime was skyrocketing, medical services were collapsing, food and fuel were increasingly scarce and life expectancy was falling for all but a tiny handful of the population; moreover, Yeltsin was increasingly getting the blame. By early October, Yeltsin had secured the support of Russia's army and ministry

and asserting that he tried this on because he was deceived into thinking that the army would join him – probably because of Yeltsin's hesitation.

We got back around 11.30, and then drove up to the University to register in our accommodation. The University is a monstrous pile, but quite graceful in a massive way, on a high bluff overlooking the city – a fine viewing point from the park in front of it – and the accommodation, which was originally for graduate students, is actually comparatively luxurious, I would have thought. One shares a bedroom and loo, but it is not *much* more Spartan than an Oxford or Trinity set, really. Stalin, who had it built after the War, plainly wished to coddle his approved intelligentsia.

We were introduced to our 'minders', two charming girls, who took our passports, and went off to register us, while we checked in to our rooms. Having done that, we drove home with Yuri, to a lunch of cabbage soup (with a lump of meat for Sunday), and *kasha* – very traditional! I learn something more about the great Losev.[117] For one thing, Madame Takho-Gody is his widow, so she would be particularly complimented by

---

of interior forces. In a massive show of force, Yeltsin called up tanks to shell the Russian White House (parliament building).

As the Supreme Soviet was dissolved, elections to the newly established parliament, the State Duma, were held in December 1993. Candidates associated with Yeltsin's economic policies were overwhelmed by a huge anti-Yeltsin vote, the bulk of which was divided between the Communist Party and ultra-nationalists. The referendum, however, held at the same time, approved the new constitution, which significantly expanded the powers of the president, giving Yeltsin the right to appoint the members of the government, to dismiss the Prime Minister and, in some cases, to dissolve the Duma."

117 Aleksei Fedorovich Losev (1893 – 1988) was a Russian philosopher, philologist and culturologist, one of the most prominent figures in Russian philosophical and religious thought of the 20th century. He had suffered considerably under Stalin, but had been rehabilitated. The conference was in his honour.

someone coming to celebrate her husband. Losev was a man of great productivity and wide interests. A pupil of Solovyev, of whom he has written an intellectual biography, he wrote about 500 books! He was interested not only in Platonism, but in the whole idealist tradition. He translated much of Plotinus, though, and Proclus' *Elements of Theology*, into Russian. He died only in 1988, at the age of 95! Yuri studied with him, in fact, but was saying that he found his superficial adoption of Marxism hard to take. I was inclined to defend the old boy, since he had spent time in Stalin's *gulags* in the '30s, and needed to survive, and Philippe adduced the case of Synesius, while I adduced Michael Psellus and Marsilio Ficino (Pico might have been a better example) as other men who had to compromise variously. The question became: 'When does the mask become the face?'

After lunch, with the sun definitely out, we took a drive in the old banger, driving past the poor White House, now blackened at the top (an impressive sight), and the TV station, also damaged, and guarded by a tank and a few soldiers. We drove on to Ostankino, the former *palazzo* of the Sheremetyev family (boyars), after whose estates the airport is named. This has been made into a fine museum, but is currently under repair, and we were only able to walk in the park adjoining.

When we came back into town, we poked our heads into Red Square, Yuri and Yelena complaining about the continued presence of the Mausoleum. There are constant plans as to what to do with Vladimir Ilyich – rather like the interminable debates about Nelson's Pillar, until the IRA solved the problem! We looked at a little church in a courtyard, in which Y and Y have a special interest, which is now being restored.

They were asking did I notice any difference from three years ago, and I must say there are striking ones. There is far more of a buzz now, I think, though the streets on a Sunday are still pretty empty. Lots of new little shops – even the old GUM seeming very modern, with concessions for Christian Dior and Benetton and so on. But the mismatch between salaries and prices is still dire. Yuri says that now a good academic salary is about 30,000 r. – but there are 1200 to the $, so that we are still talking about $25 a month, as in 1990, when it was 200 r., but 15 to the $. *Somebody* is making money, though, because the amount of Volvos, BMWs and Mercs driving around is impressive, and lots of people in the shops. Lots of reconstruction – even the roads are being repaired! Things are happening – and perhaps the putsch will help them along. There are beggars, though, and wide boys trying to sell you things, so things are plainly tough.

We then proceeded to the Pushkin Museum, for another tour (for me), but it is always a pleasure. This time I was particularly taken with the Coptic paintings from the Fayoum, as well as, of course, the French Impressionists and post-Impressionists. Yuri and I discussed the symbolic meaning of Picasso's magnificent *Acrobat on a Ball*. It is a symbol of Fortune.

Back then to more chat, and a copious dinner, laced with much vodka. We consumed the St. Kilian cheese, to much acclaim. Afterwards, I actually managed to phone home, and got Mouse and J, and asked them to call me back, but they obviously couldn't, and I couldn't get through again. But it was something.

Then around 11.00 Yuri drove us over the University, now in the pouring rain. I hope this isn't persistent, as I have no rain gear, thinking rather of cold than of wet.

DAY 3, MONDAY, OCTOBER 18TH (PONYEDYEL'NIK)

Slept comfortably enough, and woke up around 7.00 am. Since Philippe and I have to share the facilities, we have to pace each other, so I washed up early, deciding against a shower for the moment, which I may regret.

Characteristically, plans begin to change as soon as they are made. First, we are invited over for breakfast at 9.00, then a little later, and are led over at 9.15. In the hall, I meet Jim Scanlan (Irish by origin, of course), an elderly American scholar from Ohio State, and colleague of Allan Silverman[118], who is an expert on Russian philosophy, and a good man to tell

---

118 A former student of ours at Berkeley, now a rising young authority on Greek philosophy.

one about Losev. I have breakfast with him and Ysabel d'Andia, who has appeared. Very good to see her. Also J. M. Narbonne, from Quebec. Breakfast rather copious (bread, cheese, jam, buttermilk, cocoa, *kasha*, hard-boiled eggs), but in the *student* refectory, whereas Scanlan (who was a *student* here 30 years ago!) was rather hoping we would get into the *staff* refectory. He said he got very ill after a while eating in this refectory.

If I am not to put on half a stone, I will have to take serious steps. Back to our rooms, and then assembled at 10.15 to go over for registration – but plans changed again, and instead, some students took our particulars on the spot, including when we are leaving, which is important. No passports returned yet, though, and quite different students appeared to guide us.

Then Vitali Zadvornyi appeared, whom I had forgotten, but who had chauffeured us one day to the Institute last time we were here. He is Yuri's second-in-command at the Museum Greco-Latinum, as well as teaching at a *Catholic* Institute in the city (he is that rare bird, a Russian Catholic!). He brought us over to the Humanities Building to register after all – where we learned, among other things, that there is a conference fee of $150. This appalled Philippe and Ysabel, but actually it is *not* unreasonable by international standards, for board and lodging for a whole week. Anyhow, we didn't pay yet! We met *another* set of student guides, devoted once again to our service (one told me I was her *second god*, by reason of *The Middle Platonists*, which is her bible – I must get her phone number!), but no sign of Anna or my passport.

Now, however, around 11.15, Vitali proposed to take Philippe, Ysabel and myself – not Narbonne, for some reason – for a tour of the Kremlin, since our first engagement, really, is a memorial service for Losev at a church in the centre of town at 4 pm. It has been raining hard all night, but now it begins to cheer up, and we have hope.

After viewing the panorama of the city, we head off into town in Vitali's car (a Lada, again superior to that of Yuri), and park near the Kremlin. We still haven't changed any money, and Vitali insists on paying for everything. This time we visit the churches of the Kremlin (last time it was the Museum), and they are indeed magnificent. The sun came out, and lit up the golden domes, delighting Ysabel. She and Philippe have cameras – I as usual have forgotten to bring one, but a snapshot can never really capture these panoramas, I think.

We visited the Cathedral of the Dormition, the Cathedral of the Annunciation, and the Cathedral of the Archangel Michael where the Tsars are mainly buried (rows of coffins!). The frescoes and icons are quite overwhelming, and would need days to sort out, but certain items stand out, such as the iconostasis in Dormition, and the icon of the Virgin of Vladimir, though it is a copy, the original being in the Tretyakov Gallery. All these splendid buildings were put up in the early 16th century under Basil III, who employed *Italian* architects. The Annunciation Cathedral is delightful, being the Tsars' private chapel, more or less, and adjacent to the Palace.

After all this, we walked round the periphery, observing the towers, then greeted Lenin, who is still dominating the Square in front of the Presidium of the Supreme Soviet, where Mr Yeltsin is hard at work. Vitali indicated the place rather ironically, since he has no use for Yeltsin. We looked at the largest bell on earth, which broke when they tried to erect it, and the largest gun, which has never been fired, and then left to go and find a cup of coffee.

This it is now possible to do, though not in great comfort (one stands at the counter, and the coffee is not very good, but it is a start). We also had a villainous-looking bit of smoked fish on a piece of bread. At about 2.30, we drove down to Red Square, to visit the Cathedral of St. Basil – and Lenin, if we could get in to see him, but that was not possible; he has been sealed off. The Cathedral of Basil the Happy is a most extraordinary construction – built by Ivan the Terrible to commemorate his annexation of Kazan from the Tatars in 1552. It is full of little passage-ways and side-chapels, with delightful ornamentation – often flowers and vine-leaves rather than figures of saints. We spent rather too long there, and left ourselves only a few minutes to get to the memorial service for Losev in the Church of St Servius. In fact it was worse than that, since we ran into an appalling traffic jam around 4 pm, and finally parked the car and walked, arriving 25 minutes late for the service, which was about right, since it lasted an hour. Traffic is a serious problem in Moscow now.

The service was actually very pleasant. The little church was quite packed, a choir of five ladies sang antiphonally with the clergy, who looked as if they had stepped out of icons. Apparently Losev secretly became a monk in his later years (to balance his 'conversion' to Communism?), and he was being commemorated as a *monk* in this service.

After that, we set off once again with Vitali, this time to the Andronikos Monastery, last resting place of Andrei Rublev. There we strolled around in the twilight, visiting the church and his tomb, but not, unfortunately, the museum – too late!

From there we went home with Vitali to dinner, and were entertained most hospitably. He has a pleasant wife, and two daughters, of about 12 and 9, I should say. His wife is an interior designer, but speaks no French or English, so we could only make appreciative noises at her. There was also a pleasant young Jesuit, Fr François, who teaches at Vitali's institute, and has been here for some years. He drove us home, at about 10.30 or so.

A tiring, but most enjoyable, day.

DAY 4, TUESDAY, OCTOBER 19TH (VTORNIK)

We started off by heading over to the Humanities Building to see about attending the conference, getting there rather late because we misunderstood (?) Yuri and Vitali to say they would meet us at our lodgings. I proposed not waiting more than 15 minutes, and I was right. Once there, we were confronted with a problem. There is a $150 registration fee for the Conference. This includes everything, and is not at all unreasonable – for foreigners – but no one had told us, and Philippe certainly felt that Yuri had told him that there would be no charge, except our air fares. So he is not pleased. My problem is simply that they can't, or won't, accept cheques, and I don't have that kind of money. So we left the matter hanging, with mutual expressions of regret, and all went off once again with poor Vitali, who is today driving Yuri's car, because his own refused to start this morning, after its exertions of yesterday.

This time we headed off, first to change some money at a Post Office, where I changed $15, after the lady *rejected* four dollar bills, as being too tatty (very picky, I must say!), and then to Kolomenskoye, where Katerina had taken us the last time. It was lovely to see it again, though *not* in the snow, but with autumn colours. We explored all we could – one can't get into the churches, alas, but there is a small museum, and some wooden houses – after which we had a snack of tea and bangers on bread, which I hope do not prove disastrous! We also bought some presents on the way out: a matryoshka doll and a Palekh box – 6000 and 10,000 roubles respectively.

Back in town, we stopped at the Krutitskoye Podvorye, next to the Novospasski Monastery, which we just viewed from outside. It was the residence of the Metropolitan of Moscow, a 17th century haven of peace, quite neglected and seedy, but fascinating. I hope for its sake it is properly restored soon, but at present it is rather charming in its neglect.

From there on to the Tretyakov Gallery, to view the icons, and Russian painting in general. Poor Vitali is run off his feet, but very gallant. He finally got us home at 6.00, although Philippe chose to stay in town, stroll around some more, and come home on the Metro. Ysabel and I went to the refectory, and managed to cajole a dinner out of the staff for 550 roubles a head – a princely sum – comprised of sliced tomatoes, mashed potatoes, meatballs, a slice of cake, and tea. Not too bad. We had planned to get back for an early night, though when Philippe came back, we went out to find a soft drink at one of the booths in the main university building. Only next day did we discover that we had missed the showing of a film on Losev at 6.45. Ah well!

DAY 5, WEDNESDAY, OCTOBER 20TH (SRYEDA)

Today began the *serious* part of the expedition: Section I of the

Conference holds its first meeting! I went to breakfast with Philippe and Ysabel, and then straight over to the Humanities Building. The weather is holding up very well, I must say. No rain, really, since Monday night.

We arrived to find a suitable degree of confusion, but at least we are in the room we are scheduled to be in, and lots of young people have assembled to hear us. It is just as well that we visitors arrived, because the Russians are falling by the wayside. The first two speakers, Dobrokhotov (who took part in the last colloquy) and a Georgian named Djokhadze (who was to have spoken on Losev's treatment of Neoplatonism) failed to turn up, and Philippe was therefore on first.

His talk went on for about one and a half hours, and was very difficult for his *traductrice*, because he had not provided a text. Not a good idea. He spoke on the various interpretations of the subject matter of the *Categories* in the Neoplatonic commentators, which could hardly be expected to turn on the audience!

Then there was a dotty Byelorussian, with a straggling beard, who spoke engagingly, first about Losev and the Classics, and then increasingly about trends in Byelorussian philosophy! He asserted that for Losev, all Western philosophy seemed to consist of varieties of Neoplatonism — 28 varieties in all! We can't quite believe that.

Then a tall, solemn young man (A.I. Solopov) gave quite a good account of the semantic relationship of *pulcher* and *kalos* — again, rather technical, perhaps.

We adjourned, about an hour late, for lunch, over to a cafeteria in a building opposite. There we sat in solitary state, and enjoyed the normal diet — sliced tomatoes, soup (*borscht* this time), potatoes and meatballs, chocolate cake, coke and tea.

In the afternoon, a Georgian (who was to speak on John Patritsi) didn't turn up, so Ysabel spoke first, on Pseudo-Denis on the Divinisation of Man, then me, on the Ineffable in Damascius, then Yuri on *Epistrophe* in Damascius. My translator seemed very good — at least they laughed at my jokes — and we finished in just under the hour. This time we ended in pretty good time (some questions from Philippe and Jean-Marc), and then Yuri proposed a surprise visit to the Conservatory for a concert.

This turned out to be an evening of Rachmaninov Preludes, performed beautifully (in the Little Salon of the Conservatory) by a fellow called Diev, who looked rather like William Rushton[119], but played with great spirit. We had a little snack there beforehand. All was laid on because of Fyodor,[120] of course. 'We' included Philippe, Jean-Marc and Nicole Belayche.[121]

Yuri's car had developed a smoking rear tyre by the time we got to the Conservatory, but we got back safely to the University without any more manifestations.

DAY 6, THURSDAY, OCTOBER 21ST

Woke up this morning with laryngitis! Our third session was this morning, and again a Russian or two didn't show, but one lady stepped in, to give a talk on the rather dotty theme of Proclus' criticism of Plotinus' dualism in his essay De Malorum Substantia. I'll have to read the treatise now, to see if perhaps she's right.[122] Then Jean-Marc gave a useful talk on 'Self-Causation in Descartes and Plotinus', though it is a paper which has just been published. He is also just about to publish a book on Plotinus' metaphysics, and he has done a study of Ennead II 4 in a series edited by Jean Pépin.[123]

After Yelena gave quite a good paper on Homer and Plato in Maximus of Tyre, we had some questions. The whole thing rambled on until after 2.00, and meanwhile pressure was growing from our nice secretary lady, Irena, that I should somehow get hold of some *cash*, to pay the fee. It was arranged with a very efficient young man, Maxim, who spoke excellent English, that I should rush into town, to the Hotel Metropol,

---

119 British comedian, with whom I had been at Oxford.
120 That is to say, Fyodor Druzhinin, Yelena's father.
121 Distinguished authority on the religions of the Roman Empire, and a member of the École Pratique des Hautes Études.
122 She actually is largely right!
123 Plotin, Traité 25, Paris: Editions Cerf (1998).

and get money on my Visa card. However, Yuri insisted that I should have some lunch, and since I had arranged to meet Liz Cunningham at the Oktyaborskaya Metro at 4.00, the project was abandoned, and scheduled for tomorrow morning at 9.30. That will be rather tight, though.

After lunch, Vitali offered to drive me to the Metro, which was very decent, and we got there shortly after 4.00. However, there are actually *two* stations in the square (which is beside Gorky Park), and I was in confusion as to which to go to. There was no sign of her, so I spent some time at each, finally ending up at the first one at about 4.30. Just as I was giving up hope, she arrived with her boyfriend, full of apologies, very *Russian*, really! She is a graduate student under Ron Hill, but is here also as a representative of Greenpeace, and is hounding the government about dumping liquid nuclear waste into the sea off Japan.

After a glance at Gorky Park, it occurred to me that we just might go and have a coffee in the Metropol Hotel, and see if I could get my money. We took a taxi into town (for 3000r.), and entered the Metropol. It is a famous old hotel, just across from the Bolshoi Theatre, but has recently been refurbished to be super-luxurious, in the absurd way the Russians seem to do. There was *no* trouble about getting money, though there was a 5% charge. So I got $100 to add to my surviving $50, and that solved that problem. Afterwards we all had cappuccinos, at $4.50 a crack, and gossiped about the situation.

Then she had to go back to the office, and her boyfriend, a decent Dublin lad, who speaks nothing but a bit of Spanish, accompanied me to the Metro. On the way across the square, I turned my ankle on an irregular piece of pavement (of which there are many), and collapsed on the ground with an unprofessional oath, which amused him greatly. We sat on a wall until I felt well enough to hobble, and then I caught the metro out to Sportivnaya, which is the Shichalins' stop. The Metro is still in excellent shape, and I got out there in no time. After a rather grim walk, through darkened streets, I came gratefully upon the bulk of the Novodevichy Convent, and followed it along till I came to the apartment.

I arrived just before 7.00, and was welcomed warmly. My ankle was bound up by Yelena – this is now becoming a tradition – and I was given vodka and dried meat to revive me. Then the French Consul arrived – a most pleasant man (who is about to set off for Croatia) – and we had champagne and caviar and *Irish* smoked salmon, until the rest turned up, rather late. They had set off with one Yulia, a nice girl, to see a museum, but it was closed, and they shopped and walked around instead.

We had a most delightful evening, well feasted and drunk, until after midnight, when Yuri drove us back to the University.

DAY 7, FRIDAY, OCTOBER 22ND

Off to breakfast for the last time – the usual. Scanlan kindly gave me a box of pastilles for my throat, which is still bad, then Yuri came round at 11.00 to take me over to meet Professor Takho-Gody, at last. She was actually very pleased to meet me, seemed very grateful that I had come, and is quite a striking old lady generally. She presented me with a collection of her husband's essays, signed by herself, and we parted with mutual expressions of regard. I also handed over the $150 to the lady who wanted it. I hope they can digest the $100 bill!

Yuri left me back to the University, and we said goodbye, promising to be in close touch. They are a great pair, really – Yelena running the little school in her drawing-room, and Yuri battling away with his Museum Greco-Latinum. Just what Russia needs most at the present juncture!

Boris and a friend came very promptly to collect me at 11.00, and we set off on a *long* ride round Moscow to the airport, which is on the north-west of the city. I am oppressed by the endless vista of vast apartment blocks. It must be a soul-destroying way to live, especially since the surroundings of the blocks are largely undeveloped waste-lands. What a legacy Bolshevism has left!

No problem at the airport or on the plane. I viewed the Irish pub at the airport, but did not partake. Bought a bottle of vodka instead. Everything is too expensive. Once again, Aeroflot miscalculated the time, so I was an hour or so early. No great problem, though. Mouse and Mummy collected me after music, and we had a snack at the airport.

And so ended the adventure – except for the cold and sore ankle, which I expect I shall have for a while.

6. Trip to Corsica

JUNE 18 – JULY 3, 1994

This was a family holiday, designed to explore the island of Corsica, or at least the northern part of it, around the town of Calvi. We were accompanied by a friend from Howth, Elizabeth Ritchie. Jean's contributions are in italics.

DAY 1, SATURDAY, JUNE 18TH

We are leaving Ireland in rather dull, windy weather (after a few lovely days), just in time, before I collapse from multiple psycho-somatic ailments. A final strenuous day yesterday, when we appointed Roger's successor, Hazel Dodge (I hope wisely),[124] gave Roger a send-off party, and went to dinner with him in his favourite wine bar – before dropping in on the end of Mary Banotti's victory party.[125] But my pills saw me through, and I seem to be leaving in moderate shape. We had just spent the middle of the day with a pleasant Norwegian pair, the wife of whom Jean discovered in difficulties on Friday in the Bank of Ireland in Sutton. They have a splendid yacht, currently moored in Howth, and we hope to visit them some time in Norway.[126] I

---

124 Very wisely, I am glad to report! 'Roger', of course, refers to my colleague, Roger Wilson, Professor of Classical Archaeology, who had just deserted us for the University of British Columbia.

125 I think this must have been her re-election to the European parliament, for which she was a representative from 1984 to 2004. We would have first got to know her through her sister, Nora Owen, who was Fine Gael TD for North Dublin for many years.

126 This never came about, sadly.

have agreed to take *no* work with me, but I hope I will not regret that. I am bringing loads of novels and so on.

11.15, at Atwood's Guest House, Newdigate:[127] Here in the heart of rural England! We had a delightful dinner in the local pub, the Six Bells – very pleasant weather – Pimm's out in the garden. Then back to the guesthouse to watch the second half of the big match with Italy.[128] We were 1–0 at half-time, and held that score till full time, against great attacks by the Italians – and we almost scored again, in fact. The celebrations at home must have been wild!

DAY 2, SUNDAY, JUNE 19TH

We set our alarm for 4.45 a.m. I had put my back out the night before, just bending down to get something from the floor. I hardly slept, in spite of a comfy bed, but John and Ruth did. They were supposed to leave our breakfast outside our door, but someone else took ours by mistake. My back is pretty bad, so when we were taken to the airport to check in for Calvi we requested a buggy, and got it! The best thing we ever did, as it was miles to the plane. It left almost 1 ¾ hours late (at about 9.20), and we were surprised that it was a tiny plane. But we had a really comfortable journey, with hardly a bump. We flew into Calvi over a lovely coastline – though it was a little blurred, because of a slight mist.

The aromatic scent of Corsica hits you as soon as you get off the plane – all the herbs, both wild and cultivated, in the countryside![129] *The temperature is perfect, because there is a cool breeze. The hotel is cute – the St. Erasme – perched high overlooking the bay. Our balcony overlooks the swimming pool, and to reach it you pass through a lovely little courtyard filled with oleander, geraniums, pine trees and cacti. As I write this, Ruth has already found a friend – the daughter of the house, aged 10 – and is flopping round the pool with her. I suppose I'll eventually have to pluck up the courage to go down and swim, but I'm in no hurry for now – it's too nice on the balcony.*

---

127 It is not spelled out here, but we must have flown over to Gatwick, and then found lodging in this pleasant village nearby.

128 This would be the famous football match in the 1994 World Cup. That day has been remembered many times since!

129 The technical term for this is the *masochia*.

4.20: We've all had wonderful swims in the pool — except Elizabeth, who seems just as happy sunbathing. Ruth spent a couple of hours in the pool with the little girl (Marianne). We did anoint her with creams, but I hope they'll suffice to keep away the burns. I'm back on the balcony, and John is having a siesta. The back is much better, but I get the odd twinge, so I must be careful.

8.30: We're now sitting in a little pizzeria in the town, L'Oasis, which is cheerful and not expensive (about 45 fr for a pizza). It is a delightful little town, and very manageable. We walked down, and round the town, and looked at shops, and the Citadel (though without going in). We finally settled on a restaurant recommended by our proprietor, and found its pizza excellent, but its bottle of Corsican rosé, at 68 fr, rather *bad* value.

On the whole, though, this is an excellent place, and this holiday a good idea. We strolled home, resisting the temptation to stop for Corsican songs in a local bar. Perhaps later in the week!

I have already finished *The Remains of the Day* (delightful), and started on Holroyd's *Bernard Shaw* and Muriel Spark's *Memento Mori*. I find it difficult, though, to be without *anything* Classical.

DAY 3, MONDAY, JUNE 20TH

Woke up quite early, to quite a brisk wind – later identified with the *Libeccio*, a south-west wind, which we hope will drop in due course. It keeps the temperature down into the mid-20s, though, which is perhaps no harm.

We had breakfast by the pool – the usual coffee, croissants, bread. After some time, Mouse and Elizabeth emerged, and we decided to explore the port this morning. First we climbed up to the citadel and viewed the port, losing Jean in the process, since climbing is difficult for her with her back. The citadel, by the way, was built by the Genoese in the Middle Ages, and is still obviously inhabited by someone. We then went down to the port and viewed the yachts. There are some very splendid motor yachts – even American and Canadian ones. I worked my way back and found Jean near the beginning of the main street.

I bought a sausage of the country, and we went back to eat it for lunch. It is not at all bad, though I don't know what it is made of. The wind continues quite strong, but it is still delightfully warm.

After a siesta, J and I walked up the road, and discovered, first, an interesting pizzeria, open-air, with a view of the sea, and then a good swimming-place, down from the Oasis camping site, where there are flat rocks and a sheltered bay. We must return there.

In the evening, we decided to drive to the pizzeria, *U Fanale*, and found it excellent. I had the *tarte aux oignons*, J the *omelette aux lardons*, Mouse a basic pizza – all very good, and the bill came to around 240 fr, including Elizabeth's pizza.

DAY 4, TUESDAY, JUNE 21ST

Again, rose about 8.00, and roused Elizabeth and Mouse, because, after breakfast, we decided to take the little train up to Ile Rousse, and view the coastline. I also need some money, having got through the first 800 fr. We got out of the hotel about 9.15, in some fuss, and decided we must make straight for the train, and change the money later. In fact, there was no trouble about finding the train, and we boarded in good time – just as well, as any later we mightn't have got a seat.

The little train is very much the West Corsica Railway (*"Êtes vous prêt là, Michel, êtes-vous prêt?"*)[130], and rattles along from one resort to another, stopping if anyone wants to (*arrêt facultatif*), except at Lumio, Algajola, and Ile Rousse. We went all the way to Ile Rousse, to catch the morning market, proposing then to stop off on the way back at any place that caught our fancy – Algajola and S. Restitud in particular did – but we ended up sitting or lying sufficiently long on the beach at Ile Rousse that we didn't need any more diversion. The market was something of a disappointment, in that the produce seemed very expensive – honey, cheese, sausages, olive oil, all no cheaper than Dublin, really! The oddest item was a sausage made of *âne*, which as far

---

130 A reference here to Percy French's song about the West Clare Railway.

as we can comprehend means 'donkey'. Anything, I suppose, is possible, for people who eat *horse*.

Mouse wished to shop, so J accompanied her, but Elizabeth and I headed for the beach. In fact we found a quiet corner at the town end, and settled down. I ventured into the sea, which was pleasant and clean enough, but there were *bits* in it. Around 1.00, Mouse and Mummy arrived, as we anticipated, and we headed up to the square and had a coffee (and a *pastis* for me) under the statue of Paoli.[131] Then back to catch the 14.05 train. We had had enough sun, so decided not to stop on the way back. The little train lurched along, quite full, past all the resorts (including an army camp and a tennis centre), and we got home, slightly unwell, at about 3.00.

Home, then, and settled round the pool, until it was time to go down again to *U Fanale* for dinner. Watched Argentina thrash Greece 4 – 0 (Maradona scored).

DAY 5, WEDNESDAY, JUNE 22ND

I had a rather disturbed night – the oesophagitis came back mildly, probably because of a salad I ate. However, I recovered, and after breakfast walked down with J and Mouse to 'shop'. I gave up, however, after the first shop, where I was left standing in the street for a quarter of an hour, and went up round the citadel instead, which was restful. There is less wind today, and it seems to have gone round to the north, but there is still quite a swell. The yachts are out in force. It is taking time to tune oneself down, to simplify life to the level of Katounia or Fallen Leaf,[132] but I am getting there. I proceeded slowly back, and settled down to Holroyd's Shaw; an excellent work. I also sketched plans for the Ethiopian novel, and for a book on Liberalism in Irish Politics.[133]

---

131 Pasquale Paoli (1725 - 1807), Corsican statesman and patriot, who was responsible for ending Genoese rule of Corsica and for establishing enlightened rule and reforms.

132 Fallen Leaf Lake, a favourite resort of ours in the Sierra Nevada, just south of Lake Tahoe, back in California days.

133 The first plan eventually emerged as *The Scent of Eucalyptus*, published

DAY 6, THURSDAY, JUNE 23RD

Went to the rocks to swim today, John (and Ruth, a little) went snorkelling — J says it's fascinating. I swam, but won't put my face under. Ruth prefers the hotel pool. There aren't very many decisions to make in the day — e.g. pool, rocks, table in shade, visit to town (7 minutes away).

Ruth and I went to the supermarket by the back road from the hotel. There are some lovely gardens here. We stopped to admire one of them, and the lady who owned it invited us in to have a better look. She then asked us (luckily I understood French) what time we were returning from town. We said in about an hour, and she said she would leave a bunch of lavender at her gate for us. After our shopping, we found a beautiful bunch awaiting our return. Back at the hotel, I wrote her a note in my best French to thank her. When Ruth delivered it later, she was delighted, and thanked her warmly.

J and I stayed in the hotel and ate cold quiche and fruit and cheese for dinner, while Ruth and Elizabeth went to U Fanale. After dinner, Ruth, J and I went down the town to hear some Corsican music in a bar. We had a couple of beers, listened for a while (music a bit melancholic), and then returned to the hotel and watched the Italians beat the Norwegians in the World Cup. We didn't sleep well, as it was very hot, and a mosquito bothered us.

DAY 7, FRIDAY, JUNE 24TH

Rose early, and joined Elizabeth for breakfast at around 8.00. Then I went off to the rocks with the goggles, and had a splendid cruise around, chasing shoals of fish. Another very hot day in prospect, since there is no wind. Up in the 80s, certainly.

After returning, I walked down to the town and changed 1000 fr – this time at the bank, without any percentage charged. I came back with a bag of beignets (17 fr), which proved rather disappointing, and four postcards, @ 1 ½ fr. We had a little lunch, of sausage, cheese and bread (anything at the hotel is vilely expensive, unfortunately – coffee at 16 fr!), and then read for a while. I am getting through the Shaw biography – excellent, but solid going. Then a siesta, for a few hours.

Then we settled down at 6.30 pm to watch the Ireland –

---

in 2006 (2nd ed. 2019); the second plan never materialised.

Mexico match. Alas, we were not in great form. They scored just before half time (Garcia), and then again shortly into the second half – and they had other chances. John Aldrich came on and scored before it was over. But we are in trouble. The showdown is on Tuesday. We watched the second half down at *U Fanale,* where we had another good dinner. I had the pork this time, J a seafood pizza.

Another hot night. The Mouse ended up with us on the floor. She is rather burned, and feeling sorry for herself.

DAY 8, SATURDAY, JUNE 25TH

Up early. Decided not to go to the rocks, since my shoulders are a bit stiff. Am looking forward to a trip to mountain villages in the afternoon, booked by Ann Bunning.[134] Everyone else went down to an alleged market near the station, but there wasn't one. I stayed home and read – Shaw and Heisenberg. A most interesting perspective on early Greek philosophy, for one thing. J bought two plates, despite the lack of market, and some provisions. In general, though, the local produce is rather expensive. I suppose we'll end up bringing back some honey, cheese or olive oil, but I'm not sure that it's worth it.

At 2.00 we went down to the circle to wait for our bus, but no bus came. At 2.30, J went up to phone the bus company, and we learned that no message had got through that we were to be collected. I was enraged, and sent out a stiff message though to Ann Bunning's answering machine, and went off to have a *pastis* and coffee in the town. I found a game of boules in progress beneath the citadel, and settled down to watch that, but I am annoyed that my malady is coming back.[135] I bought the *Herald-Tribune,* and read that thoroughly.

When I came back, I found that Ann Bunning had come round, in great anxiety, and explained that *she* had given the message, but there was a new girl there, and she obviously hadn't passed it on properly. The bus company was also distressed,

---

134 Ann Bunning would seem to have been our local travel agent.

135 Presumably the oesophagitis; or perhaps my back.

since the driver had *known* there were three more people to go, but he didn't know where they were, and he drove round various hotels, but didn't think of the St. Erasme. Anyhow, they apologised, and have offered to take us again next Saturday, and give us one *free* trip!

Out to *U Fanale* once again – not a very enterprising choice, but an excellent dinner. We had a last collogue with our Scots friends, Alan and Tina Aird, who recommended a drive to Calenzana, and warned against one to Porto. They are off home tomorrow.

DAY 9, SUNDAY, JUNE 26TH

We had a plan to go to 10.30 am Mass in the little church, but dithered so long that we were late (Elizabeth had gone yesterday evening at 6.00 pm, and found it very stifling), and we then, since it was quite overcast, decided on a walk up the road, to the top of the pass at the base of the peninsula to the south. It was a delightful walk, in fact, and I was quite pleased that I could make it, after an initial twinge. We walked for about an hour, right out into the country, amid a succession of intrepid cyclists, RVs, and even joggers. On the way back, we called in to an apparently deserted hotel, which declared that it was "ouvert tuote l'année", but which had a tennis court (no net, though). We couldn't find anyone to talk to, so we gave up.

Back at the hotel, we had a swim and roost round the pool, since the sun had come out. Then something of a siesta. Afterwards we walked down to town for a coffee and beer in the café beneath the citadel, to watch the citizens at boules. This was most entertaining, but we were charged rather more than I expected – over 80 fr. I had been very pleased with 14 fr for an espresso and pastis the last time.

Following on this, we took a walk round the citadel, which was delightful – the *inner* part this time, not just the battlements. It is quite a little town on its own in there – and not *too* commercialised or boutique-y. People live there, and carry on their lives – though it must be quite unpleasant in July or August. Not too bad just now, though, even on a Sunday evening.

After that, we decided to stay in town and explore another restaurant, feeling a bit hidebound by *U Fanale*. We chose a little place in the open air (actually it has commandeered a public passage-way), just off the main street, called *U Fornu*, and that proved very pleasant. I had a full Corse menu, for 100 fr – *charcuterie*, a veal stew, *estofado*, and cheese-cake. J had the bean soup, Elizabeth a warm goat's cheese salad, and Mouse – wait for it! – a pizza. All proved excellent, and very filling. The veal stew was with olives and mushrooms – and lots of them!

Then up the *Crêpe Bretonne* for a crêpe for Mouse. We had coffee, and I tried a white Cap Corse, which was very pleasant – a sort of dessert wine.

And so home to bed.

DAY 10, MONDAY, JUNE 27TH

This morning we have decided to break loose with a *car*, and drive to the Roman ruins of Aleria, on the other side of the island. Down to Avis by 9.30, took out a little Renault Clio without any trouble (through Corsican Places – just provided a credit card as deposit for the petrol), and drove off. We came back to collect the Mouse – Elizabeth wouldn't come – and set off across the island.

The roads were actually fine. We headed north past Île Rousse, then across to Ponte Lecchia, then down to the east coast south of Bastia. It was a fine new road recently completed, with only about 5 km still a bit rough, and then down the east coast to Aleria, where the road is perfectly good. We first, though, dropped in to the 12th century cathedral of La Canonica, beside the Roman settlement of Mariana, some of which has been excavated. The cathedral is pretty austere Romanesque, but quite impressive. Some work is being done on it, and various workmen were having their lunch or snoozing in the sun, giving an impression of furious industry! I should say that the weather has been perfect for travelling – not too hot, and partly cloudy, though sunny enough to be pleasant.

We got to Aleria around 1.00, and had to search a bit for the Roman site, which we finally found on a hill to the south of the modern town, and rather surprisingly inland – but the coastline may have changed, and anyhow this is the *citadel*, not the port.[136] There is now a little settlement adjacent to the site, round a 14th century Genoese fort, which has become the Jerôme Carcopino Museum (was Carcopino Corsican?).[137] We had a perfectly foul cup of coffee, and then toured the site – basically the forum and baths, Capitol and Temple of Rome and Augustus. Obviously there is much more to be uncovered.

On the way back, I prevailed on J to head up into the mountains to Corte, billed as the 'nationalist capital of Corsica' (it was the capital of an independent Corsica for 14 years in the 18th century). The first part of the road was pretty bad, but it got better half way up, and the views up the valley were spectacular. Corte is a funny old town, though not *enormously* romantic. We walked up the main street, having parked in a fine square, and 'shopped'. I found a delightful old wine shop, smelling strongly of its wares, but didn't dare go in and taste. We still haven't explored the top Corsican wines, I must confess, but I doubt that they can be up to much.

While we were exploring Corte, there was a thunderstorm, and quite vigorous rain. The clouds had been threatening all day, and now we drove back to Calvi in varying degrees of downpour.

DAY 11, TUESDAY, JUNE 28TH

Ruth decided to stay in the hotel, having discovered an English couple (he a

---

136 The city was actually founded by Greeks from Phocaea in 566 B.C., but then taken over by the Etruscans, and subsequently the Romans. Most of what survives, naturally, is Roman. It is somewhat inland from the sea, since the coastline in antiquity was marshy and malarial.

137 Jérôme Carcopino (1881 – 1970) was a French historian and author. He was the fifteenth member elected to occupy seat 3 of the Académie Francaise, in 1955. He was in fact born in France, but as son of a Corsican doctor, whose family was related to Napoleon.

correspondent with the Independent, Tony Barber, she Pauline). They have a one-year-old baby girl, and Ruth likes minding her. J and I set off in the car, first of all up to see the little church perched on a hill looking across at Calvi, from where there is a panoramic view of the surrounding countryside which is quite spectacular. We then drove in the direction of the forest, in spite of clouds over the mountains. We stopped on the way to view the beautiful Auberge La Signoria, where Philo and Des[138] stayed (or at least had dinner). It is set in the most beautiful gardens. We met the chef, who is going for a spell to Ballymaloe. We then headed off to the forest, which was a nice drive, with not too many hazardous turns, and arrived in drizzle, so decided, since neither of us was dressed for rain, not to walk.

We drove back via Calanzano, which is given very little attention in the guide, but which is a very delightful town, with a lovely main square and fascinating little side streets, going en toutes directions. We tried to find the restaurant recommended to us by the Scottish couple, Alan and Tina, and think we found it, but it didn't seem to be serving food, or else we were late for lunch (2.30!).

We arrived back to the hotel around 3.00, to find Mouse away at lunch with the Barbers (!), and Elizabeth sun-bathing. At about 5.45, John dropped Elizabeth and me at the church on the hill, and we set off to walk down the hiking trail towards Calvi, and so back to the hotel. Ireland was playing Norway in the World Cup, so we went to U Fanale to see it on their telly. It started late, so we came back to the hotel to see most of it. It was a draw, but we still go through to the next round.

DAY 12, WEDNESDAY, JUNE 29TH

This morning, J and Elizabeth first drove down to Super-U, to make certain practical provisions for bringing home, and then we took the car back to Avis at 9.30. No problem, and we will collect the car (or *a* car) again at 11.30 on Saturday. It is an economical little car – we filled it up for 176 fr. (5.7 per litre), and it is a quarter full still, after 500 km or so. Petrol is expensive, though. The car is costing £75.20 a day.

We walked slowly back through the town, looking at shops, and going past the waterfront, stopping to admire the remarkable old trees at the boules ground – quite rare, it seems, and ancient. When we got back, I decided to explore the rocks

---

138 Our friends Des and Philo Peelo, from Sutton.

below the hotel. They are actually accessible, but not as pleasant on the whole as the rocks at the Oasis. I settled down on a sloping rock, and then slipped in. The underwater rocks were quite interesting, some fish, but not as well populated as the others. Rather difficult to get out of the sea, though, and the climb up was tedious.

We lunched on sausage and cheese (from the little man up the road), and then had a powerful coffee from the hotel, which precluded much of a siesta. I read the Shaw biography and Heisenberg.

Up to U Fanale again for the evening. There is a nice couple at the hotel, Pauline and Tony Barber (with baby Madeleine), he being the Eastern Europe correspondent for the London *Independent,* and a most interesting fellow. Mouse took to them immediately, took charge of Madeleine, and went out to lunch with them. Later she babysat Madeleine most of the afternoon, in and out of the pool. They went to dinner in town, and Mouse very much wanted to follow them, but we vetoed that. Once again, a good dinner (I had a kebab of lamb), and we watched some good football.

DAY 13, THURSDAY, JUNE 30TH

Everyone else up early, to go and find a market. There turned out to be no market, which was probably no loss, since it would have been either junk or very expensive. As for me, I went to the rocks, and had a very pleasant cruise around them. Quite a few people turned up, some snorkelling, but I found a shaded corner, read, and watched the life of lizards, who came and looked at me. There was black one, a green one, and an (ordinary?) striped one. They all had time to stop and contemplate me for what must have been a long time to them, before hurrying on their ways.

Then it got crowded (though chiefly with an *older* set), and I set off for home, but met J half way up the road, and so we walked down via U Fanale for a morning coffee before going back.

Mouse headed off to lunch at U Fanale with the Barbers,

who seem fascinated by her (heaven knows what she has been telling them!), and then they came back and sat around the pool, Tony in the shade as he is not a *sun* person (not a *water* person, either). I went down the town to change the last 1000 fr., succeeded in doing that without trouble, and then came back and talked a while with Tony about the future of Russia and the Ukraine, which he finds pretty awful.[139] He lived in Moscow for three years as Reuters Correspondent, overlapping with Conor O'Clery,[140] whom he liked.

For dinner we headed down to the town, to a restaurant just in front of the church, where J and I had Corse menus, and Elizabeth another goat's cheese salad. I had Corse crudités, and a rich pasta dish, J a wild boar paté and a rich potato dish – and we both felt *stuffed*. We also had a reasonably good Patrimonio wine. It all came to something more than we are used to (around 360 fr.), but not bad.

Mouse found little friends to play with, on the steps of the church, and whiled the time away in this way.

And so back to watch more football. A hot night!

DAY 14, FRIDAY, JULY 1ST

The weather has now become extremely hot. A gentleman round the pool yesterday who had a watch that measured the temperature declared that at the poolside it was 113° – a bit extreme, perhaps, but not impossible. It is certainly in the mid-90s, in the shade. I just sat under the trees, and finished off Shaw. Mouse is somewhat sunburned, but is surviving remarkably well.

It is a day when one did nothing all day, and then relaxed in the evening. We went down to town, and bought an assortment of pies and stuff, and had a dinner in our room. Even the balcony was too hot.

We ended up watching *Colombo* in French on TV.

---

139 This is remarkable, in view of what has happened much more recently!

140 *The Irish Times* correspondent, with whom I had some contact when I was there. See above, p. 30, 37, 52.

DAY 15, SATURDAY, JULY 2ND

Yet another hot day, with very little wind. We sat quite a while gossiping over breakfast, and then I headed off with Elizabeth to the rocks for a final swim. Mouse and Mummy came along too after a while, and Mouse actually got in and snorkelled, which was something of a victory. Then we realised it was after 11.00, and I had to go for the car. We hurried home, and then down to Avis, and got another Clio, but this time, unfortunately, without a sun-roof.

J and I set off (Elizabeth and Mouse wouldn't come) to see if we could get to St. Florent, and visit the wine country of Patrimonio, but unfortunately the road over the mountains proved so alarming that we gave up after about 6 km. We had just breasted the ridge, and looked down on the Désert des Agriates (which is certainly very grim), but the bad road seemed to go on for ever, and we realised that, even if we got there, we would have to *come back*. So we retreated, and found our way instead to the beach at Locari, where we had a beer and sandwich in a nice little beach bar. Lots of French children and their parents disporting themselves. Mouse would have loved it.

Then we decided to see if we could find the Ladies' Final at Wimbledon on anywhere, among the bars at the port of Calvi. Fortunately one bar had the initiative to show it, so we settled down to have a coffee and watch Concita Martinez overcome the Navratilova in a very good three-set match.

Dined for the last time in U Fanale.

DAY 16, SUNDAY, JULY 3RD

We set off reasonably early, to drive down the spine of the island to the airport at Ajaccio. Elizabeth was initially frozen with terror, but she cheered up. Fine views of the mountains on the way. We got to Ajaccio in excellent time, but it was very hot (over 100°), and there wasn't much to do. Museums and shops were all closed. We found a rather overpriced café on the seafront, and had a modest lunch. Then we drove out into the country for a while, but found little of interest except a riding stables, and it was *very* hot. So we drove the car to the airport and handed it in.

As we feared, the plane was *greatly* delayed, so our change of venue did us no good whatever. We got back to Gatwick just minutes after the gates closed for our flight to Dublin, and we had to spend another night at our nice guest-house, Atwoods, which fortunately had rooms available. And, through Elizabeth's wangling, we got onto a flight the next morning *at no extra charge*. So it all ended reasonably happily – though I almost had a heart-attack the previous night, when we missed our flight.

7. The Philo Expedition (Notre Dame, Chicago, Berkeley):

NOV 15-25, 1994

The purpose of this excursion was, first of all, to attend a meeting in the University of Notre Dame, called by Professor Gregory Sterling, to establish a new series of editions of works of the Jewish philosopher, Philo of Alexandria, for whom I have long had a special affection; then to attend a meeting of the American Academy of Religion in Chicago, in which there was a Philo section; and lastly, to return to Berkeley to attend a small colloquium in celebration of my esteemed former colleague, David Winston, head of the Centre for Judaic Studies in the Graduate Theological Union, adjacent to the university.

DAY 1, THURSDAY, NOVEMBER 15TH

Now cruising half-way across the Atlantic, just south of Greenland, at 8.06 am Chicago time. Had a good lunch. My back is very stiff, but otherwise not feeling too bad. I was up at 5.15 am, and caught the plane to Amsterdam without trouble. It was pleasant to see dawn coming up over Europe. A clear day in Holland – a good impression of the wateriness of the landscape, and of the pleasant architecture of even apartment blocks and factories.

I met David Runia[141] at the flight. As I thought, there really was only one flight – it is just that KLM and NWO are in

---

[141] David Runia, distinguished Philo scholar, was at this time Professor of Ancient and Mediaeval Philosophy at Leiden University.

partnership, and one can book with either of them. I am with NWO, he with KLM. We exchanged our papers, and are already deep in argument about the creation of the world.[142] He is now well-established at Leiden, but had to struggle for two years to bring the department back from chaos, it seems. He is suffering a bit from a groin hernia, but is otherwise in good form.

We agreed that it is good to get away for a while. I was feeling rather guilty, but on the other hand I need this sort of excursion now and again. Things are a bit fraught in the office. I need to think. The recent announcement of a job in Ancient Philosophy in Princeton is unsettling, somehow. I don't want to walk out on Trinity, but are they prepared or able to provide proper support and intellectual stimulation? It is annoying to go off just as the government may or may not be about to fall. Could Albert ever pull off a reconciliation? Only, presumably, by he himself, or Harry, or both resigning – and that's not his style. And then, will Mary have the imagination to refuse a dissolution? And if not, were Mary Banotti and Nora serious about suggesting that I go forward in Dublin North-East? Have I blown it by heading off to the U.S.? Or am I fantasising?[143]

A long haul to Chicago, but smooth enough. I couldn't even doze, unfortunately. The film was *The Mask,* which was enjoyable again. They also have a computerised projection of the route on the video screen, which is nice, except that we *crept*

---

142 David was at this time at work on an edition of Philo's treatise *On the Creation of the World.*

143 Basically, I am fantasising here, but it does indicate how seriously I was involved in politics at the time. The political crisis arose from the fracturing and eventual collapse of Taoiseach Albert Reynolds' governing coalition between Fianna Fail and the Labour Party, arising from the perceived misbehaviour of the Attorney General, Harry Whelehan, with whom we were acquainted. However, no election was called, on the initiative of the president, Mary Robinson, and as a result, a new government was formed between Fine Gael, Labour and Democratic Left, the first (and to date the only) such change in government in Ireland's history, so the question of my running for Fine Gael in Dublin NE did not arise.

across Northern Canada, so it seemed, in the latter part of the journey. The weather was excellent in the Chicago area, though, and we came in across the lake with a fine view. I am glad to say that I suffered no trouble with my ears on this trip, though I had coffee, and a Bloody Mary!

We had an hour to spare at O'Hare, so we had a beer and chatted, and then got on a small American Airlines plane for the short hop across the lake to South Bend. We were collected duly by Greg Sterling, and driven to the Morris Inn, where I had stayed before, and which is indeed a delightfully comfortable place.

We met David Winston and Tom Tobin[144] just arriving as we got there, having driven in from Chicago, so we all retired for a short wash and brush up before dinner. David is looking well and cheerful. He is going to retire in June.

I had a welcome bath, and changed – the shirt was rather smelly, I'm afraid, after a day on the plane. I also phoned home, rousing a rather sleepy Jean and a more lively Mouse. No great excitement there. The government hasn't yet fallen, anyhow. Then I went down to dinner in the Inn. A typical American Mid-West menu! We asked what was for dinner, wanting to choose the wine, and the waitress said 'salmon and beef'. So I chose white, but the salmon and beef – and a bit of *lobster* – all came on the same plate! It was actually very tasty. Various others came in to dinner: Stephen Gersh, Gretchen Reydams-Schils.[145] I was talking mainly to a young man from the Philosophy Department, David O'Connor[146], who did his Ph.D. in Stanford under Julius Moravcsik,[147] on Aristotle. He

---

144 Thomas H, Tobin, S.J., Professor of Theology at Loyola University, Chicago, and a considerable authority on Philo, among many other subjects.

145 Both members of the Notre Dame faculty, then as now – Gretchen a considerable authority on late Roman philosophy, Stephen on late Greek and Christian thinkers.

146 He is still there, I am interested to note, now as a full professor.

147 Julius Moravcsik (1931-2009) was a Hungarian-American philosopher who specialized in ancient Greek philosophy, with whom I had been acquainted when I was in Berkeley and he in Stanford. He was a great man for organising conferences , and ran a Greek philosophy reading group,

has tenure here now. Larry Cunningham, head of Theology, was also there. Greg, it seems, is coming up for tenure, so all this is *important*.[148]

After dinner I was thoroughly groggy, but survived to give my talk—just across the road, in the Centre for Continuing Education. I was not very pleased with it – rather too specialised, really, for a general audience, poor things, though OK, I suppose, for Philo buffs. Afterwards, Dimitri Nikulin, from Moscow, appeared and greeted me. It was very nice to see him. He is spending a year here.[149]

I sank into bed at around 10.00, and actually got a good night's sleep, though waking up a few times.

DAY 2, WEDNESDAY, NOVEMBER 16TH

I joined Tom Tobin, David Hay, and David Runia for breakfast – David Winston arrived just a bit later – and then went across the road to the C.C.C. for our first editorial session. Greg Sterling is certainly an efficient young man, and had prepared us a large dossier of background material. We discussed mainly the preferred *form* of commentary, and then made various choices as to what we should do. Good progress was made.

Then a pleasant lunch in the Hesburgh Centre next door, and another session till 3.00. Then I was scheduled to walk round the campus with Gretchen Reydams-Schils, but she developed a 'flu' (she had recovered by the evening!), and so I explored by myself, visiting the Church (which is rather splendid baroque, with lots of gold and Virgin Mary blue, and reasonably good murals), and then the Library, which has an impressive mural on the front of Christ Triumphant, which is nicknamed 'Touchdown Jesus', because it can be viewed from the football stadium, and seems to be celebrating touchdowns!

---

covering much of the West Coast.

148 He did in fact get tenure, but then moved to Yale, where he has flourished greatly,

149 For Dimitri, see First Visit to Moscow, above, p.35. He subsequently moved to The New School for Social Research in New York, where he flourished.

Actually, Notre Dame is not doing too well this year; it is due to play the Air Force on Saturday, and is rather apprehensive. In the library, one can visit the stacks, and their holdings of Philosophy are good – better than ours, certainly.

Then back for a short rest – nearly sprained my ankle on an irregular piece of pavement, which would be par for the course! Having excused myself from dinner, I went out with Seamus Deane[150] to the Tippecanoe Inn, former home of Clement Studebaker, whose carriage and then automobile firm was based in South Bend. I had an excellent prime rib, in marvellously quaint surroundings. Seamus is in reasonably good form, though chain-smoking, and with a shaky hand, but I think he feels a bit bereft, despite his rather sumptuous situation. We speculated at length on the Irish crisis – he had heard that an incriminating document had been found in the Attorney General's Office, showing that Cardinal Daly *had* actually intervened with Harry[151] on behalf of Fr Smyth – and that should put the tin hat on everything. It is sad to be missing this!

Seamus insisted on paying. We will get together again in Berkeley, as he will be staying over Thanksgiving with the Tracys.[152] We got back for the last bit of David Winston's talk, so I wasn't completely disgraced.

DAY 3, THURSDAY, NOVEMBER 17TH

Once again, a pleasant breakfast with the lads – in this case, Tom Tobin and David Runia. Efforts to eat less meet with mixed success – even a continental breakfast involves *two* Danish!

The second session involved a long discussion on the *form*

---

150 Seamus had been on the faculty of Notre Dame from 1992, as Donald and Marilyn Keough Professor of Irish Studies, and continued in that position till his retirement, though returning regularly to Ireland. We had first got to know him, and his wife Marion and family, in Berkeley in the early 1970s, when he was there as a visiting lecturer.

151 That is to say, Harry Whelehan, Attorney General. See above.

152 Our old friends in Berkeley, Bob and Becky Tracy. Bob was a Professor of English in the university.

of commentary, ultimately inconclusive. Theologians tend to favour commentary after each section of text, classicists prefer commentary at the end of text – but perhaps it doesn't matter.

Lunch again in the Hesburgh Center, and a final session. We appointed ourselves as an editorial board, and assigned jobs for commenting. I got stuck with the *De Abrahamo*[153]. OK!

After lunch, Greg led an expedition over to the Mediaeval Institute, and the Library generally, and then we went and visited the little Snite Museum of Art, which isn't at all bad, considering. I bought J a pair of candlesticks in the shop and went back for a brief rest. J phoned at around 4.30, giving further news of the government crisis. Albert resigned, and Harry resigned – a very sad end to his public career. The whole thing is a dismal mess, but no doubt Bertie will manage to patch everything up![154]

Then at 5.15 down to the Tippecanoe (again!) for an excellent dinner. Harry Attridge, who is Dean of the Faculty, was there, and told some dean jokes. Samples:

> "Why are deans like mushrooms?
> You keep 'em in the dark, pile shit on 'em, and then *can* 'em."
> A dean, a sociologist and an anthropologist are captured by cannibals in Papua-New Guinea. The cannibals decide to auction them. There were bids of up to ten pigs for the sociologist, five pigs for the anthropologist, but no bids for the dean. Why not? A fine fat dean – what's the problem? "OK", says one no-bidder, "he looks good – but have you ever tried to *clean* a dean?"

More prime rib – and cabernet from *Sterling* vineyards! Then back to hear David Runia's talk, which was a great success, and then out to Sterlings for a drinks party. They have a fine new house on the edge of an artificial lake, in a posh housing development. Quite astonishing, really, but his wife, Didi, is a high-powered accountant. I was driven home to bed by Tom Tobin.

---

153 My translation and commentary on this treatise, completed in cooperation with the excellent Ellen Birnbaum, finally appeared in 2021.

154 Which indeed Bertie Ahern ultimately did, becoming Taoiseach in June 1997, and continuing in that role till May 2008.

DAY 4, FRIDAY, NOVEMBER 18TH

Up in a more leisurely fashion, in time to see the lads off to Chicago by car. I stay behind, to go up with Greg Sterling tomorrow morning. I spent the morning mainly reading Gretchen's thesis, which needs a *lot* of work.

Then Greg came and got me for lunch at 11.45, and we went over to the Faculty Club, where we met his great benefactor, Jack Conway, a real estate developer from Florida who has developed a vivid interest in the origins of Christianity. He greatly admires *The Middle Platonists,* and is so distressed that it is out of print that he is prepared to finance its republication in a second edition![155] I am only delighted, and urge Greg to write to Duckworth, to release the copyright. They are not prepared to do anything, after all. Jack has Irish connections, so he may come and visit.

After lunch, I sat in the lounge of the Library for an hour or so, correcting Gretchen's thesis, and also finding my article in the Irish Literary Review on Egan and Kennelly. The puffing of Egan by Brian Arkins is grotesque. I found an article on Egan by him in Studies, and he has written a book on him![156]

When Greg finished his chores, around 3.30, he took me for a drive around the local Amish communities, which was rather charming – like similar countryside near Kenyon, Ohio[157] – and then we went back to his house. His wife Didi and younger daughter were home, and we went out to a Mexican

---

155 In fact, my book was republished by Duckworth in 1996, but I have no recollection now of Jack Conway having any role in that. However, perhaps he did, God bless him!

156 I think that I am being excessively rude here about both Desmond Egan and Brian Arkins. Egan is in fact a poet and translator of considerable stature, competent in Classical Greek, and Arkins a thoroughly respectable Classics scholar from University College Galway, specialising in the Classical heritage in Ireland.

157 Where I had visited in the past an old friend (and former fellow-graduate student in Berkeley) who taught in Kenyon College there, Clifford Weber.

restaurant. Didi may have been rather fed up with visitors by this time, but she was really rather stiff and off-hand. I did not get the impression of an awfully happy household – *too* tidy, for one thing! Anyhow, a very pleasant meal, and we came back and Greg and I retired to the basement 'den', and watched a video of *Amadeus,* which was delightful to see again.

And so to bed, for an early start tomorrow.

DAY 5, SATURDAY, NOVEMBER 19TH

We decided not to drive to Chicago, but to take the train – the South Shore Line, which I had travelled on before. A much better idea, in fact. We rose early, and *just* caught the 7.40 a.m. from the airport (Didi came along, to take back the car).

A pleasant train journey, of about two-and-a-half hours, rumbling through main streets of little towns, and areas of primeval forest and marsh, till we got to the end of the line in downtown Chicago. I grabbed the chance to read an important chapter by Tony Long[158] in Bob Lamberton's *Homer's Ancient Readers,* which is a fuller version of his talk on Stoics and Homeric Allegory. He introduces some salutary cautions, but I am still convinced that at least *later* Stoics, and Stoic-influenced persons, gave a comprehensive interpretation of Homer.

We had a short taxi ride to the Bismarck, and Greg went on to the Hilton. It was too early to check in, so I lodged the bags, had a bit of second breakfast, and then headed over to the Hilton. This is a *massive* conference – about 8000 assorted theologians milling about! Fortunately, they had my registration ready. I met Sean Freyne[159] in the registration queue, and we had a bite of lunch in the Kitty O'Shea Pub in the hotel, being served by a young lad from Foxrock. Then up to the Philo seminar.

---

158 A.A. Long, distinguished authority on Ancient Philosophy, who succeeded me in Berkeley when I returned to Ireland in 1980, and is an old friend.

159 My colleague, the Professor of Theology from Trinity, a noted authority on Second Temple Judaism and Galilee.

Tony was pleased to see me, and proposed dinner. The seminar was very well attended, and lively. Various persons popped up, such as George Carras and Bill Cassidy,[160] from long ago in Berkeley. Greg managed everything efficiently. David Dawson's book[161] I probably should get, but he seems a bit windy. I looked round apprehensively for Berchman,[162] but no sign of him. He's here, though.

After our seminar, I called across to a Neoplatonism/Gnosticism one that Greg Shaw and John Finamore were performing at, and that was quite good – though there was *too much* air-conditioning; hope I don't get pneumonia. Tony came to take me away before the end, though, so I didn't get to talk to Finamore. I must catch him, though.

Tony and I then walked to his hotel, the Stauffer, and took a cab to an excellent Greek restaurant he had found last night – the proprietor greeted him like an old friend, and we were feasted: ouzo, large bottle of retsina, metaxa! I had a good lamb dish, with avgholimeno sauce. Tony is very keen that I try for the Princeton job, but I see great difficulties with that. He would like also to consider publishing my commentary, with John Finamore, on Iamblichus' de Anima with UC Press.[163]

After dinner, we decided to pack it in. Too sloshed to go to any receptions!

---

160 Former graduate students of mine. George became a professor of Near Eastern Studies at Washington and Lee University in Virginia.

161 I have no longer any notion what this was, or indeed who he was.

162 Robert Berchman later became Professor of Philosophy and Religious Studies at Dowling College and a Senior Fellow of the Institute of Advanced Theology at Bard College, and has been a pillar of the International Society for Neoplatonic Studies for many years. I was somewhat embarrassed, as I had delivered a rather critical evaluation of a monograph he had presented for publication, arising out of his doctoral thesis.

163 I had no real desire to uproot myself, and head for Princeton, so I did not pursue this. As for the book, it was ultimately published with Brill, in the Philosophia Antiqua series, in 2002, so that didn't work out either.

DAY 6, SUNDAY, NOVEMBER 20TH

Got off to a slowish start. I had hoped to visit the Art Institute, but it doesn't open till 12.00 on Sunday. Read more of Gretchen's thesis, and Marguerite Harl on the *logos tomeus*,[164] which is most useful. Then over to the Hilton on the shuttle bus – it is raining this morning, which does not induce one to walk. I saw only Jack Conway (whom I urged to visit Ireland), had a bowl of soup in Kitty O'Shea's, and then up to the Philo session. Tony and I listened to Gretchen, and then dodged over to the Neoplatonic session to listen to Sarah Rappe, who was a student of his, and who was very good on Damascius.

We had to sit through also a rather dim man talking on Marsilio Ficino, and then Tony went off with Sarah Rappe (who seems very bright and pleasant), and I went off with John Finamore, and his Bulgarian assistant, Svetla Slaveva (a most pleasant young woman)[165], to discuss the *De Anima,* over a coffee. He really needs an NEH grant, and to get that he has to finish his previous project on Hutcheson[166], which he has got bogged down on. I am rather dubious about his prospects, but suggested he might write to John Gaskin for advice.

After a while I went back up to a Mithraic session, to hear David Ulansey on Mithras, and greeted Dieter Betz[167] – who, I

---

164 A bit technical, this – the Logos, or 'executive principle' of God, as 'cutter', or definer of things.

165 Now, as Svetla Slaveva-Griffin, Professor of Classics at Florida State University, Tallahassee, and an authority on Ancient Greek philosophy and science.

166 Francis Hutcheson (1694–1746) was an influential Anglo-Irish moralist, an advocate of moral sentimentalism, and a key figure of the Scottish Enlightenment. I cannot imagine how John got involved with writing on him, but I don't think anything came of it. John Gaskin was a colleague in Trinity, in the Philosophy Department.

167 Hans Dieter Betz (b. 1931), is an American scholar of the New Testament and Early Christianity at the University of Chicago. When I was in Berkeley, he had roped me into a project of translating the Greek Magical Papyri, published in 1986.

think, was a bit miffed at not knowing I was there, but really I didn't want to start too many hares!

Afterwards it was over to the Piano Bar for a protracted drink with Sean Freyne and some friends of his from New Orleans, whose names I forget. Then to the lobby, to meet up with Jay and Nancy,[168] and go to hear some jazz. To my alarm, they had invited Robert Berchman to join us! However, by staying off the subject of his works, we passed a pleasant evening. He is actually a perfectly nice chap, but I'm not sure that he has really learned *anything* from the criticisms that I levelled against him. The jazz was at a venue called the Blackstone – excellent tenor sax, Hank Crawford, whom Jay and I had heard in New York back in 1988, with Richie Cole, in the Village. He was backed by an excellent trio, of piano, bass and drums. We lasted till about 10.00 – the first set – and then packed it in, since I have an early start. Jay said it was like a tenor sax lesson. Crawford has a magnificent tone.

A taxi back to the Bismarck, and so to bed.

DAY 7, MONDAY, NOVEMBER 21ST

Up around 5.30 am – rather too early, in fact – and consequently had lots of time to catch the airport shuttle by 7.00. The weather is still pleasant, but changing. I got to the airport smoothly, and onto a plane for Minneapolis. Slightly delayed by headwinds, but no problem about making the connection with the plane to San Francisco. Fine views of the central plains (*very* desolate – North Dakota, etc.) and the Rockies, and down into SF about 1.45, to be met by a rather *dilapidated* Charles,[169] on a stick.

---

168 That is, my old friend Jay Bregman, formerly of Berkeley, but by this time already installed in the University of Maine at Orono, and his wife, Nancy Ogle. Jay had always been a great authority on modern jazz, and a very competent saxophone player himself.

169 That is to say, my old friend and colleague from Berkeley days, Charles Murgia, professor of Latin, and a great authority on Vergil, and his commentator Servius. He and I had shared an office when I first arrived in Berkeley, in 1966.

The poor man has a gammy knee, together with his previous ailments. His mother died back in May (he never told us!), and now he is rather alone.

First we drove out and gazed on the Pacific for a while, watching sea-birds and surfers. The weather is fine, but cool – not much warmer than Chicago, in fact – and then drove across the Bay Bridge to Berkeley. Charles left me in the Pacific School of Religion, where I have a pleasant guest room, and I arranged to meet him at 5.30 or so in his office. I had never set foot in the PSR before, so far as I can recall, but it is beautifully situated on the crest of Holy Hill,[170] with a fine view of the Bay and the Golden Gate. The room is austerely ecclesiastical in décor, but perfectly comfortable. The only nuisance is a pay phone, so I need loads of quarters. I phoned Susie,[171] and got a warm welcome. I walked down to her with a present of Barry's Tea, and was given a glass of wine, and she then drove me down to the campus, at 5.30.

We failed to get Greenie[172] to come out with us, so Charles and I went out to a Cambodian restaurant near the campus, which turned out to be very good. It is not unlike Thai food, but a bit milder – some coconut and so on. Then back to the Pritchett[173] Memorial Lecture, in the Alumni House. It was given by Emily Vermeule,[174] on 'Trojan Troubles', and was most

---

170 As we used to call the hill just north of the Berkeley campus, which housed various schools of religion.

171 Our old friend Susie Sutch, wife of Professor Richard Sutch, of the Economics Department. She had once taken a Latin class of mine, and we got to know them as a consequence of that.

172 That is to say, Crawford Greenewalt III, Professor of Archaeology, and noted as the excavator of Sardis, in Turkey.

173 In honour of Kendrick Pritchett, distinguished Greek archaeologist, and chairman of the Department when I first arrived. It was he who offered me a job in the department in 1969, on my attaining the PhD

174 Emily Dickinson Townsend Vermeule (1928 – 2001) was an American classical scholar and archaeologist. She was a professor of classical philology and archaeology at Harvard University. She had been Sather Professor in Berkeley back in 1974-5, and had been good fun. She loved visiting

entertainingly presented, though, because of the journey and the dinner, I kept falling asleep. Her position was that the *earlier* Bronze Age Greeks must already have had Homeric-style epic poetry, on the basis of the portrayal of sieges and so on. Not entirely convincing!

It was packed, though, and very well received. I greeted everybody – Bill Anderson, Kendrick himself, Ron and Connie Stroud, Leslie Threatte (!), Murray Emeneau (now 91, but very sprightly), Tom and Lilo Rosenmeyer, Ken and Marjorie Kaiser, Mark Griffith.[175] I didn't see Don Mastronarde, in fact. Greenie introduced Emily. I greeted Emily as well. All enquired after Jean and Mouse. Bob and Becky Tracy and Seamus Deane also came. There was a good reception afterwards, and then Charles drove me back to the PSR.

Everyone is being very nice about wondering when I will be coming back. The whole thing is most nostalgic. Dear old Dwinelle Hall[176] is the same as ever, same *smell*. Quite a lot of new building on campus, in fact – a lot being done to the Library.

DAY 8, TUESDAY, NOVEMBER 22ND

I decided this morning that I had better go shopping myself, since I wanted to go to the bank, and J's toe ointment might be expensive and need decision-making, so I excused Susie. I walked down to Shattuck, lodged $300 in the Bank of America, and changed our account to 'limited checking', which has no service charge. Then over to Long's Drugs and picked up most of what J and Mouse ordered – could only get commercial toe ointment, though.

---

graveyards, as I recall, and reading the inscriptions.

175 These are all my former colleagues (and their spouses), except for Marjorie Kaiser, who was the departmental secretary, and ruled us with a rod of iron, and Murray Emeneau, who was a distinguished linguistics expert, founder of the Linguistics Department in Berkeley, and actually had been a friend of my father. The exclamation mark after Threatte's name attests to his rebarbative nature, which made me surprised that he was there at all.

176 Home of the Classics Department – on the fifth floor.

Then back to the PSR, dumped the purchases, took Suzanne's package, and set off for Leroy Avenue.[177] I called tentatively on Charlotte,[178] but she was fortunately out – probably with poor old George in hospital (he is pretty ill at the moment, it seems). I sat out at coffee with Suzanne for a long time, then went round to greet Sita and Mac[179], who are remodelling their kitchen (saw John also), and then round to 1584 to see the upstairs. Was greeted warmly and shown around, viewing the fine new upstairs, and then the wife, Lorna (?), kindly drove me down to the Faculty Club, where lunch awaited me with Jock, Es, Greenie, Fred, Elaine, and Chris Simon, who is in town – a nice young man, who once sat our house and looked after Brandy.[180]

An excellent lunch, which went on till well into the afternoon, and then Fred drove me to Black Oak Books, where I went in and explored, finding two books of Plutarch's *Lives,* and Gildersleeve's *Olympian and Pythian Odes of Pindar,* which I need. All else I resisted. I walked back with these to the PSR, and then down to Wheeler Hall, to hear Seamus[181] deliver a lecture on Burke and Thomas Moore. Quite a tour de force, really. He spoke for an hour without notes, keeping the thread of his

---

177 Our old friend and neighbour, Suzanne Becker; Leroy Avenue (1584), just six blocks north of the campus, was the street on which we had lived when we were in Berkeley.

178 That is, our former next door neighbour, Charlotte Foss. She was most hospitable, and I must have feared that she might delay me. George was her husband.

179 Sita and Watson 'Mac' Laetsch, good friends and neighbours. Mac was a professor of Plant Biology, and Vice-Chancellor of the University in the 1980s. Sita was of upper-class Indian stock from Trinidad. She was a cousin of VS Naipaul, but didn't much approve of him! John was their son.

180 Jock Anderson, professor of Classical Archaeology, and his wife Esperance, with whom Jean used to ride horses; and Fred Beeson and his wife, who was part of a Classics reading group I used to belong to. I can no longer quite place Chris Simon. Brandy was our dog.

181 Seamus Deane must have been visiting the English Department at the time, from Notre Dame, where we had just been consorting.

argument (which was rather convoluted) very well. I'm not sure if I had heard Seamus speak before, but it was good.

There was a reception afterwards, where I chatted to Joan Keefe,[182] who seems in good form, to Bob[183], and to Seamus himself. Then back up to the lodgings, to wait for Colin to collect me. Colin arrived punctually at 7.00, and we went and collected a Chinese meal, and brought it back to his and Ann's apartment. He is a bit balder, but in good form, and Ann is flourishing, now with another big firm – American President Lines, I think. Andrew is quite grown up – a computer whiz, who made a prize-winning video, which we viewed (it was actually quite good – on *Lord of the Rings*), and young John is a funny little person, a great showman, very much into *swords*. I had to read him a story after dinner. Colin is still in semi-retirement, but I imagine Ann is making enough for both of them, and they are full of plans for remodelling. The cats are in fine form.

DAY 9, WEDNESDAY, NOVEMBER 23RD

At last we get to the point of the whole expedition, the celebration of David Winston (all the other delegates arrived last night). This began at 8.30, with breakfast in the GTU library, of course, they didn't tell us that, and David Runia and I already had breakfast in the PSR! It was a slightly scatter-brained meeting, really, but David seemed pleased. We delivered our papers in due order, but then David Hay and Greg Sterling had to leave for a plane in the middle of David Winston's own speech. Old Claude Welch, ex-Dean, delivered a most *inept* encomium of David, which made clear that he hadn't the faintest idea what the significance of his work was.

---

182 Wife of the distinguished physicist Denis Keefe, who had moved to Berkeley from the Institute of Advanced Studies in Dublin, and remained in Berkeley till his death. Joan herself remained on for quite a while, eventually moving back to Ireland. She became quite a successful writer. They were great hosts in Berkeley for Irish parties, and visiting Irish dignitaries.

183 That is to say, Robert Tracy, of the English Department, and a great authority on Victorian Irish literature.

Tom Rosenmeyer came up for lunch, which was nice, and stayed for my paper. Irene also came down to greet us. She is suffering from her back, and had to have lunch largely standing. Lunch was really rather peculiar – good sandwiches, but then bottles of pop, without any glasses! Some kosher fantasy, no doubt.

It was all over by 2.30; no plan for a celebratory banquet for David or anything. He just faded away. Fortunately, I am fixed up with Susie and Richard, and others have gone, but David Runia was left on his own. He and I first went down Telegraph Avenue, and visited bookstores – University Press Books, where I met up with Bill McClung, Cody's, and Moe's (where Moe is still presiding). Telegraph is very seedy, though, with lots of panhandlers.

We came back, and checked in to the end of Tony Long's seminar on the Presocratics. Afterwards we went out for a drink with him in the Faculty Club, and chatted, then he and David went off for dinner down on the Bay. I went back to the PSR, and then down to Sutches at 7.30. Charles came separately. Bill and Mui[184] were the other guests, and it was one of Richard's superb efforts.[185]

First, though, we went across the road to view Bill's toy soldiers factory, located in the basement where I lodged in 1982 – a truly magnificent sight. He is a great artist in the toy soldier area, and it seems a flourishing business. He is off to London to a Toy Soldiers Congress in a week or so.

Richard served a great *bouillabaisse*, sort of *hot*, with Mexican spices. It was a great feast – accompanied by an excellent Oregon Pinot Noir. Susie had got me gumballs, brioches and coffee – very good of her – most embarrassing. Charles enjoyed himself, but I didn't dare ask what he is doing for Thanksgiving. I hope he is fixed up. Nobody seems to be looking out for him.

---

184 Friends of the Sutches, who surname I cannot remember.
185 Richard was in general the cook in the Sutch household.

DAY 10, THURS, NOVEMBER 24TH (THANKSGIVING)

This morning I was woken by David Runia, wanting to go out and find some breakfast. PSR was dead as a doornail. No life at North Gate either, so we went down to Shattuck Ave., where we found a nice little café open, and had coffee and Danish. He is being collected by Bob Hamerton-Kelly at about 11.30 am. I am being collected by Becky[186] about noon.

Becky and Bob duly arrived at noon. I had previously dodged down to Shattuck, found a wine-shop open, got a bottle and some flowers, and also a bottle of Stag's Leap[187] to bring home. I noticed a new vineyard called *Frog's Leap* at the same time, by the way!). They drove me back to Derby Street, where we sat in the kitchen and gossiped for a while until Seamus Deane (who is staying with them), came back from a walk. While we were sitting there, Marianne[188] phoned from San Diego, looking for Seamus, and I greeted her, much to her astonishment – I hope she is not offended that I didn't try to get down to her for Thanksgiving, but I think not.

When Seamus returned, we took a stroll up to the campus, to get something from Bob's office, and take a little exercise. They had a safety scare in Wheeler Hall last year, when asbestos started coming out of the walls, and the whole place had to be evacuated and repaired.

A number of people came for dinner – Hugh (who works with a circus, putting up tents, etc.), Dominic,[189] and Lisa (a Korean orphan whom someone has adopted, and is at Cal – a nice girl) – and a cousin of Bob's, who is a nurse in San Francisco. It was a very jolly feast, with all the trimmings – and then I was conveyed by Dominic to the Durant Hotel, and put on a bus for the airport at 7.00 pm. It all worked out exceedingly well.

---

186 That is to say, Rebecca, wife of Robert Tracy.

187 One of the top California wines of the time.

188 That is to say, Marianne MacDonald, a very rich Californian lady, who was also a benefactress of our Classics Department, being a lover of the Classics, and no mean authority on Greek drama herself.

189 The two sons of Bob and Becky.

I was so stuffed that I ate and drank nothing on the flight, slept most of the way, and arrived in Amsterdam without jet-lag. A tedious wait in Amsterdam, and then a short hop home to Dublin, where I found all well, and great political excitement.[190]

---

190   The Fianna Fáil-Labour government had just collapsed, Albert Reynolds had resigned, and Bertie Ahern had taken over the leadership of the party and the government. The President, however, declined to dissolve the Dáil, and on Dec. 15, John Bruton took over as leader of a 'rainbow' coalition.

8. Visit to Trier:

July 18–25, 1999

This was a joint expedition of Jean and myself – Ruth being otherwise engaged, at a language school – for me to attend a conference on the Aristotelian philosopher Theophrastus in the fine old German city of Trier, the latest in quite a series of such conferences organised by Professor William Fortenbaugh of Rutgers University, as part of Project Theophrastus, which he had initiated back in 1979. As will be gathered from the narrative, Theophrastus is not one of my favourite guys, but I did like Bill Fortenbaugh. We decided on travelling by boat and train, which in fact worked out very well. Since Jean in fact composes the bulk of this diary, she is in normal print, while I am in italics.

DAY 1, SUNDAY, JULY 18TH

We packed everything the previous evening, having disposed of Cat to Cattery, and Benson[191] to Elizabeth (Mouse already at her Language College in Clongowes since Friday). We started out without fuss at around 9.45 am for the 11.10 boat from Dun Laoghaire in pouring rain. The rain actually lifted by the time we got to Dun Laoghaire, but it was still threatening. We had to collect our tickets, since the original ones had either got lost in the post while we were in Spain, or had perhaps been stolen from the doorstep, but there was no problem about that. The Stena Highspeed Ferry docked at 10.50, unloaded, and then loaded us, with remarkable efficiency, in about a quarter of an hour, and by 11.15 we were sailing out of the harbour.

---

191 Our dog, a vivacious and opinionated Yorkie.

The boat was pretty ghastly, with lots of people and nowhere quiet to sit. It all looked rather like a cheap casino or a McDonald's (there was in fact one on board). It is made up a series of bars and restaurants, with chairs and tables in front of them. No quiet lounges, as on other ferries. There is no necessity for any of these bars-restaurants, considering that the journey takes exactly one and a half hours, but they have obviously decided that it is a really easy way to make money.

Our journey down from Holyhead to Christine and Harley[192] in Wiltshire (6 hrs) was uneventful. We made one stop for lunch at a Little Chef restaurant, where they robbed us of £12 for dreadful soup (John) and a sandwich for me. We found Christine and Harley exhausted from the festivities surrounding their church fête the previous day, and guests in the house till two hours before our arrival. But they rallied gallantly, and we had a delicious supper of a rice dish with salmon and herbs, for which I must remember to get the recipe. We all retired at about 10.15. (The weather in Wiltshire is lovely, and we dined outside)

DAY 2, MONDAY, JULY 19TH

We rose early-ish in the morning, as we needed to leave for Dover at around 9.15 am. John headed out for a walk before breakfast, and Christine and Harley were up to have a cup of tea with us by the time he got back. Christine's garden is now looking lovely – she has done a lot of planting.

We set off at around 9.15 on a warm, sunny day. Another uneventful drive, and fairly straightforward, except for one traffic hitch nearing the area where the motorway from the North joined ours. We drove off the motorway just short of Dover to get something to eat, and found a charming farm, serving lunches and teas, with plenty of hens and geese about, a cat with a face identical to that of ours (Sasha's), and outhouses and a bakery selling their own produce. We had a light lunch, and it was very reasonably priced.

---

192 That is, Jean's cousin Christine (née Downes) and her husband Harley Patrick.

We arrived at Dover an hour before our ferry's departure, and found we could get on an earlier one (at 1.15), which we did. We also changed our return ticket for next week from a 6.00 am ferry on Sunday to one the previous evening at 6.00 pm, deciding it would be easier to stop somewhere in England that night.

Our boat trip to Calais took more or less the same amount of time as the Dublin one (c. 1 ¼ hours), but the boat was more pleasant, and we did find a fairly quiet corner. The exit at Calais is extremely well organised, in that it leads directly onto the motorway, and so we made excellent progress right away. A good cup of coffee and a Danish at an *aire* somewhere along the way – a relief to get a good cup of coffee!

Our route took us *via* Arras, St. Quentin, Rheims, Verdun, north of Metz, on a minor road (turn-off called Jarny) and stopped at a rather uninteresting town called Briey. By now we were feeling hungry and a bit tired (it was 8.00 pm) and we knew that if we ate we wouldn't feel like driving further that night. So we booked ourselves into the Hotel Commercial, which was just that. But we had a fairly decent, though not exceptional, meal, with a delicious half-bottle of Alsatian wine, went for a walk through the uninteresting town, and retired to bed around 10.45.

DAY 3, TUESDAY, JULY 20TH

We did not sleep terribly well, because of heavy traffic outside most of the night. We breakfasted at the hotel (breakfast expensive for what we got), and left at around 9.15 am, to head for Trier. It took about 1 ¼ hrs, and we finally found the Katholischer Akademie, after some minor hitches.

It is a beautiful building, set high in the hills above Trier, with magnificent views of the Mosel River from our bedroom. It was formerly a seminary, but in 1998 was modernised and turned into a conference centre. It still has a decidedly Catholic ethos, with religious leaflets and bibles everywhere. The modern sections of the building are magnificent, and the interior finishes are of very high quality. German design is as good as you can find. The bedroom furniture is economically designed to make maximum use of the space. I went for a walk up the hill behind the Centre during the morning.

The conference was under way when we arrived, but I dodged into the end of the first paper (by Stephen White of Austin TX, on the titles of Theophrastus' Opuscula*), then coffee, and then a talk by Istvan Bodnár of Budapest on Theophrastus'* On Fire — *actually most interesting, though this conference as a whole seems concerned with the most dismal aspects of Theophrastus' oeuvre: the opuscula on Fire, Sweats, Dizziness, Fatigue, and Smells! My contribution on his* Metaphysics *is distinctly out of place, but I am paired with Dimitri Gutas on the Arabic tradition of the* Metaphysics *(on Thursday morning). This is actually the tenth conference in a long line, going back to 1979 — which I was actually at, though I've only been at one since: the Liverpool one in 1983.*

Lunch was OK — except that J suspected the meat of being horse! *It was actually smoked pork, but it had a rather peculiar consistency. Then there was a slightly delayed welcoming address by the President of the University, a lady historian called Rainer Hettich. Then a discussion of* Theophrastus on Sense-Perception *led by Han Baltussen, which was not without some interest.*

Dinner was at 6.30, after which a large group of us walked down to the town (only 20 minutes or so down — *not so much fun coming* up!*) to a bistro beside the Porta Nigra*[193] *for a few beers. We took a walk around the old town, which is beautifully laid out as a pedestrian precinct, and then back to the group, which was still boozing, and took a taxi ride home with Bill and Connie Fortenbaugh (11.50 DM plus tip). The weather is still good, though there are clouds about. We slept pretty well.*

DAY 4, WEDNESDAY, JULY 21ST

John decided to go to the first talk of the morning at 9.30 am, and slip out before the second one. We took the car, and headed for town. After cruising around for a bit, we parked in an underground carpark right in the centre of the town. It was very convenient, because its exits led directly into a large department

---

193 (Note by Jean) The Roman Porta Nigra is just that – *nigra*. It is a rather ugly monument, made out of a dark native stone in about 300 A.D.

store ("Kauflot"), where we could buy the necessities we had to buy. Before doing so, however, we went to see some sights, starting with the Dom, which was built on the site of an old Roman palace in about 1300 A.D.[194] Excavations turned up many interesting things, including magnificent wall and ceiling frescoes. These are now displayed in the adjoining museum.

We didn't have much more time to explore, as John wanted to get back for the 2.30 pm lecture. So we did some quick shopping (including a coffee plunger) and stopped for a *wiener* at the tavern beside the Porta Nigra.

We arrived back just a little late for the lecture. I decided to have a siesta, and slept about 1½ hours! Afterwards, the wives (five of us) were invited to tea at the organiser's wife's house. I drove one car, with Connie Fortenbaugh as navigator (Connie is a very pleasant person). We had tea in our hostess's garden, which she tends with care, and is lovely. She gave us coffee and a delicious cherry *kuchen*. We were unable to eat much supper after that!

The evening meal is a light one, mainly cold meats, cheese, etc., and runs from 6.30 – 7.30 pm. An expedition generally goes down to the town after dinner for beers, etc – walking down and getting taxis back. This time John and I decided to take a longer walk along the river (it took about 1 ¼ hours to reach the others, who were at the bar/restaurant near the Dom, where we are to have our banquet on Thursday. At about 10.30, we headed back. The weather was cloudy today.

DAY 5, THURSDAY, JULY 22ND

My 60th birthday! John meanly told one of the organisers of the conference that it was my birthday, so I'm looking forward with trepidation to tonight! The day is overcast and cooler, and we have already had a few showers. John's talk is at 11.00 am. I took myself off for a little drive up the hills past the centre, and found some incredible views of the river. Mostly orchards

---

194 Actually, the current building was completed in 1270, but there had been various previous versions on the site.

around (plum and apple), with cows grazing. Interestingly, they don't bother much to cut lawns and verges round about, so there are lots of interesting wild flowers.

The first talk of the day was Dimitri Gutas[195] *on the Arabic tradition of Theophrastus'* Metaphysics, *which was most interesting, and then I was on, after coffee, on Theophrastus' criticisms of the Academy.*[196] *I took about fifty minutes, and it seemed to go fine, but then my respondent, a nice young fellow from Zagreb called Josip Telanga, went on to respond at almost equal length in German, reading from a notebook! This brought us to within ten minutes of lunch, and effectively stopped the show cold. No one, except for the irrepressible Hans Gottschalk, ventured to raise a question, though it was plain later than many had comments they wished to make – not least André Laks, who was presiding, and Marlein van Raalte, who has actually written a large commentary on the work – so that was rather deflating.*

The weather actually turned nasty in the afternoon, with rain showers, so there seemed little point in setting out anywhere, and I attended the last two talks, both by young scholars, Hidemi Takahashi and Todd Gambon, which were not as tedious as I expected.

I actually spent the afternoon in bed reading, as it was very damp and cool. I have tried to call Mouse at her Eurolanguages Course in Clongowes (where she is an Assistant) several times, but her mobile is always switched off. At 6.15, John returned

---

195 Dimitri Gutas (b. 1945, in Cairo) is an American Arabist and Hellenist specializing in mediaeval Islamic philosophy, now Professor Emeritus in Yale. He studied classical philology, religion, history, Arabic and Islamic studies at Yale University, where he received his doctorate in 1974. His main research interests are classical Arabic and the intellectual tradition of the Middle Ages in Islamic culture, especially Avicenna, and the Graeco-Arabica, which is the reception and the tradition of Greek works on medicine, science and philosophy in the Arab-Islamic world (especially from the 8th to the 10th century in Baghdad). In this field he is considered one of the leading experts. He is a co-editor in Yale's Project Theophrastus.

196 This was duly published as 'Theophrastus' Critique of the Old Academy in the *Metaphysics*', in *On the Opuscula of Theophrastus*, edd. WW Fortenbaugh & G. Woehrle, Stuttgart, 2002., pp. 175-87.

and we decided to take the car for a drive up river. On the way down the hill, though, we met Tony Preus.[197] He helped us change our plans, to seek out the Roman amphitheatre (about 100 A.D.). It is on the road out to the University. It was closed, but we could see it reasonably well. It also, apparently, forms one of the city gates, which is odd.

After that, we drove up to a pleasant suburb where Tony had stayed over the weekend, to see if we could find a wine shop, since it is a sort of wine suburb, but everything was shut, which seemed strange. Then we drove briefly to the University – a very new campus – and looked at that, and then back to town, to find a park.

Tony directed us to a park beside the Basilica of Constantine near our restaurant. We took a walk in the Palace gardens, and saw the Roman Baths (which were also shut, as was the museum which, according to Tony, has a marvellous collection of all sorts of treasures from excavations round the town.

We met the others at the restaurant (Palais Kesselrath), where tables were beautifully set up for us in their large wine cellar. We had a very jolly evening, with a slightly embarrassing moment when they sang 'Happy Birthday', and presented me with an inflatable birthday cake and a bouquet of flowers. We were served wine from their own cellars, and it tasted very good. The festivities broke up at about 11.30 pm.

DAY 6, FRIDAY, JULY 23RD

I woke up at about 4.00 a.m. with an appalling head and neck ache. I also felt very sick. I took an Ibuprofen, but it didn't help, and I stayed awake until it was time to get up at 7.30. John decently brought me up a cup of coffee and a roll at 8.15 am, and I managed to keep them down, and was able to appear on the front steps at 9.00 a.m. for our trip to Bernkastel.

---

197 Tony Preus is Distinguished Teaching Professor of Philosophy at Binghamton University (SUNY), and Secretary of the Society for Ancient Greek Philosophy. He has long been a stalwart of the American Classical Philosophy scene.

We were taken in a minibus on a road beside the river, through lovely little villages, with houses brimming with flowers. We stopped a little while in Piesport to see a Roman winepress, which they still use during a Weinfest in October.

In all, it took one-and-a-half hours, more or less, to Bernkastel, and we drove straight to the Cusanus-stiftung, an old people's home and library founded by Nicholas of Cusa[198] *himself back in 1450 or so, and containing his own library, including his own copy of William of Moerbeke's translation of Proclus'* Commentary on the Parmenides *– a marvellous thing to see! The Librarian very kindly took down the volume, and allowed me to handle it (cautiously). It contains Nicholas' own annotations. The chapel and cloister were also very fine. They also seem to sell wine, but we were swept off instead by Georg across the river to Bernkastel itself, which is a lovely old town, to a very pleasant restaurant in the town square.*

Unfortunately, we had no time, either before or after dinner, to explore the town, which is cobbled and quaint, but just outside our restaurant there was a lovely chocolate shop, where I bought a present for Mouse. We then boarded a boat for our return trip to Trier. The view of the hills from the river is fantastic, with patchwork patterns created by the vineyards on very steep hills. We noticed that some rows of vines were planted closer together than others. Apparently those placed farther apart produce better grapes, because they ripen better. The soil has a great deal of slate in it, which produces minerals necessary to grow these types of vines well. When one sees signs saying "... Bruder', it means a co-op, which most of the vineyards are.

We left Bernkastel at 3 pm, and it took two locks and 4½ hours to reach Trier. We were all very tired by the time we got back. We said goodbye to most of the company at the pier (only a few staying overnight at the Academy), and wandered up the

---

198 Nicholas of Cusa (1401 – 1464) was a German Catholic cardinal, philosopher, theologian, jurist, mathematician and astronomer. One of the first German proponents of Renaissance humanism, he made spiritual and political contributions in European history. A notable example of this is his mystical or spiritual writings on "learned ignorance," as well as his participation in power struggles between Rome and the German states of the Holy Roman Empire.

town to find a pizza with Pamela Huby.[199] We found a modest Italian restaurant, and had quite a good pizza and some very good ice-cream. Then took a taxi back.

DAY 7, SATURDAY, JULY 24TH

John was up during the night with what felt like a cold, but could be allergies, from which a number of people seem to be suffering. It could be because of the preponderance of uncut meadow round about.

We rose at 7.30, and went down to breakfast, where we found that *one* pot of coffee had been provided for eight people. Sandra Sider stomped her foot, and went about cursing and complaining. Finally, someone came out and presented me with a pot, and I realised it was only half-full. I said so, and the girl, without apologies, went and filled it up – *more or less!*

Then we went to settle up the bill, and got a bit of a shock. It came to 600 DM in all – 110 a day for J, including the Monday night that we weren't here, and charging for both of us for Friday night. Not cheap – but I suppose for full board not so bad. Anyhow, it was a nice place. Plainly, it is still thoroughly Catholic in ethos, despite giving up as a seminary.

We said goodbye to remaining colleagues – met Stephen White's wife for the first time, as she had just arrived – and set off a little after 9.00 am – first into town to see if we could find an independent wine shop, but the one we had picked put, opposite the Porta Nigra, was hermetically sealed, and really looked like a wholesale place, anyhow. So we just drove on.

This time we decided to take a more northerly route, from Luxemburg up to Lille, via Namur, and it proved significantly shorter. We flashed through Luxemburg, and then up through Belgium, where we stopped for a coffee – paying (extravagantly) in German Marks (90 DM!).

We should have come this route on the way down – it is

---

199 Pamela Margaret Huby (1922 - 2019) was a distinguished authority on Greek philosophy, and Reader in Philosophy at the University of Liverpool, for whom I had a great liking. She actually published a book on Theophrastus in 1999 (*Theophrastus of Eresus*).

shorter, and it is *free!* We paid about £40 in tolls by the other route, as we were mainly in France. The Belgian and German freeways are excellent. As soon as we were within reaching distance of Lille, the road disimproved and became winding and full of local French traffic, with pushy drivers trying to outspeed each other. It was pretty bad for about 10 km.

We were making good time, so we decided to go off the motorway to a little mediaeval walled town called Bergues, where we had an excellent lunch of *Flammkuchen,* and bought a case of wine at a supermarket. We managed to get on a ferry at 5.00 pm, instead of the one we had booked at 6.30 pm. (Note: it is really not necessary to book a place on the Dover-Calais ferry ahead of time.)

The climate in SE England is amazing. It is really hot (28c), with lovely blue skies. I believe that the rest of the British Isles is covered with patchy cloud. And Dublin was 16-17° yesterday, when it was 26° in London. Maddening!

We drove to Woburn (NW of London) off the M 1, and found a delightful hotel, *The Bell Hotel,* which gave us as very favourable rate of £60, for two single rooms.

DAY 8, SUNDAY, JULY 25TH

The rooms were very small, but comfortable enough, The weather is still excellent. After a good breakfast in the inn opposite, we took a cruise around Woburn Abbey grounds, seeing a number of odd animals, and a remarkable folly called the Paris House, which is now an exclusive restaurant.

Then we set off for Holyhead. Our only error was to get off the Motorway for a while, which led to our being bogged down in various kinds of traffic, but we had lots of time. We rejoined the good road at Chester. We took a short break, to walk in a nice little park at the Menai Bridge. At the boat, we were invited to book dinner, which we did, and that turned out to have been a good choice – a delightful experience, with a very jolly gay waiter, and good food. We reached home unscathed.

9. Trip to Warsaw,

MARCH 16–22, 2000

This was an expedition provoked by my former student in Trinity, Barry Keane, who was now settled in Warsaw, and beginning an academic career there, and who had conspired to get me invited over to Poland to lecture on Joyce. He had actually studied Latin and Italian at the university, but while on a year abroad in Northern Italy, had taken a bus trip to Poland, and fallen in love with the place. He subsequently made his career there, as lecturer in English Literature at the University of Warsaw, with special reference to comparative studies between Polish and English literature, on which subject he has since become a major authority.

DAY 1, THURSDAY, MARCH 16TH

Up at 5.00 am, to catch the 6.45 plane to London. It is surprisingly easy to get up when one has to. We had a pleasant evening yesterday. Brian[200] to dinner (after a long interval), following a game of golf in the Deerpark, where I performed *very* moderately, though he professed to think I am improving. Then some frantic packing – I hope effective. I am now on the plane (British Midland), approaching Heathrow, at 7.46, after a pleasant breakfast, and in bright sunshine. However, I am feeling distinctly apprehensive now about posing as a Joyce expert in Poland – these fellows sound pretty serious about Joyce, and Barry seems to have promoted me as a great authority! I am conscious now that I have no address or phone number for him, which is worrying. He is due to meet me at the airport, but...

---

200 My colleague Brian McGing.

11.45 pm (local time). Now at last tucked up in a comfortable bed in Barry's flat, after a most adventurous day. The Warsaw flight was not full (about 30 passengers, in fact), and arrived on time (12.25), in cool but sunny weather, though with snow showers, and Barry was there to meet me. We got a taxi back to his flat on the other side of the city – avoiding *mafia* taxis, which have no phone numbers! – had a cup of tea, and then I took a rest until 3.00. The flat he and Agata have bought, which is plainly a good idea (Warsaw prices for rental and buying are even worse than Dublin, he says), and they have done it up very nicely (it is the northern suburb of Zoliborz, which is very pleasant and well-treed). I'm afraid I've put him out of his bed, though (Agata is, perhaps fortunately, away in London on business).

At 3.00, we got another taxi downtown, to the Old Square, and began a tour of the Old Town. It is certainly marvellous how it has been reconstructed. Hitler had ordered it totally demolished after the 1944 Rising, and his orders were enthusiastically carried out.

We walked from the Plac Zamkowy up to the Ulica Swietojamska to the Old Town Square, where we visited, first, the Mickiewicz Museum, to see photos and relics of Barry's poets, the Skamander Group;[201] then over to the Historical Museum, to take in bits of the history of Warsaw. The latter museum is an extraordinary rabbit-warren of a house, which leads one from prehistoric times (not much here before the 9th century AD, though), up to the destruction of the city by Hitler, over three or four floors. We sampled it, and then walked back down to the Krakowskie Przedmiescie, where we had a beer and snack in the Literary Café, attached to a little library where Barry mainly works. Then on down to the Grand Opera, to see if there was anything worth seeing. A very impressive programme, but some obscure Polish thing is on tonight, so we went to a film instead – a very sick one, but good, called *The Bone Collector.* The Poles have to subsist on subtitles.

We walked on after that down as far as the university, which

---

201 He had written a book about them.

we may visit tomorrow. Then home in a taxi, and so to bed. A most stimulating first day – cold, but quite bearable.

DAY 2, FRIDAY, MARCH 17TH (ST. PADDY'S DAY).

Barry got up early to go and teach a few classes, and was back by 9.30 am. I got up before that, and had a bath. Then a fine breakfast, after which I went for a walk for my regulation 40 minutes or so[202] in the adjacent forest. His situation is pretty pleasant. With a loan from AIB, he and Agata have bought this apartment in the pleasant suburb of Zoliborz, near to this park, and not far from the centre of town, and are doing it up very nicely. He has to teach most mornings for a number of hours, and gets paid in sterling, to a bank in England, and then he has his graduate fellowship. It serves. He got some work done, and I went through his translation of, and commentary on, the Threnodies of Jan Kochanowski, which is very good, and to which I wrote a short introduction.[203]

Then, in the afternoon, we headed out to town, to meet an Australian friend, Anthony Byrnes, in the Literary Café. As we started out, though, it started to snow gently. I have not been very fortunate with the weather. It *could* have been spring-like, it seems! We got a bus pass, and took the bus into town. The public transport is excellent. Anthony turned out very jolly. They teach together in the school. He is a lawyer back in Adelaide, but is around for a bit of adventure. We had a good lunch, at very moderate cost. We then went off to find the Chopin Museum, but it was closed, and then headed for the National Museum, now in a driving blizzard, but found that *it* was closing, an hour earlier than the guide book said (the *Rough Guide*, by the way, is pretty good, but not accurate on things like this). In frustration, I roared at the doorman, but it wasn't his fault.

Then we went off to a traditional working men's bar, and had a few beers, waiting for the Ambassador's St. Patrick's Day

---

202 Prescribed since my heart attack back in 1995.

203 This was duly published the following year (2001), as Jan Kochanowski: The Threnodies and The Dismissal of the Greek Envoys, Biblioteka Slaska.

party to begin. It was fun in the bar – mostly an older set, and one has to wonder what anyone over sixty has seen and put up with in this country. It is etched on many people's faces. A beer in these places is only 5 zloty – less than a £ (the rate being 6.2 zt to the £). I didn't see any more sights, then, but got more of an idea of the city as a whole.

We headed off then for the reception – not in the Embassy, but in a commercial club. It was a really big affair. We were greeted by the First Secretary, Brian Earls,[204] in the reception line, and then by the Ambassador, Patrick McCabe, inside – both very hospitable. Earls will come down to Katowice with us tomorrow. At first the crowd was daunting, and the music too loud, but we met a number of pleasant people, and the diplomats thinned out after a while, so things improved. I had a nice chat with the ambassador about the possibilities of starting a lectureship in Polish in Trinity.[205] I met a fellow called Wawrzyniec Konarski, who is a student of Irish politics, and lectures in Warsaw, and he knew of both James Dillon and John Dillon. A sound man!

The party lasted till about 9.00 – lots of good food as well as drink – and then we were wrecked. We refused the suggestion of going on somewhere for more, and got a taxi home. There will be an early start in the morning.

DAY 3, SATURDAY, MARCH 18TH

Up early, to get down to the station by 8.00, to meet Ernest Bryll – former Ambassador to Ireland, and distinguished poet (I had entertained him once to lunch in College when he was in Ireland) – and Brian Earls from the Embassy, to take the train to Katowice, to take part in a celebration of St. Patrick and Ireland organised by Bryll's wife Magda, who is a great connoisseur of Ireland. It was certainly a remarkable effort.

---

204 Brian Earls (1947-2013), though a career diplomat, was also a scholar who specialised in the study of folklore, and was an authority on the works of William Carleton among others. I found him a most stimulating companion.

205 There is one there now, but I can't claim any credit for it.

Katowice is a pretty dismal place, it must be said, in the midst of a vast, decaying complex of mining and heavy industry, but the Silesian Library, where we were meeting, is a beautiful building, and the Director, Prof. Jan Malicki, most welcoming and jolly. He himself is a Renaissance scholar, and anxious to publish Barry's book. We were met first, after a coffee, by an enthusiastic crowd of schoolgirls, dressed in green or white or orange, who gave us a great cheer, and we then turned to some welcoming speeches, by the Mayor and others. After that we spoke – Brian Earls on Ireland in 2000, myself on Joyce and the Classsics, then a harp recital, and then Ernest Bryll on Irish mythology. It was a large hall, and well-filled. I was much afraid that my talk would be too specialised, and indeed it surely was, but they took it manfully.

We then retired to a copious lunch (starting with steak tartare, which was pretty daring!), while the festivities continued – a rendering of Molly Bloom's soliloquy in Polish, then some (very good!) Irish dancing by folk dancers from Krakow, then a film, *Snakes and Ladders,* which we didn't see. Brian, Barry and I went off instead to see if we could find the 'old' town of Katowice, but no such luck! There is a kind of centre, but really no *'there'* there! We walked around, had a beer, and came back to face more beer – and wicked nibbles, including an old Silesian speciality of *pure fat* spread on bread, offered to me by Bryll, who has himself just had a *quadruple bypass*! It was very good, unfortunately, but I certainly will need the Lipostat after that!

I slid out of that around 10.00 pm to bed. Brian Earls is an interesting fellow. I found out that he and Barry had lived around the corner from each other, off the South Circular Road. Barry was sent off to bed with a tray containing 14 pints of beer – an excess of hospitality!

DAY 4, SUNDAY, MARCH 19TH

We rose around 8.30 am, and headed out of Katowice as fast as possible. It is an unfortunate place, and a light snowfall didn't help. The weather has *not* been very kind to us so far, sadly. We had coffee and doughnuts at the station, and caught a train at 9.45 to Kracow.

We arrived there around 11.00, still in mild snow, and walked to the university hotel, *Dom Goscinny*, on Florianska Street (No 49). It is very central, and pleasant. Costs 177 zt a night – somewhat high by Polish standards (around £30), but not by Irish! I'll pay for Barry, since I got him into this. We lodged the bags, and took a stroll around, up to the main square, down past the University buildings to the Wawel Royal Castle, where we bought a ticket for a concert this evening, and then back *via* the Marianska Church, where we looked in on a very crowded mass. Then we found a Greek restaurant for a rather copious and very cheap lunch, and so back for a bit of a siesta, as the snow had now become a blizzard. We must hope it lets up!

Fortunately it did, around 4.00 pm, and we headed out to see things – back to the Marianska, and admired the High Altar carved by Veit Stoss and various other treasures – choir stalls and suchlike. We keep missing the trumpeter in the tower, though. He blows on the hour – breaking off suddenly, because once, long ago, he was shot through the neck, while in mid-blow, by a Tartar arrow![206] Then down past Wawel Hill (which was just closing) to the old Jewish Quarter of Kasimierez, cleared out by the Nazis under the awful Goetz, of *Schindler's List* fame. We wandered into some churches on the way, but ended up in a pleasant Jewish coffee house in a little square, where there has been some rebuilding and revival going on, and had a coffee and vodka.

After that it was back to the hotel, and, after a hasty Big Mac at a neighbouring MacDonald's, out again to a concert at the Concert Hall by the NDR orchestra. The event featured an excellent American pianist, Tsimon Barto and a programme of Slavic music – Dvorák, Prokofiev (Piano Concerto 2, and Symphony No. 8 (I got a CD of him playing Chopin). It was all preceded by speeches from dignitaries, as this is part of Krakow's

---

[206] During the Mongol invasion of Poland in the mid-12th century, to be exact!

European Capital of Culture celebrations. Tickets cost 50 zt. Excellent auditorium.

And so to bed (phoned home, where all is well, except that Elizabeth is in hospital with a bad back. On the other hand, Ireland beat France 27-22!).

DAY 5, MONDAY, MARCH 20TH

We rose around 8.00, and had breakfast. I managed to get in contact with Mme Staminovska, who had actually e-mailed me last Tuesday, but I had not gone into the office to check email, of course! She has unfortunately booked me into another place for tonight – I would really have liked to stay here. However, an assistant will collect us for lunch at 1.20 – the lecture is at 3.15pm.

All museums are closed on Monday (as normal, so we set off for the Wawel, in the hope that that might be open. It was, and so was the Cathedral, so we had a good explore. Barry is very sentimental about his days in Krakow, and I can see why. In summer weather all this must be truly delightful. Even now it is lovely, but certainly cold. We viewed the courtyard of the Palace – fine Renaissance loggias, and so on, but all currently under repair – there *is* a lot of repairing going on, which is good, if inconvenient. For the Cathedral, Barry engaged a guide, who was a very jolly fellow, and showed us *everything*. Of the 45 kings of Poland, 41 are buried in the Cathedral, either upstairs or in the crypt, and I think we viewed *all* of them. I was feeling slightly faint when we got through, but it was certainly a great trundle through Polish history. The Swedes had actually been quite destructive, one may note, in the 17th century. Poland, it must be said, has quite a tradition of toleration, both of Jews and of dotty Christian sects, down through history, and quite a democratic tradition as regards *electing* kings, which is interesting in view of its current rather intolerant Catholicism.

We had a coffee in a fine old writers' café on the Florianska, and got back in time to be collected by the young lady designated. I paid the hotel, and we set out across town. The young lady is very pleasant – a Doktorant, or doctoral student, but teaching already – available as a dogsbody! Happily, Barry was asked to lunch as well, so six of us repaired to the cafeteria in the basement of the rather dismal building that houses the Humanities – a new, rather than old, part of this ancient university – and had a moderate lunch. An interesting Englishman was there too, whose name I forget. He knows my colleague John Scattergood, Professor of English in Trinity, though.

There was a great turnout for the lecture – lots of students – but how much they really can have understood I dread to think. Anyhow, they seemed appreciative. Afterwards, however, it being about 4.30 pm, Mme S. just lined up a group of students, and said that they would show me round the town. We explained that we had actually seen the town, and Barry suggested they just show us where to have a drink. They seemed much relieved at this, and four of them (three girls and a lad) brought us to a very jolly student pub, where I stood them a beer, and we chatted pleasantly. Their English was excellent (one girl had actually been in America for four years – including at Champaign-Urbana!). However, at the end of an hour, Barry just suggested I come on back to Warsaw, and I agreed. The hostel that I was assigned to was dismal, and not near anything I wanted to see, and it would have spoiled the aura of Krakow. So we just went back there, got the bags, checked out, and fled. We got the 7.00 pm train back to Warsaw.

DAY 6, TUESDAY, MARCH 21ST

The weather has warmed up a bit, but it is still overcast. Barry decided to cancel his classes, to my slight confusion, and proposed a visit to a fine park, the Lazienki, for a walk. We set out about 10.00 am, on the bus, stopping off on the way to visit the University. First, up to the OBTA, where we met a nice lady, who sent us over to the Classics Department, where we met another nice lady – Professor Helena Cichocka, who herself specialises in rhetoric, but said there were *two philosophers*, neither in that day, one rather old (75), Julius Domanski, one younger, Mikolaj Szymanski, whom I might contact.

The walk round the Lazienki Park was delightful – preceded by a coffee and plum cake in a rather posh café overlooking the park. A light drizzle had started , but that didn't faze us. Lots of schoolkids were converging on the park in expectation of a rock concert (which was in fact warming up), in celebration of the first day of spring – we were presented with a tulip each in its honour outside the university. The Chopin Monument, where concerts are held in the summer, is very striking. We didn't bother with the Palace, and came back on the bus for a bit of a siesta, before setting out to the great adventure of the evening – if not of the whole tour!

This was a party out in the country, at the *dvorek,* or country house, of the actor Wojciech Siemion.[207] We took a taxi over to the Irish Embassy, situated in a pleasant quarter on the south of the city, and joined up with Brian Earls. We drove out in a chauffeured Embassy Mercedes about 20 km into the countryside, past pretty dull, though not unprosperous, farms and villages, till we reached the *dvorek*. This turned out to be an Aladdin's Cave of treasures, mainly of a folk-art nature, but lots of paintings by friends of Siemion, as well as some old pieces of furniture, all over the house, including the attic and basement. We got a guided tour, with various stories about individual items.

---

207 Wojciech Juliusz Siemion (1928 – 2010) was a Polish stage and film actor. He studied law at the Catholic University in Lublin from 1947 to 1950. At the same time, he attended acting classes at a local theatre. He enrolled at the State Theatre Academy in Warsaw, and after just one month, was able to skip two years of studies. Upon graduation in 1951 he began acting in several theatres and cabarets including Pod Egida. In 1983, he became a member of the council of the Patriotic Movement for National Rebirth, and in 1985–1989 served as a member of the Sejm from the Polish United Workers' Party. After the fall of the communist regime in Poland, Siemion became a member of the Polish Peoples' Party and served in the regional legislature of the Masovian Voivodeship. Siemion was awarded many cultural and state awards, including the Order of Polonia Restituta. He was killed in a car crash in April 2010.

By this time, quite a large company of friends and neighbours had assembled, and we had some (rather doubtful) Polish (?) wine, but basically, it seemed, they had come to hear *me on Joyce* – this all concocted by Margaret Bryll – though also Barry reading some poems of his. *And* I was not to speak about the *Wake!* A nice challenge! So I decided just to talk about the Parnellite Split, leading up to a reading of *Portrait of the Artist* – the Christmas dinner scene. I didn't want to exhaust them, though. Then Barry read, very well, and Seimion gave a very dramatic recitation in Polish.

And then a copious dinner was laid out, and we tucked in. Various people wanted to talk, but I was ultimately ambushed by a very voluble lady, who kept me standing so long that I really felt faint,[208] and had to sit down. Barry got me some water, and we made our escape, in the embassy car, which kindly gave us a lift home.

A good evening, though. One interesting fellow there was a poet and translator (of Shakespeare) called Siko, who had been ambassador to Denmark – like Ernest Bryll to Ireland!

DAY 7, WEDNESDAY, MARCH 22ND.

Here the diary breaks off. But we must assume an uneventful return, first to Heathrow, and then to Dublin.

---

208 Since my heart attack in early 1995, I have suffered from what it called 'orthostatic hypotension', which means that my capacity to stand around without moving is limited.

10. Trip to Greece
(The Peloponnese)

AUGUST 27 – SEPTEMBER 7, 2000

The occasion for this expedition was a conference on Plato's Academy in Athens organised by my old friend Paul Kalligas on Plato's Academy, but we took the excuse to make it a bit of a holiday as well. Instead of our usual destinations of Katounia, or one or other of the Aegean islands, we decided on this occasion to explore a part of Greece that we had never ventured into, the southern section of the mainland known as the Peloponnese, which is not a major tourist destination, despite possessing much of interest from virtually all periods of Greek history, from the Mycenaean to the mediaeval and Renaissance – all of which, I am glad to say, we had occasion to enjoy. In this case, my contributions are in ordinary print, Jean's in italics. Our daughter Ruth, as it happens, was at this time enjoying a post-Leaving Certificate holiday in Mallia, on the island of Crete, with her cronies.

DAY 1, SUNDAY, AUGUST 27TH

The adventure began promptly at 4.00 pm, when my sister Katharine came to collect us for the airport (poor Elizabeth, who had offered, was out of commission, because Liam died of a heart-attack, while in Galway). The airport was not too crowded, and Ryanair was very efficient – got us to Luton right on time. Then we had a three-hour wait, though, for our Easyjet flight to Athens. We had a burger at Burger King, and phoned around local hotels (from a list supplied by the airport) for somewhere to stay on Sept. 6th, hoping we arrive back reasonably on time! Found a pleasant-sounding one (Brache Travelodge), and booked in. The mobile phone, one has to admit, is a great invention. Then J sent a message to Mouse, which seemed to go through. We haven't quite mastered the mystery of phoning from a foreign country to a foreign country, but we hope this will be revealed. Then we moved over to Bewley's for a good coffee, and met three jolly young persons, all black, who were, remarkably, heading off for the Peloponnese as well, and ultimately for Pylos. How very discerning of them!

Easyjet, with true Swiss efficiency, got us off more or less on time. All very austere on the flight, though. No food, and any drinks you had to pay for. But what does one expect for £47? Also, no pillow on which to rest the head!

DAY 2, MONDAY, AUGUST 28TH

Nonetheless, we managed to snooze a bit, and in no time at all we were coming in to land in a darkened Athens, at 4.55 am their time (just 2.55 am Irish time!). It was lovely, though, to feel the warm air greeting one, even at 5.00 in the morning!

The car representative cheerfully met us and provided us with a small air conditioned Toyota, which is satisfactory (but without power steering). After what seemed an endless, one-and-a-half hour drive right through a tacky and dirty Athens, we began to smell familiar herbal smells and see brown hills with olive groves. Now the journey begins to be beautiful. The temperature is ideal for sight-seeing – about the mid-20s.

Our first stop was Nemea, to view Steve Miller's[209] progress in excavation. It is an impressive sight. The site is beautifully laid out, with gardens at the entrance and very extensive excavation. While we were there, we saw a group (Greeks) reconstructing a pillar – we felt they were using quite a lot of artistic licence, and making pieces fit which did not look too comfortable together! We had a (bad) cup of Greek coffee in a café in the town.

We passed Corinth, and about half-way between it and Tripoli we found a beautiful valley, with a rather smart café facing down the valley (Travel Break Café). We had a good cheese and ham pie between us, and rather innocuous coffee – 1380 drs.

---

209 My former colleague in Berkeley, where he was Professor of Classical Archaeology.

We left the autoroute after Tripoli – or it left us (not finished yet!) – and turned off it to Sparta, still on quite a good road. We decided to call in to Tegea, which was just off the road, to see what there was there. In fact, a very delightful village, largely unspoiled. The only antiquity was actually a very ruinous temple to Athena – lots of pillar-drums, but basically down to the foundations – and a bit of an old church. As we were pottering around, a rather dotty priest drove up, parked outside the church, his radio blaring religious chant, seemed to shout something at us, and then vanished down a side-street. A small mystery!

We came over a pass into the vale of Lacedaemon, Mount Taygetus rising mistily to our right. We were now thoroughly exhausted, afraid of going asleep at the wheel, but suddenly Sparta popped up, at around one o'clock. We drove in to look for a hotel, but were depressed by the volume of traffic, and the apparent featurelessness of the place. It is a new town, of course, only re-founded by King Otto in the 1830's, and is said to have a pleasant main square, but we didn't wait to find out.

There was mention in the guide-book of an hotel at Mistra, so we headed up the road to see what we could find. As we drove into Mistra (only five miles away), our hearts sank: all out the road there were cars and trucks parked – but then we saw that it was just a very popular local market! Further up the hill, on the main street, we found the Hotel Byzantion, which had been recommended, and it proved excellent value, at 18,000 dr a night for two, including breakfast (and an air-conditioned room).

The first thing one sees of Mistra is the extraordinary rock which rises above it, crowned by its castle. However, our first concern was to flop down for a siesta, which we accordingly did for two hours. We roused ourselves around 4.30, when things were a bit cooler – though in fact the temperature was never unpleasant (probably high 20s) – and headed up the hill to visit old Mistra.

It is indeed a marvellous site. Only the churches are now well preserved, but one gets an excellent feel of the whole town. We went round the Metropolis, the SS Theodora (two Theodoras seem to share this!), and the Hodêgêtria – all with very fine, if fragmentary, frescoes, and interesting architecture (though the fine points escape us!). Some good restoration has been done. We then toiled up towards the palace, pausing to watch some ants, and didn't in fact quite make it to the Palace, but called into the Pantanassa church, which is still inhabited by a convent of nuns. We descended again a little before closing time (7.00), and had a pleasant *Mythos* beer at a delightful restaurant just down the hill, with a fine view of the valley, all the way back to Sparta and beyond.

After a little rest back at the hotel, we had some trouble in rousing ourselves to go out to dinner in the restaurant across the road (Taverna *To Kastro*), which only started filling up around 9.30 (as usual), and served an excellent dinner. J had pork *souvlaki*, I had liver and onions – all very good. No dessert, as we had *tzatziki* to start. Instead of a coffee, we had chocolate and water on the verandah.

And so to bed. The temperature is perfect – mid- to high 20s.

DAY 3, TUESDAY, AUGUST 29TH

We slept heavily and arose later than we wished, at about 8.30 am. The breakfast at the hotel was rather boring – Nescafé, plastic ham, plastic cheese and bread, orange juice (not fresh – which, given the fact that the countryside is covered with orange trees, is pretty ridiculous!). But John ordered some yoghurt and honey, and it was delicious. We set out at about 10.00, to drive to a coastal port, Gythion. The drive was very pleasant – olive trees, orange, lime, and lemon trees, and eucalyptus. We parked at the port and strolled about the town, which had pleasant little back alleys and a prosperous waterfront, with an antique shop and many thriving restaurants. We stopped at the local supermarket to buy ingredients for a picnic (salami, cheese, orange drink, pears). Before leaving Gythion, we decided we would like to see the little island where Paris is supposed to have married Helen after he stole her from Menelaus in Sparta!! John was a bit sceptical about the 'marriage', and as a result got his punishment from

Helen by stepping on an uneven bit of pavement approaching the island, falling down, and spraining his ankle!

We found ourselves at the local health centre, with a very nice English speaking doctor, who wrapped his ankle in a bandage.

He was most conscientious, and felt it should be x-rayed, but his radiologist was on holidays (for which he apologised). He suggested we call into a health centre at Vlachiotis, on the way to Monemvasia, and wrote us a chit. When we got on our way, though, we decided that it really wasn't broken, and we wouldn't bother, but it was good of him to suggest it.

A fine drive along the coast east of Gytheion, then inland and over the Parnon range to Monemvasia. As the guide book remarks, the approach is misleading. One sees this massive rock (very like Gibraltar) sticking out into the sea, apparently barren and uninhabited, and a modern, pleasant, but unremarkable fishing village on the mainland. But then one drives across the causeway, round the rock to the sea side, and then one comes upon one of the most marvellous sites of Greece – a whole mediaeval town in excellent shape, the counterpart of Mistra (in fact, Guillaume de Villehardouin captured Monemvasia in the same year that he constructed the castle at Mistra – 1249).

With the ankle, it didn't seem possible to visit, but I just couldn't give up then. So J parked the car, leaving me at the gate, and we tottered through the gate, and up a narrow cobbled street to a little square with a Turkish cannon in the middle of it, and had a coffee frappé. Then J went to investigate a little museum in the square. It was beautifully laid out, so she brought me down. Just bits and pieces from the town, but they have made the most of it. On our way back up the street we found a wine shop, and bought a bottle of Malvasia (Malmsey) wine from a nice lady, discussing the fact that King John drowned in a vat of it. She was of the opinion that he was drowned in it (by his nobles). Very possibly![210]

I had planned to swim, but this was out of the question, so we headed back to Mistra. Just before Sparta, though, we

---

210 It seems to have been rather George Plantagenet, Duke of Clarence, who was drowned in a vat of Malmsey wine!

decided to check out the precinct of Apollo at Amyclae. It was up a little side road to the right, and turned out to be on a hilltop with a fine view, flanked by a little church. There was a young man sitting on what remained of the sanctuary (which was not much). He addressed us in English, wondering if we spoke it – perfect American English, actually. He turned out to be a young Greek-American lawyer, John Psichogios, and he was most interesting. A great enthusiast for orthodox theology (he was clutching a volume of Gregory of Nyssa, and impatiently awaiting Paul Kalligas' completion of his Plotinus translation), and even seemed to have heard of me. I gave him a brochure of the Centre, in case he ever wanted to enrol! His family comes from Sellasia, just north of Sparta, so he says he comes here often, to read. His office, though, is in the Piraeus (he is a shipping lawyer!).

After that, we drove home, too late for much of a siesta. Dark clouds were massing over Mount Taygetus, and it really looked like a thunderstorm, but it never came. We went back to the restaurant across the street, but got a rather surly waiter this time, who actually forgot my main course (pork), and had to be reminded. He also tried to sell us the most expensive wine, and otherwise chatted to his friends. He rather spoiled things.

The *panegyri* is still roaring on. Our hostess says it goes on all week – in honour of St John. Used to be an animal fair, it seems, but is now general. Loads of gypsies and blacks, all trading away. A funfair, and an ongoing religious service, blared out of the church. Sounds like the muezzin calling – except that this fellow never stops calling!

DAY 4, WEDNESDAY, AUGUST 30TH

We arose about 8.30 am, and were treated to a nicer breakfast of that delicious yoghurt and honey again, and hard-boiled eggs. We checked out, and set off right away on our journey through the Langada Pass in the Taygetus mountains. It was quite a spectacular drive, with large overhanging rock formations, a deep gorge, and a variety of vegetation, most of which I am unable to name, except for figs, plane, pine, and olives on the lower plains.

The tops of the mountains were fairly barren, but every now and then we would see a little stall selling tomatoes, honey and suchlike.

It took about one-and-a-half hours to reach Kalamata from Mistra. We were not tempted to visit Kalamata, as our eyes began to smart as soon as we approached its environs.

We drove next towards Korone, down the eastern side of the peninsula, past a series of holiday settlements and campsites. Suddenly, by the side of the road, we saw something that looked like *Dermot McAleese*.[211] We ground to a stop, and I went back to check. It was indeed Dermot – and his wife – who had signed on for a two-week holiday in a villa there, and were, like ourselves, just in their third day of residence. To us in our car, it seemed a rather limited existence, but no doubt for them it is just the ticket. We drove on, after exchanging mutual good wishes.

Korone, in fact, has not a lot to be said for it, Crusader castle notwithstanding. It is quite a modern town, pleasant enough, but unremarkable, and rather touristy. We had our picnic, availed of the toilet facilities, and drove on over another range of hills, to Methone. This was a pleasant drive, through more olive groves and some vines, until the sea appeared again, and we arrived in the resort of Fenikoundas. We actually left Methone aside for the moment, and decided to drive straight to Pylos, to find somewhere to stay.

We failed to find the two hotels mentioned by Baedeker, the Castor and the Nestor, and found instead the Karalis, which is quite pleasant, but on the main road of the town, and rather noisy. But it has a lovely view across the bay. We tried to take a siesta, but failed, and at about 5 pm set out to find a suitable beach to swim – at least John wanted one! We eventually found a rather dirty beach, with water full of bracken, but it was lukewarm! John had a swim, and I put my feet in.

Sadly, Navarino Bay is not great for swimming – rather shallow, and rather clouded with floating seaweed (I hope nothing worse!). Where we stopped to swim, an old wreck was keeled over just off-shore, which wasn't very encouraging either

---

211 My colleague in Trinity – the Whately Professor of Political Economy. Dermot was a great authority on the Irish economy, and much in demand. to sit on commissions and suchlike.

– presumably *not* part of the Turkish navy wrecked in the Battle of Navarino! The island of Sphacteria, which closes in the bay, is a most extraordinary sight – an enormous slab of rock rising to a series of crests, and rather difficult to distinguish from the mainland.

We drove on, and found a delightful little settlement at Khora, and there were our friends from the plane, ensconced in a café! We greeted them, and learned that they had based themselves in Methone, and driven up here in a car. They have invited us down to join them for dinner tomorrow or the next day, if we're free. Melinda has given us her mobile number.

We found a pleasant little hotel on the beach, the *Zoe*, and have provisionally booked for tomorrow. The clientele seems to be mainly German, but none the worse for that, no doubt! Then we drove on again, to check out the site of Nestor's Palace, and an interesting wild-life lagoon which is advertised as needing saving, and in the process found an absolutely splendid hotel, the *Navarone*, complete with pool, which we hope to move to on Sept, 1 – only 15,000 dr. Hard to believe!

J has mastered the mobile now, just about, and we got onto a rather miserable Mouse, who is in bed with an asthma attack – may be psychosomatic – dissatisfaction with her company – but still disturbing. We hope it clears up in the next day or so.

Back to Pylos in the evening, and went strolling. We still haven't found either of the recommended hotels. Perhaps they've changed their names! Had another good dinner, at a seafood restaurant – I had calamari, J grilled chicken. It came to less than 4000 dr. We met some rather brash returned Canadian Greeks. Then a coffee and ouzo in the main square, before retiring. Will have to cut down on the feasting!

DAY 5, THURSDAY, AUGUST 31ST

Again, rose a little later than we should – around 8.30 am. There was an excellent breakfast on offer in the hotel, but we just stuck to yoghurt, honey and fruit. Then we decided to head for the Castro, at the other edge of town. We drove up to it, and found *another* Karalis Hotel, in a beautiful setting overlooking the Bay, but it was in fact full. We then walked up, through pine trees, to the entrance of the castle, which is a magnificent pile, but apparently of Turkish foundation (though there is a Byzantine church in the precinct). It must have been the ancient acropolis, but there seems to be no signs of ancient remains.

Then we set out north to find Nestor's Palace.[212] *The temperature was pretty high today, so we were rather dreading getting out of the air-conditioned car to view the Palace. But we remembered that it had been covered with a plastic roof, and that was a blessing. The most impressive parts of the site were the hearth (circular) in the throne room, and the decorated bath, in almost perfect condition. (We picnicked under a tree, on delicious peaches, pears, ham pasties and tyropita, prior to viewing the site).*

We drove back to check into our hotel at Gialova, called the Hotel Zoe (13,000 dr for two, including breakfast – not air-conditioned, but O.K.). It is quite a find, basic but clean, with its own beach front, planted with palms, oleanders and fig trees. We had a 2-3 hour siesta (!!), then John had a swim in the bay, where the water was lukewarm.

We went round the corner to the Café Marco for a coffee frappé (John) and Greek coffee (me), and read for a while. Then roused ourselves for an evening drive to some tholos tombs. We visited first the restored one just north of the palace, then a collapsed one a bit south of the Palace, in somebody's orchard. Not unlike Irish passage graves, in fact, except for no carving on the stones – and 2000 years later, of course!

On our way back, we called in to view the Gialova Lagoon, where we saw an egret, and quite a number of RV's, proposing to camp for the night, despite the mosquitos. We might do a more serious tour of it tomorrow. It is a fine situation, certainly, no doubt plotted against by local Greek gombeen men and cowboy developers!

I must say that the visit to Nestor's Palace puts Telemachus' visit to Nestor in an interesting perspective.[213] There is an

---

212 (Note by John) First, however, we visited the very impressive museum in the neighbouring town of Khora, where quite a proportion of the finds from the Palace and neighbouring tholos tombs are preserved.

213 This refers to a passage early in Homer's Odyssey (Book 3), in which Telemachus, son of Odysseus, goes to visit the aged and wise King Nestor of

excellent view of the north entrance to the Bay from the front of the Palace – probably a five-mile walk up – but one could see any ship coming in round the north end of Sphakteria. Very well placed to anticipate visitors, hostile or otherwise!

For dinner, we decided to snub the rather rude fellow who runs the Oasis, and patronise another taverna a little down the way. It was perfectly good. J had moussaka and I had 'little fishes', and we shared a *saganaki*. Various cats attended me closely, as I was distributing fish tails. Then a Greek coffee with Marco, and so to bed.

DAY 6, FRIDAY, SEPTEMBER 1ST

We slept not too badly, despite no air-conditioning, because there was a slight breeze from the sea. They served a good breakfast – fried egg, fresh bread, jam. Then we set off to visit the Gialova Lagoon. This is just round the corner, really, but a bit of a bumpy ride. There is a nature trail, which we followed, which is well laid out, and deals with the various flora and fauna in the salt water and fresh water environments. Then we drove to the end of the trail, to see if we could find the castle of the tholos tomb – identified by Pausanias[214] as that of Nestor's son! We got to the end of the road, where the end of Sphakteria creates a narrow channel separating it from the mainland, but everything unfortunately required climbing, and the ankle is still not equal to that sort of thing, so we took a little walk along a path at the base of the promontory.

There was a beach, with a coffee shop and umbrellas, but we decided we might as well be back on our own beach, and went back for a coffee frappé at Marco's, after which I took a very pleasant swim, before the afternoon breeze got up. Then a bit of reading, a bit of lunch – cheese or cheese and ham pies at Marco's (rather too rich!), beer, and coffee. Then a siesta. It is becoming rather hot!

---

* Pylos, in the hope of learning news of his father.
214 An ancient Greek geographer, who wrote a Description of Greece.

We headed for Methone, at about 6 pm, to view the Castle. It is a magnificent sight, which once enclosed a whole town, founded by the Venetians in about 1200, until it was sacked by the Turks in 1500 or so. It has an enormous, sometimes seemingly double, moat. The castle was about to close just as we arrived, so we unfortunately had only a quick dash through its interior.

We had arranged by phone to meet some people we had originally met at Luton airport – two Afro-Englishmen, Danny and Roy, and an English girl, Melinda – for a drink in the main square. We met in the main square, and finally found out what our friends do for a living. They are all social workers in Birmingham. Melinda is a court representative. After a nice chat, and having directed Danny to a health centre for treatment of prickly heat, we came back to Pylos. There we had dinner at the same restaurant, **Ta Adelphia,** *where we had dined last in Pylos, and very good it was: stuffed pepper and tomato, tsatsiki, grilled pork chop, écrevisses, and the local rosé, which we have been making a habit of. Then back to Gialova. We have omitted to mention so far that this area is almost wholly dominated by German tourists, with just a sprinkling of Italians and English.*

DAY 7, SATURDAY, SEPTEMBER 7TH

Spent a rather uncomfortable night – very hot, and *no* breeze. The Hotel Zoe does not run to air conditioning. After another pleasant breakfast, we paid (26,000 dr), and set out north, for Bassai. Clouds were about, looking a bit threatening, but no rain came, and it was very hot and humid. We turned off the coast road at a place called Tholo, and headed into the hills (our guide did not feel that there was much of a road, but it has been improved).

We came first to Lepreon, and found a sign to the Acropolis. A granny assured us that we could drive up, and she was right. It is a magnificent site – not much left but foundations, but most impressive nonetheless. There are the remains of a fine temple, overlooking the valley, with a view down to the sea. We also found a fine fig tree, and liberated a handful of ripe figs for lunch.

Then on to Bassai – a wonderful drive, if a bit slow. The temple itself is magnificently situated, but rather sadly encased in a plastic cover and scaffolding, until repairs can be completed. Still, impressive enough! There are remains of other buildings just below it.

After leaving Bassai, we had a picnic by the side of the road, with remains of breakfast and the figs. After that, we drove through Andritseva, to the magnificent mountain village of Karytaina, nestling under its Frankish castle. J was not too keen to drive up to the castle, but we did, and were glad of that. It is a bit dilapidated, but plainly being repaired. There is a lovely little Byzantine church also.

For at least half an hour of the drive, we went through mountainside after mountainside of thoroughly blackened farms, the result, seemingly, of tremendous fires which we seem to remember having happened around July. Since this is all very steep country, I dread to think what will happen when the rains arrive. We met a man walking down the road with a flock of goats, and wondered how on earth he managed to feed them.

We came down to Megalopolis on a reasonably good road, stopping for a look at the remains of ancient Megalopolis on the way. The ruins were actually closed, apparently for repairs, but one could see a theatre, the council house of the Arcadian League, and a temple of Zeus. Then down into town, and we had a cappuccino in the square. A very nice waiter, but very expensive – 700 dr each! Better stick to *kafé ellêniko!*

We decided then to head on to Tolon, or perhaps Nafplion. However, having viewed the crowds in Nafplion, and tried one pension (which was full), we decided to drive on to Tolon, and stay either at the Solon (recommended by the Boydells)[215] or the Hotel Flisvos (where we had stayed back in 1977!).[216] The Hotel Solon appeared first, and because it was already 8.00 pm, we were tired, and, as they had a room, we took it. As it turned out, it is a very forbidding room, with a plastic floor, furniture too small for its scale, and not attractive at all; but we have decided to take it. At least it has parking outside, and back steps from a terrace onto the beach.

We helped ourselves to beers from the fridge – no one there

---

215 Our friends from Howth. Brian Boydell was Professor of Music in Trinity College., and quite a distinguished composer.
216 See Being There I, p. 26ff.

to help or hinder us – and contemplated the sea for a while. Then we wandered out to find dinner. We saw an advertisement for what seemed to be an Italian restaurant a little up the hill, but it turned out to be just as Greek as anything else – run by a great operator, who attended to us personally. In fact, he served excellent food, though the atmosphere of rip-off was pervasive. He and his young waiter 'treated' us to a performance of a Greek dance!

We returned to our hotel, and because the key wouldn't turn in our bedroom door, we had to ask the assistance of the large woman at the desk. As an aside, when she was leaving us, she mentioned the beer! We were rather dishonestly not going to say anything, because we felt we were being greatly overcharged for the room. Oh well!

DAY 8, SUNDAY, SEPTEMBER 3RD

Next morning, before breakfast (about 8.30 am), John had a lovely swim off the back steps of the hotel. Good, clean, lukewarm water. After breakfast, we headed for Nafplion, and by day it is a really lovely town. Sunday morning was a good time to visit, because all the visitors of the night before were either in bed or at church. We climbed as high as we dared, with John's gammy foot, the huge Venetian castle overlooking the bay and town. It was rather hot by this stage.

On our continued journey towards Athens, we decided to take a walk in Ancient Corinth, and we were rewarded with an amazing site, with quite a lot standing of the Temple of Apollo and the Fountain of Peirene. It is an amazing structure, with a stream pouring in one side, and six round arched openings which were added by the Romans (but the original structure can be seen behind the newer one). After another little while, we got a bit hot and tired and John a bit dizzy, so we returned to the car and sat in the air-conditioning for a while. Then we sat on a bank at the edge of the car park, and had some breakfast sandwich which we had preserved, and some fizzy orange.

We arrived in Athens at about 4.30 pm, and managed to park just around the corner from our Hotel, the Plaka, which is very conveniently placed near Monasteraki, on Mitropoleos, and dumped the bags. They assured us at the desk that it was a tow-away zone, so we didn't linger long (lots of people parked, nonetheless!). *The hotel seems excellent – air conditioning and pleasant rooms.*

We then drove the car up to the American School, and parked on Souidias, as the gates were closed. We got in through a side gate, but could find nobody to give the key to.[217] We wandered then into the British School, and found Rebecca's[218] boyfriend, William Boyd, holding the fort. He obligingly took charge of the key, and said he would leave it in the office for collection. Then we got a taxi back to the Hotel Plaka.

I called Andrew Smith[219] (who had been visiting Eleni Perdikouri[220]), and fixed up to meet him for a drink and dinner at 7.30. He duly arrived, and we set out to find a venue in the Plaka. We settled on a restaurant beside the Tower of the Winds, where we had a pleasant dinner – *mezes,* and lamb with pasta, in my case. Then up to the Irish School,[221] for a bottle of retsina. It looks pretty good, with new bookshelves and George Huxley's books. As we were finishing the bottle, Pat Cronin[222] and his wife arrived, and we chatted for a while before going back to the hotel.

---

217 This is not made clear earlier, but I must have somehow rented the car through the American School.

218 That is to say, Dr Rebecca Sweetman, daughter of my first cousin David Sweetman, Professor of Classics at the University of St. Andrews, and at this time Assistant Director of the British School in Athens. A major authority on the archaeology of Greece in the Roman era, she has subsequently (from Sept 2022) been appointed Director of the British School.

219 Professor of Classics in University College Dublin, and a distinguished authority on Neoplatonism, who was also attending the conference.

220 A former visitor to the Plato Centre in Trinity College, and now Assistant Professor of Philosophy in the University of Patras.

221 The Irish School of Hellenic Studies in Athens had been founded a few years earlier, in 1996, mainly at the instigation of George Huxley, Professor of Classics in Queen's University, Belfast, and a great promoter of classical studies in Ireland generally. At this time it was based in rather humble premises on the northern slopes of the Acropolis, but moved later to more spacious premises in Odos Notara.

222 Our first Director, Professor Patrick Cronin, of University College Cork. I myself became Director from 2003 to 2012.

DAY 8, MONDAY, SEPTEMBER 3RD

Up at 7.30 am, enjoyed a good breakfast of yoghurt and honey. Then phoned Motorent, and gave them information on the car. They *seemed* to me on the ball. Then walked up to the Museum of the City of Athens to begin our little conference. I found Andrew, Paul Kalligas, and others – including the redoubtable Judith Binder, a feisty old girl – in attendance, but the chief speaker, Mme Ligouri, of the Academy excavations, was *not* present. When contacted, she claimed that she had received no invitation (!), but agreed to be around tomorrow, to show us the site. This lady will be trouble, I should say.

A good talk was delivered, however, by another archaeologist, Mme Choremi, on her dig at Hadrian's Library – a fascinating structure. The only problem is to know how it was administered, and who used it. There seems to be no answer to that! After coffee, at which I communed with Polymnia,[223] who had popped up, I presided over talks given by Elias Tempelis, on 'Proclus' House and the Closing of the Academy', and his wife, Christina Manolea (who is currently working under Gerard O'Daly in London), on 'Rhetoric and Philosophy in Syrianus' – both very sound, though Elias perhaps a bit optimistic about Proclus' House, and controversial as to what Justinian was up to in 529.[224]

We then retired for a 'light lunch' to a very pleasant restaurant not far away. This consisted, in my case, of a *mikrê poikilia*,[225] which turned out to be a vast plate of *mezes*, washed down by ouzo. I had an interesting further talk with Judith Binder. Then back to the Museum for a business session at 3.00, in which we hammered out the form of a possible collective volume on Philosophers in Athens (with the proviso that the

---

223 That is, Polymnia Athanassiadi, formerly wife of Garth Fowden, and a considerable authority on later Greek philosophy. For an earlier encounter with her, see *Being There*, p. 109.

224 That is to say, the Roman Emperor Justinian, who closed the Academy in that year.

225 Sc. a 'small variety'.

archaeological evidence seems pretty thin on the ground, as things stand), after which the Director of the Museum gave us a tour. This was actually most delightful, as it is laid out in the form of an upper-class 19th-century townhouse (which is what it is), replete with memorabilia of King Otto and his wife Amelia.

I went off on my own for most of the day. I decided to visit the Agora, and walked to it via Ermou, which is a really nasty street, full of scruffy little shops and lots of smelly traffic. I arrived at the Agora to find it closed (Mondays), so instead I visited the Greek Folk Museum beside Hadrian's House. It is a lovely little museum which had once been a church. It houses the private collection of a Professor of Ceramics, gathered from all over Greece. This man travelled far and wide to meet the individual craftsmen. Some of their stories are extremely sad, they having come to Greece as refugees from Asia Minor, and having died in awful poverty in spite of their talents. [226]

I then visited two delightful Byzantine churches, both within walking distance of our hotel, one at Kapnikarea Square, which had wonderful frescoes well preserved, and one at Mitripoliou – this one incorporating many wonderful pieces of stone from previous Greek and Roman buildings.

Then I went back to rest at the hotel. John and Andrew arrived at about 6.30 pm.

We went for a beer up the road, within sight of the Tower of the Winds. Then Andrew went off to get some wine for the reception,[227] and we went back to the hotel for a while. At 7.00, we set off up the hill to give a hand at the reception. The Institute was looking quite well, as I have remarked earlier, with a new bookcase containing the Library, with both George Huxley's books and a consignment from the Embassy.

About twelve people came to the reception, including the rather jolly head of the Canadian School, David Jordan, and his wife Jan, who works in the Agora for the American excavations. Jordan has been here thirty years, and seems set to go on. He is making an edition of *defixiones,* and plans to re-edit Preisendanz's

---

226 This must actually have been the Tzistarakis Mosque in Monastiraki Square, which is one of the annexes of the Museum of Greek Folk Art, housing the "V. Kyriazopoulos Collection of Folk Pottery".

227 This seems to have been a reception that we were staging at the Irish Institute.

PGM.²²⁸ He has quite an interest in magic. Polymnia and her husband John were also there, as well as Pavlos²²⁹ and his wife Themeli, and some students – a young fellow who wanted to study with me among them. We agreed on a thesis on Plotinus' concept of *Zoe*.²³⁰

Then all off to a fine dinner at the *Xynos* restaurant – quite an old taverna, apparently. Good *mezes*, and lots of retsina drunk. I sat beside Polymnia, and she discoursed unrelentingly – but interestingly – about, among other things, her encounter with Seferis²³¹ in her youth. I talked to David Jordan also, about Myles na Gopaleen.

Michael Telford²³² had turned up in time for the reception (he is to give a lecture on the Book of Kells tomorrow evening), and after dinner we entertained Andrew and himself to a nightcap on the roof garden of the hotel, which has a fine view of both the Acropolis and Lycabettus, both illuminated.

DAY 9, TUESDAY, SEPTEMBER 4TH

This was the day for tramping round ruins, and we all assembled at Hadrian's Gate at 9.00 am, to visit, first, the Houses of Proclus (?), and of Damascius (?)²³³. Fortunately, Judith Binder was not in attendance!²³⁴ First we walked round to the south slope

---

228 That is to say, the *Papyri Magicae Graecae*, a comprehensive collection of Greek magical texts preserved on papyri. Defixiones are curse tablets. Jordan published the curse tablets in a series of articles in the Classical magazine Phoenix, but he never re-did the PGM.

229 That is to say, Paul Kalligas.

230 I have no recollection of who this might have been, or of the thesis, so it must never have come to anything.

231 The distinguished Greek poet, George Seferis (1900-1971).

232 Headmaster of John Scottus School in Dublin, and quite a lover of things Platonic, but I don't know how he became involved in the conference.

233 Proclus (412-485 AD) and Damascius (458-550) were heads of the Platonic Academy in late antiquity.

234 I cannot now remember the reason for this remark. Perhaps she had strong views on the identity of these two sites.

of the Acropolis to view the sad traces of the 'Proclus House'. Now immured under Dionysius the Areopagite Street (very ironically!).[235] It is certainly in the right area, but so are various other villas, and there is very little, really, to identify it as the right one.

Then round to the north side, to view the 'Damascius House'. This is far more promising. We were shown round by a nice young lady from the Archaeological Service, and Polymnia was also voluble on the subject.[236] Certainly it is a fine villa, of the right period, which seems to have been taken over by an important Christian (Polymnia thinks the Bishop of Athens himself) in around 530 AD, which would fit well.

Then straight on (unfortunately) to look at Hadrian's Library, in broiling sun. I was beginning to fade anyhow, but Mme Choremi began to give her lecture all over again at the front façade, instead of just showing us round, and I had to give up, and go back to the hotel to rest. Just as well, as we got out of the 'leisurely lunch' that Andrew had planned, which would have finished me in any case. Instead, we had a nice sandwich in the hotel bedroom.

I rose again, though, to be driven out to the Academy at 3.30 by Pavlos, to be shown round by Mme Ligouri. She came up trumps in the end, but the pickings in the Academy are sadly, pretty slim. There is a Roman gymnasium and another peristyle structure – nothing faintly connecting to Plato or the Old Academy, or really to any philosophical activity at all. It actually began to rain while we were out there, which was rather pleasant, but it remained warm. Mme Ligouri drove us back to the Plaka around 5.30. There we met up with J and had a beer, preparatory to attending Michael's lecture in the Goulandris Horn Foundation.

This proved an excellent occasion – very lucid lecture

---

235 That is because the Christian theologian who sheltered behind the pseudonym of 'Dionysius the Areopagite' borrowed a good deal of his theology from Proclus.

236 Polymnia had actually recently produced an edition of Damascius' *Philosophical History*, a most entertaining work of late antique gossip.

by Michael, well illustrated, a good audience, and a pleasant reception afterwards. I met the Irish ambassador – a rather dim man, I thought – and a jolly civil engineer called Andy Fahy, prominent in the Greek-Irish Association. We went on to dinner in the Restaurant Plato with Rebecca and Mike, and had excellent vegetarian *mezes* – came to 10,000 dr for the four of us.

DAY 10, WEDNESDAY, SEPTEMBER 5TH

Rose about 9.00 am, not quite clear what we wanted to do with ourselves. We packed up, but don't have vacate the room till 12.00, so we decided to *walk* up to Motorent, at 71 Vasilissas Sophias Avenue. This proved not such a great idea, as it was rather far along the avenue (the individual buildings being rather big), but we made it, and collected the bill, which came to around 133,000 dr, or $325, which seems tolerable for unlimited mileage, air-conditioning, and full insurance. Then we walked back, intending to stop off at the Benakis Museum, but instead found the Goulandris Museum of Cycladic Art, which is hosting the fascinating exhibition of finds from the Metro excavations, 'The City beneath the City'. We spent the best part of an hour at this, and then caught a taxi back to the hotel.

    Then we thought to phone Andrew, to see what he was doing. He was in fact at the Institute, surrounded by half-empty bottles of wine, lots of nibbles left over from the reception, and slightly at a loss. So we left the bags, and went up to join him. That proved very jolly. We came upon a neighbour across the street, who is a prosperous banker (the Alpha Bank boss in Romania, in fact!), and is restoring his house, and was rather concerned as to who *we* were, and what our plans were. So we explained our situation, and he might turn out to be helpful. Certainly, Bob McCabe has to be gently urged to clarify our situation. In particular, we would like the house of St Nectarius, just down the street, which he also owns. If O'Reilly/Goulandris[237] would

---

237 That is to say, the major Irish entrepreneur Tony O'Reilly, who was married to a very rich Greek-American lady, Chryss Goulandris. Nothing came of this, I regret to say!

buy that for us, perhaps, and set us up with an endowment, then all would be well!

Pat and Ann Cronin arrived while we were finishing off the wine, hoping to take a rest (George Huxley had been at them since early morning!), and we and Andrew went back down the hill to have a coffee frappé, and look at Hadrian's Library again. This occupied us pleasantly till 5.30, when our taxi came to take us to the airport.

In fact, Easyjet came up trumps again – only around 40 minutes late in the end. We arrived in Luton less than a half-hour late, so we were able to get a taxi to the Brache Travelodge before 11.30 pm. This turns out to be a rather new and mildly tacky Americanised erection, costing £55 or so for bed and breakfast, but it served OK, and proved a pleasant enough end to the holiday.

DAY 11, THURSDAY, SEPTEMBER 6TH

Ryanair got us home next morning just on time. All in all, the holiday was characterized by everything going *right*, which is quite remarkable. The only thing wrong was my sprained ankle, which no one else can be blamed for.

(Meanwhile, over in Mallia, the Mouse was having troubles with respiratory diseases, but ultimately that all came right; we had had some anxious phone calls, though, between the Peloponnese and Crete!)[238]

---

238 As has been mentioned in the introductory note, our daughter Ruth was at this time celebrating the taking of her Leaving Certificate by spending a holiday in Crete with her cronies!

Porta Nigra, Trier, Germany

Old Warsaw, Poland

Temple of Apollo, Corinth, Greece

View of the sea from Nestor's Palace, Pylos, Greece

Town Hall Square, Riga, Latvia

The Temple of Sanjusangendo, Kyoto, Japan

Temple of Kiyomizu-dera-Kyoto, in Kyoto, Japan

Sydney Harbour, Australia

11. TRIP TO RIGA, LATVIA:

MARCH 25 – APRIL 2, 2001

This was the result of an invitation by Edgars Narkevics, of the University of Riga, to give a series of lectures to his Classical Philosophy group, Ad Fontes – stimulated, as I recall, by a recommendation from my friend Eyjólfur Emilsson, of the University of Oslo, who had been invited there previously. I was somewhat apprehensive about this, as can be seen from the early entries, but it in fact all worked out rather well, and gave me a fascinating insight into a gallant little nation that has endured much.

DAY 1, SUNDAY. MARCH 25TH

6.46 am: On my *SAS* flight, just waiting to pull away from the dock. This is possibly one of my dottier expeditions ever. I am heading off for a week to a country I know nothing of (though I have been boning up with an excellent guide book that Hodges Figgis managed to provide), to people I know nothing of (Is Edgars Narkevics a university person, or a private enthusiast for Greek philosophy? And what are the AD FONTES group?), to talk off the top of my head – I have brought no texts of talks – about the development of Platonism in general. The only talk I've brought is the one on Joyce, which may be way over their heads. All this has to be in *English*, of course.

    The plane is more or less on time, but it has only a 40 minute overlap time in Copenhagen, so I foresee disaster at that end, for the bag at least – and I have had to put *everything* in the big bag, as I have brought the briefcase. Ah, well!

    I leave a household racked by illness – Mouse has been out

of action since last Tuesday with a virus, and got *worse* yesterday. I actually woke up this morning in a lather of sweat, feeling I had the flu, but that *seems* to have passed off, as of now. The weather has certainly been miserable – fog for the last two days – but perhaps our very pleasant dinner in the Citrus with Pat and Jim Coffey last night was the primary cause.

I leave also a country in crisis, not knowing where Foot and Mouth will strike next, and waiting to see what the US – and world – economy is going to do. Our much-vaunted boom could dissolve more or less overnight, leaving everything half-done and half-built, and many young people over-borrowed. Indeed, the next week should reveal a lot. When I return on April 2, things may be clearer.[239]

9.43 am: Just landing in Copenhagen – still on time. Weather is fine, cold (1°), but the fields look rather flooded. We flew over water from the west of Denmark to get here. I hadn't grasped that previously. I must study the map!

10.23 am: I am just now on board flight BT 134 to Riga, after a furious rush across the very *largest* terminal. It could hardly have been farther away. SAS was most irresponsible in leaving only 40 minutes to get from flight to flight – especially as passport controls are extremely slow, for an EU country! I ended up in a fine lather, sweating and shaking – *not* good for me – and my bags are certainly lost. I note that there is slightly *more* than an hour's grace on the way back. It still needs everything to be on time, though. The airport is fine and modern, though I was in no mood to appreciate it – *endless* bloody cafés and boutiques!

At this moment I am wondering what in hell this is all about. Why am I spending a whole week preaching about Platonism to these people in Latvia?

10.57 am: In the air. Funny how behaviours of airlines are more or less identical the world over. The cabin crew are now serving a second breakfast – I'll have to consider my position;

---

239 I was being excessively gloomy here. The boom romped on, as we know, until late 2008, when all that I fear here came to pass.

I've just had my first! I'm reading the *Baltic Times* – very readable and interesting. The man beside me is reading a Russian paper. It's quite a *little* plane – an Avro RJ70. I am trying to bone up on a bit of Latvian from the back of my guide book:

> 'Please' is *Lūdzu;* 'Thank you' is *Paldies*
> *Vai Jus runājiet Angliski?* 'Do you speak English?'
> *Es nerunaju latviski,* 'I don't speak Latvian.'

So, *es* is 'I', *Jus* is 'you', *runaj* – 'speak', *-et* – 2nd person ending, *-u*, 1st person ending; *ne-*, negative prefix. This is fun!

10.30: The end of an eventful and very pleasant day! The bag did in fact get through, and was there by the time I had cleared immigration. Edgars and Janete Narkevics were there to meet me – a very delightful young couple! Edgars is rather like a younger Mario Rinvolucri, an old friend of mine from Oxford days, and Janete is a pretty, delicate person with excellent English. We went by taxi to my hotel in the Old City, *Rudi m Dragi* ('Friends and Relations'), a pleasant, modern hotel, apparently founded by Latvians from England. I have a room on the 6th floor, with a view, over roofs, to the steeple of the Cathedral.

We went out for a bite of lunch, and worked out procedure for the next week – two-hour sessions, with a break in the middle. Then back to the hotel, and I rested until 5.30 pm, when they came back to collect me. We took a walk round the Old Town, coming to the Cathedral, where we stopped for part of an excellent choral concert – in commemoration of the deportations of 1949 – flags hanging out everywhere with black ribbons on them. The weather, by the way, is fine and clear, but temperature hanging round about *zero* – so I need to wrap up. At least it's not *damp*, though.

After more perambulations, during which we viewed a bust of Herder, who taught here for a while, we stopped in to an excellent restaurant for dinner. I introduced them to *kir*, and paid for the wine (Edgars has presented me with 200 lats as expenses, while I'm here). We had an excellent dinner, and much interesting chat about the state of Latvia, and the goings-on under Communism. It sounds as though things in Classics, or even Greek philosophy, are under threat, though, in the university now; one needs 15 customers to put on a class in anything, as in many parts of our own system, indeed!

I phoned Jean when I got in, on the mobile. Mouse is somewhat better. I thought it was two hours *on*, but it is actually two hours *back*, of course, so only really 8.00 I was exhausted enough, though, so had no trouble going asleep.

DAY 2, MONDAY, MARCH 26TH

I was up a bit during the night. Thought I was getting the flu, and indeed I have a bit of a cold, but got back to sleep, and woke at 8.45 am. A comfortable bed and room, I must say. Breakfast in the café next door, for which I have a voucher. I had a tomato and mushroom omelette, toast and coffee. Then I decided on a walk round the Old Town, following a route recommended by the guide book,[240] up to the Powder Tower, and down to the Castle. Lots of interesting things to see, though all museums are closed on Mondays. Churches were open, though, and I called into the Catholic Cathedral (St. James's), where lots of old ladies were either saying the rosary or doing the Stations of the Cross. It is *not* a very spectacular building, but old enough. I found also the English Church, looking over the Daugava River, and the Guildhall, which has concerts. I am now sitting in a pleasant café, having a coffee. I changed 20 Lats – this didn't even cost one Lat, for coffee and cake!

I had lunch in the hotel café – a curious but tasty cabbage schnitzel with mushrooms, and a beer, and then Edgars came to collect me at 2.00 for the lecture. We walked across the canal into the New Town, and round a corner from the main university building to where Philosophy and kindred disciplines are housed. There is redecorating going on, though, so we had to go by devious routes to the lecture-room. A large crowd

---

240 Latvia – The Bradt Travel Guide, by Stephen Baister and Chris Patrick (1995), which was indeed excellent, and which I still retain.

greeted me, including many students. Quite a surprise! I was worried about just talking off the top of my head, but in fact found no lack of things to say. There was a short break in the middle, and we stopped about 4.20, having more or less covered the development of Platonism from Plato to Numenius. Then Edgars and a colleague (Arvins, I think) took me off to a pub in the Old Town, and we sat there over beer and *mezes* for about *four hours*, talking philosophy. There is quite a hunger for talk here, I think. I was told that I was the first Irish scholar to visit the university, but also the first person to talk on Platonism since before the War!

After that, I simply went home to bed, without any dinner. It is really only early evening, but I am exhausted.

DAY 3, TUESDAY, MARCH 27TH

I woke up, once again, in the middle of the night – around 3.00 – but having had probably enough sleep. I do definitely have a cold, and a cough – must get some cough mixture. I read for a while – *Outerbridge Reach*,[241] and then Zeyl's translation of the *Timaeus* – but I got to sleep again, and only woke up at about 9.20 – no time for breakfast, just a quick instant coffee in the room, before Edgars collected me.

The class today seemed to go well. I talked on First Principles – didn't quite get to the end of the story, but covered a fair bit. They are recording me, and want to transcribe and publish the results. I wonder if that will work. After the lecture, I was taken off to coffee by half a dozen of the students, who were very pleasant – they all seemed to be working on Plato, and all spoke English very well. I had a cake with my coffee, since I hadn't had any breakfast, but it was well after 1.00 when we broke up the party, so where did that leave lunch? I went out for a *Bummel*, and found my way into the Museum of the Occupation, a very grim black box of a building adjacent to the Cathedral, but it was a most interesting, if very grim, exhibition – first the Commies, then the Nazis, then the Commies again, one worse than the

---

[241] A 1992 novel by Robert Stone. I can't imagine why I was reading it.

other. Half the nation was wiped out! We have no conception of what these people had to go through. It is so splendid that they have been able to rise again, still speaking their own language – though there is still a *majority* of Russians in Riga (as there used to be a majority of Germans in the old days!).

On the way back from the Museum, I stopped off at an Irish pub, 'Paddy Whelan's' (God forgive me, but it's just beside the Hotel) to have a beer (*not* Irish) and a good hot sandwich. Then back to the hotel, to find Janete waiting for me, to take me on an excursion to Jurmala, the seaside resort of Riga, about 25 km out of town to the west. We drive with an interesting fellow, Uldis Torons, who is attending the lectures. He helps to edit a monthly magazine, *Rigas Lailas* ('Riga Times'). We drove in his Volvo, with his young son Arturs, to Jurmala, and took a pleasant walk along the beach and through the town. The weather seems a few degrees warmer, so it was not unpleasant. It is a rather fascinating town, a bit reminiscent of Carmel, or a New England seaside resort, with rather dilapidated, but sometimes magnificent, modern houses, and tree-shaded avenues. It had great days before the War, it seems, but got run down in the Soviet era – only party functionaries and visiting Russians could come here, it seems. Now it is being revived, but the old houses have to be preserved as such, which is causing difficulties. After the walk, we went to a pleasant pub/restaurant for what for me was afternoon tea (I had tea and a stuffed pancake – apple and pear), but for the others seemed more supper. I stood the company, which came to about 14 Lats!

And so back to Riga in the twilight. I am now sitting in a pleasant restaurant – the back end of the Dickens English Pub – again, more or less opposite the hotel, at 21.47, having had a substantial soup, and a mess of veal and mushrooms – good, but some most interesting mushrooms in the mix; I trust they aren't psychedelic! A large party of rather noisy English at a table nearby. The whole place is really pretty cosmopolitan, and it should be able to take its proper place in Europe pretty soon.[242]

---

242 Latvia succeeded in joining the EU in 2004.

And so back to the hotel, after a short stroll. I called home. Mouse is still in bed! Got a very bad dose, I'm afraid. The weather is foul, apparently. At least the weather here is clear.

DAY 4, WEDNESDAY, MARCH 28TH

Today I got up in good time, had a shower and a shave, and got to breakfast. I tried the porridge, which was very vile, so really just had toast and coffee. Edgars and Janete collected me for my lecture at 9.30 am, and we strolled up. I gave Janete a Xerox of my ticket yesterday, and money is apparently in prospect, but no sign of it yet. I can always claim it back from Trinity if necessary, though. The lecture seemed to go well enough, though there was no real reaction. No coffee afterwards, since we were going to lunch, before going off to the Outdoor Museum, but a girl did ask me a good question in the corridor, which she had been afraid to ask in the lecture: was there a constant number of souls? I urged to her to come to coffee tomorrow.

We had a sandwich and a beer in the café of the hotel, and then caught a taxi to the Museum, which is out of town, along Freedom Boulevard. Unfortunately, the driver – a Russian – had just started the day before, and hadn't the least idea where he was going, so it took a bit of time. I felt a bit sorry for him, since he seemed honest enough, and gave him an extra Lat. He didn't charge us for all the wandering.

The Museum is a sort of theme-park, and quite fun, though *most* of it was closed (it is really a summer place). We got shown round a few of the houses, though, and a rather fine church, and I bought some hand-carved souvenirs. They have gathered houses and barns and churches from all over Latvia, and grouped them in regional villages, and it really is quite delightful.

We got back a bit after 5.00 pm, for a newspaper interview with a friend of Edgars', who was quite a character, and apparently writes for a local newspaper, though is himself a philosopher.[243] We talked about more or less everything, for

---

243 This was in fact Arnis Ritups, with whom I had quite a bit of contact in the following years.

nearly three hours – again, Latvians love to talk – consuming beer, brandy and coffee. I had an idea to take in a Latvian opera, if I were at a loose end, but no chance. Had a modest dinner in the hotel, and went to do my homework, and then bed.

DAY 5, THURSDAY, MARCH 29TH

Slept reasonably well. The weather continues fine and bright here, foul in Western Europe. My maladies seem to have largely cleared up – perhaps the result of a few shots of Black Bottom.

Once again, up to the university, to talk, this time, on Ethics. After that, went for a coffee with a large group of students. They are all quite ready to talk on an informal basis, and full of sensible questions.

Then, after a little rest and some lunch, I set off for the Art Nouveau district, along Elizabetes iela. It really is most impressive – more or less whole streets of very imaginative façades, some rather dilapidated now, but many being restored. I called in to the Rozentals[244] Museum, and was warmly welcomed, as the only customer, by the lady curators. The museum is simply his apartment, with a nice selection of his paintings and drawings. I was sat down with a book on him, and read up on him a bit. He is certainly an excellent artist – about comparable with Osborne or Lavery[245], I should say, and contemporary with them – and he had an interesting life. He died in 1916, having returned to Finland, where his wife was from.

Back from there in time for a rest, and then off at 6.00 pm to talk on Joyce, again to a small but enthusiastic group, who seemed to follow most of what I was saying. Some distinguished Latvian literary figures came along!

After that, I took Edgars and Janete out to dinner at the Dickens – was rather extravagant, and splurged 51 Lats, but I think I can afford it. It was good, but wine is always expensive; one should stick to beer.

---

244 Janis Rozentals (1866-1916), one of Latvia's most distinguished painters.
245 Walter Osborne and Sir John Lavery, distinguished Irish artists.

Phoned home again, to find Mouse still ill, and J with a headache – a gloomy scenario.

DAY 6, FRIDAY, MARCH 30TH

Last lecture today – not too happy about this one, on epistemology; a troublesome story! I had bacon and eggs for breakfast, which was naughty, but I felt like it, and it was good. I survived the last lecture, though a bit confused. One odd thing is that there is no *applause* in Latvia. The lecture just ends; yet they seem to appreciate it.

After the lecture, I went to coffee with the head of the department, Professor Marta Rubene, who is a very pleasant lady, and has come to most of the lectures. She is herself in the area of modern continental philosophy, and aesthetics.

Then Janete joined us, with a ticket for the opera this evening, and we had another coffee. Arnis then brought me to a bookstore, to buy some postcards, to send to the usual recipients. I went off to have a sandwich and write the postcards, back at the hotel, then found my way to the post office and posted them, and then went off to the Museum of Modern Art – a splendid building of rather Stalinist proportions – to see a bit of art, preferably some more Rozentals. In fact, Rozental was about all that was worth seeing. It was all *Latvian* art, and much of it *very* mediocre, especially the 1930-60s segment. Apparently the Museum once had a good collection of French and other artists, but a director in the 1920s, himself an artist, scrapped it, and went for Latvian!

Then back for a bit of a rest and a read, and then down to the hotel café at 6.15 pm for coffee and bun, and then off to the opera, to see *The Magic Flute*. The Opera is a fine building, and there was a great crowd. I was actually *just* fitted in, in the back row of a box at one side, so the view wasn't great, but still it was a memorable experience. This was a controversial presentation – a very futuristic set – Papageno uses a mobile phone instead of magic chimes, a washing machine pops up from the floor at one stage – but it actually worked superbly well, as *The Magic Flute* is a surreal opera anyhow. And the music and singing was superb, so it was indeed a memorable occasion. The director's name is Viesturs Kairiss; stage designer, Ilmars Blumbergs.

DAY 7, SATURDAY, MARCH 31ST

No more morning lectures, so I rose at a leisurely pace. Breakfast about 9.00 am – apple pancakes – and then I decided to take a walk round the Old City, before facing an interview with Arnis Ritups on film. Arnis is a dear man, but I feel that I am in a false position here – I know more or less *nothing* about film. At any rate, we had a lively discussion for about two hours, in which I revealed my almost total ignorance of films and their significance – Arnis recording everything faithfully.

A short break, and then Edgars came to collect me at 3.45, to go along to the Disputation. The Disputation took place on the premises of Latvian Cultural Foundation, just at the edge of the Old City, a short walk away. It worked out fine, in fact – all the students of *Ad Fontes* turned up, including Edgars' and Janete's nice old lady Greek teacher, who is composing a Latvian-Greek Dictionary, among other things. She had let herself out of hospital for the occasion, where she is undergoing tests for high blood pressure and stress. Edgars stated his position on the question of *influence* (by Platonists on Christian thinkers), and I responded, with reference to the particular case of the Cappadocian doctrine of the Trinity. I rather think I won on points, though various most interesting details emerged. Arnis asked some pertinent questions, but no one else dared to intervene. I think it is a rather hierarchical society here still.

Then Edgars, Janete, Arnis and I went off to dinner at another pleasant place in the Old City, and were joined there by Arnis' girlfriend Anna, a beautiful and very smart cookie, who is a film director – which explains his great interest in film, perhaps! One has, overall, the impression of a very lively culture, and lots of people waiting for half a chance to show what they can do.

Rain has arrived, sadly. Perhaps better tomorrow?

DAY 8, SUNDAY, APRIL 1ST

Today we are to go for an expedition up to Sigulda and its environs by car. The day dawned overcast, threatening rain. I rose fairly late. At more or less 10.00 am Edgars and Janete arrived, having borrowed *her* brother-in-law Valerij and his car, a dependable Opel. Valerij is *Russian*, a fine-looking young man, who teaches fencing to the Latvian junior team, and is married to Janete's sister Diana. His English was fairly minimal, though he can understand some, but he drove cheerfully enough. We started off by heading up the coast north of Riga to the resort of Saulkrasti, stopping just before that to look at the sea. Then we had a coffee there, and headed inland towards Turaida and Sigulda, mainly through forests of birch and fir. There is more snow and ice still up there, whereas it has almost vanished from the Riga area.

We arrived first at the Castle of Turaida, where I bought a rather nice walking-stick (to replace my Kenyan one, much-lamented). They have been restoring the old castle in *very* new-looking red brick, but it will doubtless weather in time. We walked round it, and visited the little museum, and the grave of Maija, 'the Rose of Turaida', whereby hangs quite a tale[246] – it is favourite place for couples to visit on their wedding day – as did Edgars and Janete!

Then we walked round the remarkable Sulphur Park, dedicated to Krisjanis Barons, the collector of *dainas*, or folk-songs. It features a series of works by the Latvian sculptor Indulis Ranks, each depicting an aspect of Latvian folklore from the collection of songs made by Barons.

It began to rain quite strongly as we finished this. We drove across the river to Sigurda, and took the cable car back and forth over the gorge of the Gauja River – a fine view, despite the weather! Then we visited the castle of Sigurda, which is also being restored, and where there takes place an important opera festival in the summer. It is also a popular venue for

---

[246] Essentially, she chose death rather than enforced marriage or rape. This goes back to 1601, and the Polish-Swedish Wars.

the Midsummer Festival, which Latvians still celebrate pretty seriously!

After a pleasant lunch, we headed off, lastly, for the Ligatne Nature and Educational Park, which has enclosures featuring all the wild animals of Latvia. Unfortunately, at this time of year, the park is a bit of a cod, as it still beset by snow and, above all, *ice*, on the paths, and we were simply not equipped to negotiate that. We set off bravely, but just got stuck before we got to any animals – not worth breaking a leg! Edgars and Janete were indignant – Janete said that they would make a *scandal* – and they complained. They received sympathy, but no satisfaction.

That wasn't much of a success, then, but the expedition as a whole was delightful. We came back to Riga by the inland route – almost a freeway – and I got back to the hotel around 5.00 for a short rest, before being collected again by Edgars at 7.45, to come out to dinner at their flat. This was out in the suburbs, in a rather grim (though only three-story) Soviet-style apartment block, but very pleasant, if small, inside, and Janete provided an excellent meal of pork, then cheese (including my contribution), and cake. We talked of the possibilities of at least Edgars coming to Dublin to give a paper. And, more broadly, of his getting some sort of grant for a sabbatical. We broke up about 11.00, and I took a taxi back to the Old City.

DAY 9, MONDAY, APRIL 2ND

5.32 Now sitting in the departure area of Riga Airport – almost deserted, I must say; I hope they haven't cancelled all the planes – waiting for a 6.05 pm flight out of here. There are just three German businessmen (all on mobile phones) waiting with me. Is it worth running this plane?

I have had a strenuous, if enjoyable, day – and it certainly isn't over yet. After breakfast, I went for a last constitutional around the Old City, finding a few new corners, and noting rather more cats than before. The weather has returned to excellence, after its one bad day – sunny, and now positively warm! I phoned up SAS on my return, and learned that the flight was actually at

6.05, not 5.05, which depressed me rather. Then I phoned up our Honorary Consul, Mr Michael Burke, to see if I could have a chat with him, but only got a rather unwelcoming secretary (Edgars and Janete said he was a philistine, interested only in pub culture, so I probably missed nothing). A pity – the Irish Embassy in Warsaw was most culturally aware.

Janete came round to collect me a little before 11.00, and we went on a shopping tour. I found various things of beauty or value, which I hope will be appreciated. Then back to the hotel café, to meet Edgars for lunch. Janete had to go and teach about 2.00 pm, so Edgars philosophised at me till it was time to catch the taxi to the airport at 4.00. I couldn't persuade him that I could look after myself! Anyhow, it was thoughtful of him.

I have just managed to come down to the wire on Lats. After giving 8L plus 1L tip to the taxi, I now have 1L and a few centimes left. Edgars and Janete were appalled at my extravagance, I think, but one can't take Lats with one, after all, so I got through 200 in a week.

Now a few more people have arrived, but no sign of any attendants, and it's 5.45 pm!

And here the diary ends, but I returned safely, despite my misgivings. My ordinary diary records that I reached Dublin, via Copenhagen, at 7.40 am

12. VISIT TO JAPAN:

MAY 9 – 18, 2001

This expedition had the purpose of accompanying our daughter Ruth to check out in advance the Japanese University, Senshu, which would be the base for her designated period of study, in the third year of her degree at Trinity College in Business and Japanese. I managed to justify the expedition in part by giving a lecture or two, at the invitation of Prof. Sachiko Sakonji, head of the Department of Philosophy at Gakushuin University, whose acquaintance I had made through the CNRS in Paris, but our purpose was really tourism, and the support of Ruth in what was a rather daunting adventure. This diary is in fact entirely composed by Jean.

DAY 1, WEDNESDAY, MAY 9TH

Having flown from Dublin to London Heathrow at 8.40 am, we then boarded, at 12.40, our British Airways flight for Tokyo. We are now into our last hour of the flight, and are kept well informed of our position by our individual TV screens, with a map and a little plane giving us our exact location. Mouse has settled very well and quite enjoyed her vegetarian meals, as we have ours. The crew are very polite and kind, and the flight itself was extremely comfortable. It has actually seemed extraordinarily short, in spite of its eleven and a half hours. We had a very nice view of Siberia for a while. It looked friendly enough from the air, with many seemingly well-cultivated areas, and a few lakes.

John had two interesting finds on the journey. First, at London airport, he came across – on the ground – a whole family's tickets to Australia, which of course he handed to a security guard. Then, on the flight, he found a diamond ring in the bathroom at the back of the plane, which of course he handed to a crew member. I hope it found its way to its owner.

DAY 2, THURSDAY, MAY 10TH

We were met at the airport by Mme Sakonji's[247] sister Nabuko and her daughter Aiyoko. She kindly drove us all the way to our accommodation on the edge of Gakushuin University. She bravely battled the most awful traffic – which we really only came upon as we neared the very central area of the city. The journey took us approximately 1 hour and 40 minutes. When we arrived it had been raining, and a mist still remained. We were greeted on arrival by Ritsuko Nakaoji (who had visited us in Dublin about four years ago). Our apartment has two main rooms, a kitchen, bathroom and lavatory with a basin. The two main rooms are pleasant, with tatami mats on the floor.

After the formalities had been gone through, and Mme Sakonji had visited us at noon, we were left alone for a while to get some sleep. We found that the soft mattresses provided were quite comfortable. John and Ruth slept soundly for a couple of hours, and I dozed. Ritsuko returned at 5.00 pm, and led us to a local supermarket, and to the university, which is very pretty. The paths are lined with (clipped!) azaleas and exotic trees, only some of which I recognised – platanus, gingko, pines, etc. I hope I will be able to identify more of them eventually.

At 6.30, Mme Sakonji met us on campus, and led us to a Chinese restaurant nearby for a large feast. There were many other guests present, all wishing to do everything possible for us. The Japanese really go out of their way to help us, almost to the point of embarrassment. John will have to list here the scholars present:

---

247 Mrs Sakonji was the head of the Philosophy Department of the university, who had invited me to visit, and give a number of lectures.

Satoshi Horie (Keio University), Hirojuki Ogino (Sophia) – also included in the party were two Sakonji daughters, Ritsuko, another female student, and an Irish student called Russell Mallon, who was originally from Northern Ireland, but settled in Scotland. He is a 'Christian', according to himself, so we wonder if he is planning to join the ministry. He is studying Japanese language, and is here for one year.

Mme Sakonji, we gather, is a great lover of cats, and has 26 of them at home! Oko Sakonji accompanied Ruth and me to a local food market to buy some very basic items to get us by for breakfast and a couple of snacks for Mouse. The items filled two bags, and cost $64! This was our first mistake, as these 24-hour shops charge much more than regular supermarkets. By the time we were leaving, the heavens had opened, and there was a huge downpour, with thunder and lightning. We were thoroughly soaked. Luckily, our air conditioning seems to dry things pretty well.

DAY 3, FRIDAY, MAY 11TH

Mouse is holding up very well, and seems to be over her illness. We slept until quite late, using my mobile phone as an alarm clock. We had a leisurely breakfast of coffee and dry toast with honey (as we had forgotten to buy butter!). We had bought what we thought was yoghurt for John, but turned out to be a rather revolting gelatinous concoction with strawberry flavouring.

The weather is still very changeable, but warm, so we went around with umbrellas. We headed for the local station – Mejiro. As we stood at the ticket vending machine, a very nice girl came over and asked if she could help. She showed us how to read the map, figure out our fare to be paid, and to use the machine. Very simple it was, too! Our local line is called Yamanote, and it does a complete circuit of Tokyo – so if you miss your stop, you can just go round again! We got off the train one station later than we intended, to visit the Imperial Palace, which was visible from the outside, but the bridge and gate leading to the palace grounds was quite charming. The gardens are quite extraordinary. Though full of the most lovely trees and azaleas, they seem to find it necessary to prune everything into exotic, asymmetrical shapes. I only recognised the gingkos by their leaves.

I spoke too soon about Mouse's health, as her allergies are returning, and with them the usual painful joints – the poor little thing! She was very brave, and battled on as we made our way to the nearby Idemitsu Museum of Art, stopping along the way, with great relief, in a 'Pronto' café, where we had sandwiches, coffee, and Mouse a croissant. The museum was showing a special collection of Chinese ceramics, gathered by the man for whom the museum was named. It was a truly impressive collection, with some 5000 to 6000-year-old pots in almost perfect condition. I would have preferred to see Japanese ceramics, but only a few were included. The space was lovely and peaceful, and included an area where one could sit and drink tea (free of charge), with a view of the palace grounds and what appeared to be the roof of the palace itself.

We are quite amazed at the lack of concessions to tourists, who are extremely few in number. While they make an effort to translate a title or subject into English, that is as far as they will go (apart from the usual introductory piece at the beginning of the exhibition), and none of the details are translated. Poor Mouse made a great effort and battled her way around, and then sank into a chair until we had finished. She revived enough for us to be able to stop at one of the well-known department stores, called 'Dori'. Its rival store, Seiji, is directly opposite, and they are owned by rival half-brothers. Apparently they were the sons, one legitimate, the other illegitimate, of a wealthy commercial family.[248] The Seiji stores were dotted around Japan,

---

248 Jean has got onto an interesting story here. I quote from the Britannica Money entry:

Tsutsumi Yasujiro fathered numerous children by three successive wives and various mistresses. Tsutsumi Yoshiaki (b. May 29, 1934) inherited the bulk of his father's fortune, becoming president of Seibu Railway Co. and the principal shareholder in Kokudo Keikaku. The owner of the largest private

but in addition the father owned multiple properties, including golf courses. When he died, he left the bulk of his estate to his illegitimate son. The illegitimate son set up the Dori department store, and it was an instant success. Ever since, the legitimate son has competed with his brother for business. We only managed to visit the Dori store, which is a massive enterprise covering 15 floors, each floor almost a city block on its own.

Mouse is in search of 'Hello Kitty' objects[249] and is managing to find them everywhere, but was a little disappointed at the selection in Dori. We had some dinner at a mediocre Italian restaurant, Mouse had spaghetti alle vongole, and I had spaghetti with shrimp. Oh well, it was fairly inexpensive, at least! On the way home, we stopped at our local supermarket and bought a few provisions for the morning. Tomorrow we leave for Kyoto.

---

railroad company in Japan, Yoshiaki built many hotels, amusement parks, resorts, golf courses, and sports centres adjacent to his network of railway lines radiating from Tokyo. By the early 1990s he was the largest private landowner in Japan and, owing to the spectacular rise in Japanese real-estate values, one of the world's wealthiest people.

The other prominent son of Yasujiro was Seiji (b. March 30, 1927), who in 1964 received only a single department store as his share of his father's inheritance. But Seiji was able to parlay this property into the Seibu chain of luxury department stores, which by 1990 had become Japan's largest department store chain. Seiji also built up The Seiyu, Ltd., a large chain of discount department stores, and he diversified into an array of other retailing, financial, and leisure-time services. His more than 100 companies were unified in the Saison Group conglomerate, which in 1988 purchased the Inter-Continental luxury hotel chain in the US, Europe, and the Middle East. An unconventional and artistically inclined businessman, Seiji was also a well-known author of poems and short stories under the pen name of Tsuji Takashi. Yoshiaki and Seiji kept their corporate empires separate and in fact were said to be intensely competitive rivals of one another.

249 Our daughter Ruth had picked the 'Hello Kitty' enterprise as the subject of her undergraduate thesis, in her Trinity College degree course in Business and a Language.

DAY 4, SATURDAY, MAY 12TH

8.00 am: We were called for at the apartment by a male graduate student and his wife, who led us to the station. We had quite a time dragging our heavy bags, but managed to make it to the train just in time. Our seats were reserved, and the numbers were in English, so it was easy to find our places. We set off at *exactly* the specified time of 9.00 am.

The train was immaculately clean, and was so smooth that it was difficult to believe we were travelling at 250 mph. The scenery along the way was fairly unspectacular, though interesting. All along the train route has been built upon, with occasional little rice paddy fields, sports grounds, factories, and mostly houses in Western styles – at least they seemed so from outside! We passed Mount Fuji in the far distance not too long out of Tokyo, and Mouse photographed it through the window. We arrived in Kyoto at 11.14, and were met by Ayoko Sakonji, who led us out to our hotel, which is reached by literally walking out the exit of the station, up a few steps, and into the Hotel Keihan.

Mouse was absolutely thrilled to find that, adjacent to our hotel, was a seven-storey department store called Avanti, with every kind of 'Hello Kitty' object one could imagine. Our hotel is very comfortable, large and more or less in the middle range – perhaps the equivalent of Jury's at home! We have two rooms, so Mouse and I took the double, and John the tiny single one. Ours had a table and chairs in front of the window, with a nice view towards some hills in the distance, where one could see some shrine/temple roofs.

Kyoto really surprised us. We expected, I suppose, a small town, surrounded by gardens and temples, but it is in fact a major city, with an incredible railway station, designed by the leading architect Hiroshi Hara. It is a magnificent piece of architecture, viewed both from the inside and the outside. Alongside the station are other hotels and a theatre, also of very imaginative design. No one area of Kyoto seems to be either new or old, and one often sees tiny little traditional houses alongside shiny new office blocks.

We deposited our bags at the reception desk, and were hoping to settle into our rooms right away, but were told we could not have them until 1.00 pm. The weather in Kyoto is lovely, about 25-27 degrees and sunny. Ayoko led us off to see our first temple, Sanjusangendo. It is the longest wooden building in Japan, housing 1001 many-armed deities, and the chief deity Kannon, Goddess of Mercy. Each of the deities (or rather, manifestations of Kannon) is gilded and divided into 33 sections. The carving of the statues was overseen by the famous sculptor Tankei. Originally built in 1164, it was burned in 1249, and rebuilt in 1266.

Mouse at this stage was beginning to feel rather awful, and we decided to find a sandwich bar, which we eventually did. But half way through lunch, of which she did not partake, she became upset, and we had to abandon any more sightseeing for the day. It was actually a mercy, as we would much prefer to explore on our own. Mouse retired to bed, and I stayed with her. Dad had a little rest too, but then decided he would like to explore another temple before nightfall. He had read about a charming one on the 'wrong side of the tracks'. So off he went, and he enjoyed seeing it. It was the Toji temple, Japan's tallest wooden pagoda.[250] By the time that John got back, Mouse felt sufficiently well for us to go in search of a pizza or something. We compromised, and first we went to a sort of tempura bar (very down-market!) for shrimp tempura, and John had pork.

---

250 Toji Temple, literally "East Temple", was founded at the beginning of the. Heian Period, just after the capital was moved to Kyoto in the late 700s. The large temple, together with its now defunct sister temple Saiji ("West Temple"), flanked the south entrance to the city and served as the capital's guardian temples. Toji Temple is one of Kyoto's many UNESCO Worlds Heritage sites. About thirty years after the temple's establishment, Kobo Daishi, the founder of the Shingon sect of Japanese Buddhism. was appointed head priest of Toji, and the temple became one of the most important Shingon temples besides the sect's headquarters on Mount Kova. Kobo Daishi also added many of the large wooden buildings that stand on the grounds today.

Neither was good. Then we went across the foyer (this was all in the basement of a department store) to what turned out to be a very good pizza and coffee restaurant. We sat while Mouse had a dish of plain spaghetti and a very good pizza – with a chocolate frappé, which she said was very good.

Before we retired for the night, we booked ourselves into a bus tour for next morning, a half-day one, which we felt would be sufficient, as it was to cover four sites – enough for one day, we think! We hope Mouse will be well enough. During the earlier part of the night –12.00-1.00 am. – I couldn't sleep, and got up and had a luxurious bath, at 12.30 am.

DAY 5, SUNDAY, MAY 13TH

We had a troubled night. Mouse was up practically all of it, having taken a laxative. We started our tour at the Higashi-Honganji Temple, one of a pair of temples built by a rival of the owner of nearby Nishi-Honganji. It had to be completely rebuilt after a fire in 1886. It has a wonderful, large central hall. Many Japanese women sacrificed their long hair to make ropes strong enough to hoist the beams. Some ropes are still on display.

We next visited Nijo-jo, which has magnificent screen paintings. By the time we had got through this, and were already on the bus, Mouse had to suddenly jump up and, without explanation to the tour guide, rush back into the castle lavatories, ignoring security persons and all. I raced after her, and told the tour guide in passing that we would follow to the next site by taxi.

Mouse took two *arrêts* and, after a little rest on a bench, we hailed a taxi (the tour guide had told me how to say in Japanese "Kinkaku-ji", which was the Golden Pavilion). It was a long and expensive taxi ride, but worth every bit of it. It has the most spectacular garden we have ever seen, and, to one side of the central lake, the most beautiful pavilion. The main attraction of the garden is the use of really spectacular maples and azaleas and other delicate trees, including gingko and platanus, and a clump, at one of the corners of the lake, of some lovely iris. It was unfortunate that Mouse and I had to see it so fast in order to catch up with the tour bus, but we did find them, and went on to the next site, which was a Crafts Centre specifically aimed at tourists. They had a Western-style cafeteria, which we made the most of, and a shuttle bus service, which took us back to our hotel.

Mouse shopped for an hour and a half or so at Avanti's, buying more 'Hello Kitty' goods, while John and I rested. At 4.00 pm, we met Ayoko down in the foyer, and we ordered some tea. John had a cake (which was actually quite good – marzipan-ish in texture) and a cup of tea, and Ayoko and I had a green tea-flavoured ice-cream. Miyako Nakagawa, wife of Sumio, who is at present in Dublin, arrived at 4.45 pm or so, having invited us all to dinner. As a safety measure, while she was having a coffee frappé, I took Mouse down to the Italian restaurant for a pizza, knowing the food would not suit her.

We then went, in two taxis, to the Gion district, which quite fascinating, and very good for shopping, with many traditional houses, and paper lanterns hanging outside shops and restaurants.[251] We bought some spices in attractive little bamboo containers, a little linen cloth, and I found some good handmade paper for about $1.50 a sheet – not too different from at home. I only bought four pieces.

At about 7.00 pm, we arrived at the restaurant Miyako had chosen, the Minoko. It was in the most adorable little traditional wooden (they look like redwood) houses, with private dining rooms divided by screens.

First we were ushered into a reception room for frothy green tea and two little sweets (*higashi*). One takes the bowl in

---

251 Gion is Kyoto's geisha district, with hostesses in colourful kimonos often sighted on the wooden Tatsumi Bridge, or amid upscale Japanese restaurants and boutiques on Hanamikoji Street. Gion Corner hosts traditional Kyomai dances, while Kennin-ji Temple is known for its Zen garden and Yasaka Shrine has seasonal festivals in a lantern-lit courtyard. Nightlife ranges from quiet sake bars to buzzing, pub-like izakayas.

one hand, and with the other one turns it clockwise two-and-a-half times. You should drink all the tea in three sips if possible, and eat two sweets.

Then we were taken to the dining-room, which was lovely. The floor was sunken beneath the table, so one could sit with one's legs hanging down, which was a relief. Facing us was a lovely little glassed-in garden, with bamboos and other plants set in stones. The hostess came through a low door in the wall, kneeling as she did so. Dinner is served on lacquer trays. When finished with a particular dish, one puts one's chopsticks horizontally on a chopstick holder.

We had numerous courses, including duck, which I had asked for and it was delicious. The tempura was very good, as were some pickled vegetables, including ginger – also very good. The miso soup had some pond life in it which was rather slithery, and I hope was not tadpoles. I had difficulty in not reacting to that! All in all, though, it was a memorable evening, and Mouse really enjoyed it, taking many pictures.

DAY 6, MONDAY. MAY 14TH

I rose about 8.00 am, and washed my hair. It has been good to be able to take a bath in a normal bathroom with a hair-dryer (ours will not work properly here). John and I went downstairs to the second-floor café for toast and coffee, which was very good. The Japanese have excellent European-style bakeries, and their toast is just like our own. We brought the remainder of our toast upstairs for Mouse. We packed our bags, and Mouse went back to the department store for three-quarters of an hour or so, while we spent the time sitting with our bags in the lobby (we had to vacate our room at 11.00 am).

Our train was at 12.10. We had a pleasant and uneventful journey back. We rested, and then set off at 5.00 pm for a reception at the Irish Embassy residence, to a celebratory party in honour of Donal Doyle S.J. (whom I grew up with in De Vesci

Terrace!).[252] He is being presented with Lafcadio Hearn[253] Gold Medal for his role in Irish-Japanese relations. Mouse looked extremely smart in her new suit, and coped very well with her first Embassy reception. We met many interesting people there, including Sister Ruth Sheehy, Ruth Casey's sister-in-law, who is a Sacred Heart nun based here. They are a large presence here in Japan, as are the Jesuits. Frank Doyle was also present, and seemed to know everyone, many of whom he has entertained in Dublin. Donal looks wonderful, and was extremely friendly. John talked a good deal to a theologian called O'Leary,[254] who has hit the headlines recently with some fairly controversial notions – about which, of course, I know nothing!

John was feeling rather mouldy, and we raced home, where he had a rather nasty attack of the runs. We suspect a sandwich we bought before boarding the train. On the way through the university grounds, as John was rushing to get to the flat (with a tummy pain), he fell on a bit of uneven pavement, and twisted his ankle and grazed his knee. Some students helped him to his feet, and when Mouse and I caught up with him (we had stopped at a local shop), he had slowly managed to hobble to the periphery gate and was standing holding it open for us (as it had been locked), the poor dear! He was in a pretty awful state, and has wrecked the trousers belonging to his suit, so he will have to wear his sports jacket to his lecture.

---

252 The Montgomery home in Monkstown, south of Dublin. Donal, as I recall, was stationed in Sophia University in Tokyo.

253 Yakumo Koizumi (1850 –1904), born Patrick Lafcadio Hearn, was a Greek-Irish writer, translator, and teacher who introduced the culture and literature of Japan to the West. His writings offered unprecedented insight into Japanese culture, especially his collections of legends and ghost stories, such as *Kwaidan: Stories and Studies of Strange Things*. Before moving to Japan and becoming a Japanese citizen, he worked as a journalist in the United States, primarily in Cincinnati and New Orleans His writings about New Orleans, based on his decade-long stay there, are also well-known.

254 This would be Professor Joseph O'Leary, also of Sophia University, who is indeed a theologian of interesting views.

DAY 7, TUESDAY, MAY 15TH

We phoned Russell Mallon[255] first thing, and asked him about getting bandages, etc., for John, as he has to give a lecture in the afternoon a couple of hours away from here. They were to go by train, but at the moment there is no way he can walk any distance. Russell kindly met Ruth and me at Mejiro station, and he had already shopped for everything, which was marvellous! We brought the goods back, and bandaged J's foot. He had a pretty awful time with diarrhoea all night, and it hasn't reacted to the pills yet.

Madame Sakonji arrived to take him to the lecture at 11.30 am (having said she would arrive at 12.00), and they went by taxi the whole way. It cost approximately €120 – 13,600 yen each way. The lecture seems to have been very successful, and a buffet dinner was served.

Mouse and I went shopping, did some clothes washing, and explored Mejiro, which is quite pleasant and has many different shops, bakeries and pharmacies, and I discovered a lovely little gallery with a show on of delightful ceramics and paintings. I want to go back and buy some things before we leave here. Mouse and I ate some of the food we had bought at the supermarket – me a chicken wing (good) and a tempura of shrimp and veg (not so good), and Mouse a disappointing dish of macaroni with an equally disappointing sauce. But the baguette was very good. Unfortunately, Mouse does not like the Japanese rice, which is too sticky for her. She is so used to basmati.

DAY 8, WEDNESDAY, MAY 16TH

Mouse and I set off for Senshu University, south-west of Tokyo, This is Trinity's exchange university, to which she would come if she studies Japanese. We took 55 minutes to get there, not having read her instructions properly. It is in a hilly suburb, with fairly nondescript buildings and plantings, unlike Gakushuin,

---

255 Russell Mallon was a student of Madame Sakonji's, whom we had met with Madame on our second day.

but it has one extremely large and interesting modern central building, which was fascinating. We ran into a Canadian man who told us how to find the dormitory for foreigners. It was down the hill, on the way back to the station. Just as we reached the building, we found an American from Columbia University who showed us around. He knew it well, because he brings groups of foreign students there. He comes over once or twice a year to teach Economics. He was very informative about everything. We stopped at a Mister Doughnut in the town, and I had a good frankfurter in pastry and sugar doughnut, and Ruth had two iced doughnuts. We came back on the Express, which got us back in 25 minutes.

We bathed our feet and relaxed, and then set off to find the rival department store, Seibu, to find some dinner. We found no suitable restaurant there except one very expensive one, which we declined. So we went back to Tobu and found California Bay, which didn't faintly resemble anything Californian. I had an OK hamburger with tomato sauce and a sort of risotto. Mouse had an OK pizza. John was being dined.

DAY 9, THURSDAY, MAY 17TH

John saw a student called Kaori at his office, to whom he explained that he wished to see a doctor about his tummy. She fixed an appointment for him to come to campus at 1.00 pm, which he duly did, and he was prescribed medication. We hope it works!

After lunch, all three of us set off to find Mary Boydell's[256] contact in the Museum of Glass, Suntory Museum. We had a gift of Waterford glass from her to a professor there, which we handed over to a nice student, and then got into the museum free (saving ourselves about $20). We saw no glass, in fact, because there was a special exhibition of Chinese ceramics – one beautiful bowl in perfect condition about 4-5000 years old!

---

256 Mary Boydell was the wife of the distinguished Irish composer Brian Boydell (1917-2000), Professor of Music in Trinity College, with whom we were friendly in Howth. Their son Cormac is a distinguished potter, a number of whose products we possess.

Afterwards we went to meet Ed Seidensticker[257] for dinner in his district, called Ueno. It is a street market area, very colourful, which also has a famous park, with museums and shrines. Our train was delayed almost an hour, because some mad chap threw a bicycle onto the line. Poor Ed was still there when we arrived. He took us to a delightful restaurant (Indian) called Samrat, where we had a very good dinner. Mouse was delighted. We had intended to treat him, but he would hear none of it. He did, however, allow us to buy him and us some hot chocolate and coffee at a cute little bar afterwards – 'The Marble' coffee bar.

DAY 10, FRIDAY, MAY 18TH

We had intended to do some sightseeing, but our visit to Dr Kato and his wife was arranged earlier, and we had to leave the house around 3.00 pm.

And here, sadly, Jean's diary ends. I can give some account of the rest of the holiday from my much briefer diary notes:

Dinner with Shinro Kato[258] *Prof. Kanzaki came along. We went with Mme Sakonji. A very jolly evening! They have a nice little house in the western suburb of Setagaya.*

---

257 Edward George Seidensticker (1921 – 2007) was a noted post-World War II American scholar, historian, and preeminent translator of classical and contemporary Japanese literature, and a remote cousin of John's, through his mother, Mary Dillon, of Denver, Colorado (to which my grand-uncle, William Dillon, had emigrated in the 1880s). His English translation of the epic *The Tale of Genji*, published in 1976, was especially well received critically and is counted among the preferred modern translations. Seidensticker is closely associated with the work of three major Japanese writers of the 20th century: Yasunari Kawabata, Junichiro Tanizaki, and Yukio Mishima. His landmark translations of novels by Kawabata, in particular *Snow Country* (1956) and *Thousand Cranes* (1958), led, in part, to Kawabata being awarded the Nobel Prize for Literature in 1968.

258 Shinro Kato was the doyen of Japanese authorities on Ancient Philosophy, and a fellow member of the organising committee of the International Plato Society.

DAY 11, SATURDAY, MAY 19TH

My Patristics lecture – seemed to go down fine. Ed came along, and was received rapturously, to his displeasure! Reception afterwards.

DAY 12, SUNDAY, MAY 20TH

Tea ceremony, 10.30 am – preceded by trying on of kimonos, and followed by a copious lunch.

DAY 13, MONDAY, MAY 21ST

We decided not to go to Nikko[259] today – just too far and too strenuous. Went to Asakusa, and viewed Senso-ji, a distinguished Buddhist temple; then down the river on a ferry to Hama-rikyu Gardens,[260] but we were too exhausted and hungry by that time to enjoy it that much. Home by train, and then revived enough for an Italian dinner in Ikebukuro, which was fine.

DAY 14, TUESDAY, MAY 22ND

Gave my lecture on Plato's Timaeus at 1.00 pm. Ed came again, and this time we all met up and went out for a coffee.

At 4.30, I went off to meet Satoshi Horie[261] for a French dinner, at a very posh restaurant called the Côte d'Or. The chef was Masao Seisu, a pupil of Bernard Pacaud.

---

259 Nikkō, a city 140 km. north of Tokyo, is a popular destination for Japanese and international tourists. Attractions include the mausoleum of shogun Tokugawa Ieyasu at the Nikko Tosho-gu shrine, and that of his grandson Iemitsu along with Futarasan Shrine, which dates to the year 767 AD. There are many famous hot springs (onsen) in the area. Elevations range from 200 to 2,000 meters.

260 Hama-rikyū Gardens is a metropolitan garden in Chuo ward, Tokyo. Located at the mouth of the Sumida River, it was opened to the public on April 1, 1946. A landscaped garden of 250,216 m² includes Shioiri-no-ike (Tidal Pond), and the garden is surrounded by a seawater moat filled by Tokyo Bay. It was remodeled as a public garden on the site of a villa belonging to the ruling Tokugawa family in the 17th century.

261 Another professor of Ancient Philosophy in Tokyo, but I no longer have his details.

DAY 15, WEDNESDAY, MAY 23RD

Spent a bad night after my gourmet dinner, but revived sufficiently to be collected by Ritsuko's Dad at 7.00 am for the drive to the airport. An excellent fellow! He got us there at 8.45. It is at a distance equal to that of Drogheda from Dublin.

An uneventful flight home!

13. VISIT TO KATOUNIA:

SEPTEMBER 9-23, 2001

This diary is sadly truncated, fading out in the middle of Day 9 (Sept. 17th), for what reason I know not, but it seems worth preserving nonetheless. We were accompanied on this visit by old friends, Michael and Dinah Cunningham, and their daughter Sarah, who was a little older than Ruth. There had been a hiatus of fully ten years between this and our last visit in 1991, largely by reason of my participation in the Westminster cruises, as evidenced in a number of comments made. Some details of the last portion of the visit are recorded in my ordinary diary, and will be listed at the end. One notable feature of this trip was that it coincided with '9/11', the attack on the World Trade Center (see record of Day 3).

DAY 1, SUNDAY, SEPTEMBER 9TH

We were collected with perfect efficiency by Elizabeth[262] at 6.50 am, to catch Ryanair flight FR 332 to London at 8.30. The absurdity of getting an early morning flight in order to catch a late night flight from London is lessened by arranging with the Garnseys[263] to come and batten on them for the day. Peter has gallantly offered to meet us at Luton and drive us to Cambridge. It is a fine clear morning, but cold.

---

262 That is to say, our friend Elizabeth Ritchie, with whom we had travelled to Corsica in 1994 (see Ch. 6 above).

263 Our old friends from Berkeley days, now resident in Cambridge, where Peter was Professor of the History of Classical Antiquity, with whom we had gone on holiday to Aix-en-Provence back in August 1986 (see *Being There* I, Ch. 10). His wife is Elizabeth.

Later: Peter was in fact there, as good as his word, when we arrived (on time) in Luton, and drove us back to Cambridge, where we met Mark Franklin, Elizabeth's brother (whom we had actually not previously met, despite much talk of him). He is currently head of the Political Science department at Trinity College, Hertford, Connecticut, and knows Michael Marsh, head of *our* Politics Department. Peter, as usual, is being house-father, as well as running all errands. At 12.00, he and I went and collected Monica[264] from the station, interrupting his making of an excellent lamb stew for lunch, while Elizabeth rather flubbed around. After lunch, we had a rest, and then Mark and I took a walk with Elizabeth and Monica in a magnificent university property some way out of Cambridge, while Peter took J and Mouse to find some make-up for Mouse.

Then we all assembled back at the house and chatted, until Michael and Dinah[265] arrived at about 6.45, to drive us to the airport. This we did without trouble, left their car at a parking complex, reclaimed our luggage, and settled down to have a bit of dinner, and wait for Sarah, who was coming up from London.

Sarah duly arrived, in fine form. We checked in (discovering in the process that J had checked in Ruth *twice* – must check whether the refund for that comes through on her credit card), and boarded the plane, which (once again to Easyjet's credit) departed virtually on time.

The weather in England had been distinctly brisk, with squalls of rain, so we are glad to be heading for the heat, and very happy to be doing it with Michael and Dinah after all these years!

DAY 2, MONDAY, SEPTEMBER 10TH

The plane arrived, if anything, a bit early, at 4.30 am, after a

---

264 Their eldest daughter, and my god-daughter.

265 My old friend from prep-school days, Michael Cunningham, and his wife Dinah. He was now a GP in King's Lynn, somewhat north of Cambridge. As mentioned in the Introductory Note, they, with their daughter Sarah, were accompanying us on this trip.

smooth flight. We got the luggage pretty promptly – lots of bits and pieces to worry about! – and headed for the Europcar desk. There was a nice young man to greet us there, but his computer was down, and he really took an inordinate time to check us through. Then he sent us off to *find* the cars in the rental car lot! We actually did find them without too much trouble, but it was 6.30 am before we were properly on the road.

The new airport at Spata is actually out behind Athens to the north-east, rather than simply north of the city, so it is not that convenient, really – especially until they build a proper road to it[266] – so we slogged through the suburbs of Kefissia and Maroussi, in an intensifying rush-hour, until we reached the freeway, after which things were easier.

We filled up before the bridge, but didn't stop for coffee until well past Chalkis, up into the mountains, at a fine *kafeneio* by the side of the road. The heat and characteristic aromas were delightful. J bought a large bottle of pine honey.

We reached Limni at around 12.00, found it busier than we remembered, but otherwise familiar, and then headed out the road to Katounia. We found that rather *narrower* than we remembered, especially around the point, but reached our destination safely. Found Liadain in her house, confined there for the moment by tending to her mother, who is obviously in a bad way with Alzheimer's, but she showed us the Cobbold villa, which is just beyond her sister Selga's studio, and is very charming – old-fashioned in a Mulu Farm sort of way,[267] but very spacious, and with a verandah giving a splendid view. We hauled up the bags, and settled in – meeting Selga at the gate on her scooter, who warned us not to block the gate.

It is magnificent to be back, though it is somewhat windy just at the moment. Everyone went to sleep, though not before Dinah and J went shopping at Roussos', and stocked up on

---

266 As they have now done!

267 This a reference way back to my days in Ethiopia (1961-3), where one used to go out of town to visit the Sandfords on their farm in the countryside (cf. *A Scent of Eucalyptus*, passim).

supplies. Liadain had said that Garth Fowden[268] was about, and would like to call on us, so I suggested 5.00 pm.

I slept in fact for about three hours – Michael slept for almost six! – and I was the only one upright to greet Garth when he arrived. But we had an interesting chat over a beer, and he invited us all to dinner on the 15th – so that solves my birthday problem! We must bring a bottle, though.

Garth said that Peter Brown[269] had been ill again in August – a thrombosis – but he has pulled through, and is recovering. It is disturbing, though. He also said that Philip Noel-Baker's wife has written a history of the family's involvement in Prokopi, which is available at the little museum in Limni.[270]

For dinner, we went down, about 9.00, and renewed our acquaintance with David at the taverna. He was in excellent form, but remembered us really only when Jean mentioned the incident of Yiota falling into the pool at the big villa, and he recalled that well. She is now, of course, eighteen, and going to the University of Athens. Big Yiota has graduated from Aberdeen, and is now running an English Language School in Limni, with her Scots husband! Advertisements for it are all over town. Dinner was excellent – pork or meat-balls for us (very good), omelettes for Ruth and Sarah, the vegetarian ladies.

DAY 3, TUESDAY, SEPTEMBER 11TH

We got going fairly slowly, with a breakfast of yoghurt and honey, and bread. Weather a bit windy, so the sea choppy, and somewhat infested with jellyfish. We went up to visit Denise around 11.00 – calling first to the little church that Philip constructed, and to his grave. There is also a little guest-house. It is a delightful

---

268 Distinguished scholar of Late Antiquity, formerly married to Polymnia Athanassiadi.

269 The distinguished authority on Late Antiquity who was his teacher, and had been my colleague in Berkeley for some years in the late 1970s.

270 This would be Barbro Noel-Baker, *An Isle in Greece: The Noels in Euboea* (2000), a copy of which reposes on our shelves. I bought it for my birthday at the Museum (see below).

spot. Denise greeted us warmly, offering coffee, but we had just had that, so she invited us back for a glass of wine at 7.00, to watch the sun go down.

After lunch and a swim, we went into Limni to shop, and were confronted with extraordinary scenes on the TV in more or less every shop and café that we passed – terrorist suicide bombers have flown commercial aircraft into the World Trade Centre in New York, demolishing it, and are said to have attacked the Pentagon and the White House as well![271] It is quite unbelievable – an extraordinary coup – but I trust that it will rebound severely on the perpetrators, presumably Osama bin Laden and his colleagues.

Back for drinks with Denise, at which we learned much that I had forgotten – e.g. the mine that Philip and his friends originally bought the valley from mined *magnesite*, a clay useful for insulating electrical things; Jane, in the house on the road, is the daughter of Philip's friend with whom he bought the valley.

Sarah had found a bottle with a message in it during her swim a little down the coast, and we appealed to Denise for help in deciphering it. It is an appeal for spiritual help from a distraught mother of a son, Stilios, who is suffering from a brain tumour, and she was hoping that it would reach a monastery in Rhodes, which might intercede for her. Denise undertook to speak with her friend Fr David of the Monastery of David 'the Old Man', inland from Rovies, a little north of Limni, since St. David is quite a good healer. We must go up and visit on Friday, and bring the bottle. It had a 1000 dr note in it, wrapping the message – a most pathetic document.

We went out to dinner, this time, to a pizzeria in town, in deference to Mouse. It wasn't too bad, in fact.

DAY 4, WEDNESDAY, SEPTEMBER 12TH

Still somewhat windy, but we bathed, read, slept, dined at home on spaghetti. Tomorrow we have decided to go to Delphi via the

---

[271] In fact of course, they did not manage to get to them.

ferry at Aidepsos – though J and Mouse are doubtful, as Mouse's weakness has recurred.

DAY 5, THURSDAY, SEPTEMBER 13TH

We set out shortly after 7.00 am, in one car, leaving J and Mouse behind, and reached the ferry at Loutra Aidepsou, with five minutes or so to spare! We backed the car on, and had a smooth crossing of 50 minutes to Arkitsa. It cost 3600 dr for the car, and 400 for each person – not too bad. No other foreigners that we could see.

We set off up the freeway, Michael driving to Thermopylae, then turned south through the mountains to Amphissa, where we had coffee and *large* baklava in the main square. It is a pleasant little town, with a crusader castle, mainly famous for goat-bells, it seems. Then on to Delphi, where we arrived at the ruins around 11.30. It is therefore quite easy to get from Katounia to Delphi and back in a day, it would seem!

We climbed straight up to the stadium, where a fierce old lady guard was on the watch for misbehaviour and unsuitable dress, and then down to the theatre, the Apollo temple, the Treasury of the Athenians, and so on. Michael much admired the polygonal masonry of the Temple of Apollo and elsewhere. Then we went to the Museum, and saluted the Charioteer. I also found an inscription in honour of Plutarch, and two statues of philosophers, one of whom I have decided is Polemon, the other Calvenus Taurus.[272]

Then off to lunch in Arakhova, which seemed a better bet than Delphi, and was indeed pleasant – Taverna Parnassos, up to the right. We had some of their excellent fried cheese, among other things.

Then on to the monastery of Hosios Loukas, via Distomos – a rather longer drive than I remember it being – and then we decided not to retrace our steps, but to press on, which involved

---

272 The former the last head of the Old Academy, about whom we know virtually nothing, and the latter a distinguished Platonist philosopher from the second century AD, who came from Beirut, but operated in Athens.

us in much wandering through the hills, on third-class roads, but at last we rejoined the main road, and headed, through Orchomenos, to the National Road and the boat. We were just in time to catch the 8.15 pm ferry. The TV on the boat was still full of the U.S. disaster.

We drove straight on from the ferry, and got back just on 10.00 pm, which was when we had said we would!

DAY 6, FRIDAY, SEPTEMBER 14TH

The main event of the day was a visit to the monastery of St. David 'the Old Man', to deliver the message in the bottle. An interesting drive up to Rovies, and then into the mountains for half an hour or so. Lovely upland meadows, interspersed with woods – indeed a fertile and fortunate land!

We were received very warmly by Denise's friend, Father David, quite a young fellow, with just a little English, who showed us round the church and the relics – including the skull of Saint David (which he said on occasion becomes moist, and gives off a heavenly odour). Then we partook of coffee and preserves in the guest room, and handed over the bottle that Sarah found. Father David discovered that the lady who wrote it was actually in Athens, and was hoping that the bottle would float to Rhodes, to the monastery of the Archangel Gabriel at Archangelos (on the other side of Rhodes). Instead, it floated up the Euboean Gulf, and found its way to another wonder-worker, Saint David. He promised to phone and ask what the lady, Maria, wanted done with it, and we parted on the understanding that he would communicate this to Denise. We celebrated the event with a group photograph.

And so home, for a rest and a swim, and dinner at home. We have not been down to the taverna again, by the way, because, unfortunately, David has disgraced himself by making some sort of a pass at Sarah, when she was down making a call to Max.[273] She was distressed about the bombings in New York, and he consoled her with wine, and, it seems, went rather too far.

---

273 Sarah's boyfriend, as I recall.

DAY 7, SATURDAY, SEPTEMBER 15TH

Some pleasant present-giving over breakfast – coffee-making equipment from J and Mouse, and a paraffin lamp from Michael and Dinah. Lovely – though I suspect that when we get back from this magical place, not much use will be found for a paraffin lamp!

We went into town to the Museum, which is a delightful little enterprise. Antiquities only on the ground floor, including even a Mycenaean pot or two, wherever they found them (the lady guide said that ancient Elymnion was up the hill a bit). The other two floors are devoted to folklore, and portrayals of Euboean life in the last few centuries. On the way out, I bought a book for my birthday, *An Isle of Greece: The Noels in Euboea,* by Barbro Noel-Baker (Swedish wife of Francis), and published by herself. I have started in to read it, and find it fascinating. It explains a great deal. The original Edward Noel was a cousin of Byron's by marriage, and an idealistic philhellene also. The story of his struggle to survive on the estate of Achmedye is remarkable.

Home, then, for lunch, and some rather nice birthday cake. Then a swim, and a lovely dinner with Garth and Elizabeth Fowden, to which we brought Denise, and sent the girls out on the town to find some pasta. They served an excellent dinner of chicken, and much interesting conversation. The second Mrs Fowden[274] is a girl from Texas, who, however, has totally adopted Garth's clipped tones, to the extent that I thought she was perhaps Greek.

Before going home, Denise walked us from the carpark to a delightful little Byzantine shrine, remains of an old cathedral (built, in turn, on Roman baths!), still open at midnight, and quite unscathed by vandals. It is a nice country in that way, though a very dirty nation, at the same time!

---

274 The first, of course, was Polymnia Athanassiadi.

DAY 8, SUNDAY, SEPTEMBER 16TH

Today we had an expedition up to Prokopi for lunch, to meet Philip Noel-Baker – and his girlfriend Leah, who is Greek, and about to have a baby. This was fixed up last night by Denise from Garth's. The invitation came very promptly, because they are about to receive a group of Australians for a cooking course, and a further five power-boat enthusiasts, so this was a good time.

It was very fascinating to see the place, especially now, after reading about it. Philip himself is a jolly fellow, looking no more than thirty, though the family tree says he was born in 1958. He is obviously committed to the place, but fairly outspoken, which might get him into trouble. He showed us round, and then we settled down to an excellent lunch in the garden (having declined a swim in the fine pool). He would like to sponsor a Classical course, but it is plain that I would have to organise every aspect of it, and I don't think I'm up to that. On the other hand, a little conference or reading group in Prokopi would be delightful.

After leaving the estate, we (J, Mouse and Michael) drove down to check out the ancient site of Kerinthos. A fairly grotty beach, it must be said, but the old site is still there, untouched (to all appearances). We jumped across a tiny rivulet, and took a walk on the promontory. The old harbour is silted up, from where the fire-breathing Abantes set sail for the Trojan War.

We were back in time for a swim before dinner, which we took at a fish restaurant in town. We were lashed by waves, beating against the plastic sheeting. We then dropped into Garth and Elizabeth, to deliver a copy of a book from Prokopi.

DAY 9, MONDAY, SEPTEMBER 17TH

Mouse and I went up to Denise's to sort out her computer, which Mouse did, to the extent of giving her an e-mail she can use. We had coffee, and wine also, with her workman Simon.

And here, sadly, the diary breaks off. My ordinary diary has the following entries, evidencing just one more adventure:

SEPTEMBER 18TH:

Took a tour of the northern coast. Coffee in Orei. Couldn't find any ruins in Histiaea or Artemision, but the Bull of Orei was in good form.

SEPTEMBER 20TH:

Took Liadain and Denise to lunch in town.

SEPTEMBER 21ST:

Lunch with Denise at the little church.[275]

SEPTEMBER 22ND:

Drove down safely to airport, via the Amphiareion (closed).

---

275 Presumably the one on the estate, up the valley.

14. The Australian Trip:

JULY 11 – AUGUST 7, 2002

The focus of this visit to Australia was a conference (from July 15th -18th) on the theme of 'Plato's Ancient Readers', at the University of Newcastle, a coastal town in the middle of New South Wales, organised by my old friend Harold Tarrant, who had made his academic career In Australia. Happily, we had a chance to travel a bit following on the conference, but only around New South Wales, viewing merely a fraction of that great continent. My contributions are in italics, since Jean is the majority author on this trip.

1, THURSDAY, JULY 11TH

11.30 a.m. Frankfurt Airport. Now waiting in the departure lounge for Singapore Airlines flight SQ 317 to Singapore. It looks pretty full! We just met up with John and Breda Cleary,[276] who had come over on a 7.20 am flight from Dublin – we were content with the 8.20. Compared with going to the U.S., there is very little fuss, so we had lots of time, in fact. Botsy and Betsy[277], who are minding the house while we're away, drove us to the airport (I having initiated them into the mysteries of my car!).

DAY 2, FRIDAY, JULY 12TH.

It is now 5.30 pm (Singapore time), and we are sitting by the rooftop pool of the Hilton Hotel, after a pleasant swim. The temperature is in the 80s,

---

276 John was a professor of Philosophy in Maynooth University), and a considerable authority on Aristotle, and Breda was his wife.

277 Our old friends from the US, Robert Meagher, and his wife. This was our daughter Ruth's name for them, which we adopted.

but perfectly pleasant – quite humid, though. Our flight yesterday was OK, but no more – not quite what one is led to expect from Singapore Airlines – though Upper and Raffles Class looked most luxurious! Mainly, the electronic controls for TV and lights didn't work properly, so it took a very long time before I found a movie (though then I did see 'Iris'), and the lights wouldn't turn off, so I got no sleep.

But we got here, no bother, at 7.50 am this morning, and then everything was most pleasant and efficient. There was coach transfer to the hotel: a very pleasant drive into town – impressive modern architecture, and fragrant foliage. The Hilton is a Hilton, but very comfortable and welcoming. Our porter turned out to be quite a fan of the Irish football team, and most concerned about Roy Keane.[278]

We slept, in fact, till 2.00 pm. (from about 10.00), and were only woken by a call from David Sulzmann,[279] whom J had left a message for earlier. We arranged to phone him again at 6.15 pm or so. Then out to the bank, where I got $200 Singapore out of an ATM machine with no problems, and we had a snack in Starbucks. The hotel is up on Orchard Street, where most of the top hotels are, and surrounded by shops of every sort – but entirely modern and cosmopolitan. We will have to get downtown if we are to sample old Singapore! Too late for any tours today, so we retired to the pool on the rooftop.

At about 6.45, we hailed a taxi, to meet David at Club Street. He wanted to show us a furniture business he was thinking of tying in with, with a view to importing into Ireland. We had to be rather frank about its possibilities, as it was in a rather heavy Indonesian style, traditional, and really too bulky for Irish houses, which tend to be rather small – except for the very grand houses, which I don't think this furniture would suit either.

We then made our way to Raffles, which was restored to its former glory in 1991. It is a splendid old hotel in colonial style, with courtyards dotted about, sporting exotic vegetation, and with balustraded balconies overlooking them from above. We had a Singapore Sling in the old Long Bar, before dining in

---

278 This would be a reference to the 'Saipan Incident' of May that year.
279 Jean's nephew, who lived and worked at the time in Singapore.

Doc Cheng's Restaurant within the hotel. We had rather hoped that David would have chosen some more interesting (and reasonable) restaurant in some other area of the city. Instead, we had a good but enormously expensive dinner – $311 Singapore (about €187), which included a bottle of Australian wine for $95. It is taxed at about 80% in Singapore. We returned to the hotel at about 11.00 pm.

DAY 3, SATURDAY, JULY 13TH

We booked ourselves on a Bay Cruise at 10.30 am, having had a good breakfast at Coffee Bean Restaurant down the road. The cruise took us approximately two hours, including a pleasant visit to Kusu Island, and fine views of the skyline, despite the rain. After this, we returned to the hotel, packed our bags, and left them at reception.

We headed downtown next, using the hop-on/hop-off bus, and re-visited Raffles with John and Breda Cleary (who are staying at the same hotel with us) – they had not yet visited it. We had a pitcher of beer, and wandered about the hotel. Next we visited the Art Museum, which was featuring an excellent Rodin exhibition, based on the Burghers of Calais and the Gates of Hell from Dante's *Inferno,* from the collection of Cantor.

We intended to visit the Botanic Gardens, but the last bus was at 6.00 pm, and we arrived too late to catch it, so we got a taxi to our hotel, and spent the rest of the evening at the hotel roof pool, which was very pleasant.

We left for the airport at 9.15 pm.

DAY 4, SUNDAY, JULY 14TH

We arrived at our Sydney hotel, *The Four Points,* at about 9.45 am, after an uneventful flight on which, once again, John's TV didn't work. The *Four Points* is a Sheraton hotel, and they accommodated us immediately. We were given a very pleasant room overlooking Darling Harbour (one of the harbours of Sydney), but not the Opera House harbour. We had a long sleep, which we didn't really mean to do – only waking about 2.30 pm. We had a very good coffee and Danish out at the hotel's snack bar, and then headed down for a walk around the harbour (we met John and Breda walking around in the opposite direction at one stage).

Having toured the harbour and its 'sights' of cafés and shops, we ended up at the aquarium, which is quite extraordinary. The platypus is an adorable creature, though much smaller than we had imagined. There was one display of different kinds of jellyfish, featuring the most deadly type, called 'box-jellyfish', which leaves its tentacles on the body, and within minutes the body's airwaves are affected. In the bowels of the aquarium is a magnificent replica of the Great Barrier Reef, with specimens of sharks, giant ray and many other types of fish and turtles. The tank even extends over one's head as you walk around. The roof of the walkway is made of glass, and the fish are very happy to pose for photographs. It is really amazing to see a shark at such close quarters. At one point one walks on a glass floor under which the fish are swimming, and it is an uncanny experience.

We met John and Breda back at the hotel at 7.00 pm, and took a taxi up to The Rocks, which is the oldest area of Sydney, and which has been restored, and has cafés, restaurants, chic shops, etc. – rather in the manner of Temple Bar. This is also the part of the harbour which houses the Sydney Opera House, which we viewed from the quay-side. Unfortunately, it was dark at this time, and the Opera House was much less well lit up than we had hoped, so we will have to view it properly on our return.

We (John and I) decided to eat at a restaurant/wine-bar called Phillip's Foote. It was set out in small courtyards leading from one to the other, with benches and patio heaters (luckily, because it is really quite chilly – about 6° at night, and only rising to about 14° during the day). They have large barbeques on which one cooks steaks of one's choice, and a large salad bar, from which you help yourself. We chose sirloins, which were really delicious, and drank a bottle of red wine (house Shiraz, $22). The place had a great atmosphere, but by the time we were finished (about 10.00 pm), it was almost empty, because their drinks licence expires at 10.00. Apparently, there are many different kinds of drink licences here. John and Breda joined us later, having eaten at an Italian restaurant down the road. We had decided to walk back to our hotel, but because we were not properly dressed for the cold, we weakened and took a taxi.

DAY 5, MONDAY, JULY 15TH

Our train for Newcastle was to leave the station at 10.15, so we rose early-ish (me at 7.30 to wash my hair), and breakfasted in the hotel café – appalling coffee! The train was a double-decker, on the lines of the TGV in France. By the time we were underway, and a few miles outside Sydney, the rain (which had been forecast for Tuesday) had arrived, but was still just a faint drizzle. A very pleasant woman, in a seat opposite, described the places of interest as we journeyed on. For the first time I saw mangroves, which are really just low shrubs on the edges of swamp lands. The Hawkesbury River runs along here, and is apparently the longest river in Australia (I think).[280] By the time we reached our destination, it was raining properly, and because our hotel was 500 metres away, it was too close to take a taxi, and we had to drag our luggage up in the rain.

The hotel (Noah's) is quite pleasant, though not in the same league as the Hilton or Sheraton. It is situated overlooking the ocean, which has large waves and is popular with surfers.[281] Because J and I hadn't slept well the night before, we were very exhausted, so I went to bed and slept for about three hours! John had to go to his first talk at 2.00 pm., which was being given by

---

280 We were misinformed here. The river is actually only 120 km. long. The longest river in Australia is in fact the Murray (2508 km.), spanning NSW, Victoria and South Australia.

281 Newcastle is a harbour city in the Australian state of New South Wales. Its plentiful beaches are linked by the Bathers Way, a coastal walk stretching between Nobbys Beach and Merewether Beach. The walk provides access to Bogey Hole, a convict-built ocean bath from the colonial period. Also on the path is the 1880s Fort Scratchley, a historic site and a viewpoint for spotting migrating whales.

Hayden Ausland.[282] The rain was by now pouring down, and there was very little point in exploring – which is why I slept instead.

At about 5.00, Breda phoned to say the men were tied up 'til about 10 pm. So we agreed to meet and go and find some dinner. By now the rain had stopped, but it was *cold*. We found a pizzeria down by the harbour, and had a good meal – pizzas at a special price of $11 (about £8) on Monday nights! We returned to the hotel at 10 pm, to find them all assembled having drinks in the lobby. I met for the first time Lloyd Gerson, Kate and Richard Sorabji (the only other wife here, I think, apart from Breda and myself), Hayden – as interesting as ever, and looking more and more like Uncle David![283] Still the caustic sense of humour and laid-back attitude. We all retired about 11 pm.

DAY 6, TUESDAY, JULY 16TH

John went down to breakfast at about 8.30 am, while I took my time. I took my breakfast at a local (very good) café, called the Bogey Hole, where I had coffee, toast and bacon, and am now sitting writing this before I go across the road to use the Internet.

My efforts at the Internet were laughable, and I finally gave up after about half an hour. Instead, I took a stroll around the town, which in itself is not interesting, but had lovely views of the bay from an obelisk atop the hill at the highest point.

At lunch in the hotel (a beautiful and delicious spread provided by the University), I met John Finamore – as jolly and good fun as ever, and he had been looking for an Internet café, so said that after lunch (they had a free afternoon) he would come to the café and show me how to work it. We were joined (John came too) by a very pleasant Dutch girl, whose name I can't remember.[284] Of course John F. worked it out, and there

---

282 A former student of mine from Berkeley, who was now professor of classics in the University of Montana.

283 That is, my uncle, David La Touche, who had lived with us for a while in Drumnigh in the 1980s.

284 This may have been Marija Martijn, from the University of Leiden.

was an e-mail waiting for us from Mouse, asking had we reached our destination, but with not too much other news. So we sent her a reply. John had thought of checking his university e-mail, but couldn't remember his password or his ID! He eventually got fed up, and went for a walk, while I practised a little more.

Then I walked down to the wharf, and back to the hotel, via a series of little streets which seemed to be the oldest end of town. The houses are all wood cladding, very like California, but often with decorative wrought-iron balconies and trellises – very picturesque, but quite poor-looking, really.

When I arrived at the hotel, I read for a while, and then had a lovely long bath. After drinks in Lloyd Gerson's room with Hayden and Sarah Rappe (an odd but interesting girl, who grows on you), John Cleary, Breda, Lloyd Gerson, John and I went to Scratchley's Restaurant on the harbour, where we had a good meal (except for mine, which was a perfectly good piece of veal, but spoiled by being smothered in melted cheese and a rather awful sauce). Lloyd took charge (!!) of ordering the wine, and ordered two bottles of local wine, one priced at $78 and the other at $65, which we didn't know until we got the bill. He also ordered a platter of Tasmanian cheeses (which no one else wanted), and when it came to paying, he produced $40 – said he had no more, and we in fact each owed $64. We never got the money back. We will be very cautious of him in the future! The others all ate at the pizzeria, which we would have done if we had known.

DAY 7, WEDNESDAY, JULY 17TH

We had to be out of our rooms by 11 am. The conference continued through the morning, and I went out to my café (Bogey Hole) for breakfast, accompanied by Breda. I had already packed our bags, so I had nothing to fuss about, and I continued down to find Boots, to buy a pocket mirror (which they didn't have). On my way, I found a delightful shop run by the Wildlife Society, and bought three really interesting, colourful tea-towels.

At about 2 pm, we all packed up, and were collected by our

shuttle bus to take us to the wine country – the Hunter Valley. It is a very pleasant drive, very reminiscent of Napa Valley,[285] but with eucalyptus instead of holm oak. Along the way, we encountered our first kangaroos, who were gathered in an olive grove. We all got madly excited, and jumped off the bus to take pictures.

The weather has been perfect ever since that one rainy day. The temperature goes down dramatically at night, to about 6-8 degrees, but the days are 19-20 degrees, with gorgeous, clear blue skies. Our hotel, The Polkobin Inn, is in fact a kind of inn – one-storey buildings dotted around a gorgeous garden, with palms and a swimming pool. Ours has two bedrooms, a bathroom and a verandah, with table and chairs outside – plus a kitchenette with a microwave. We were given an enormous lunch on arrival (portions are always huge here). I had bangers and mash – not as good as Irish bangers!

We did a wine tour in the afternoon, visiting Lindeman's, McWilliam's, and the Mount Pleasant wineries. Then back to the hotel, and at 6.00 pm the conference had a discussion. There was another large meal at the hotel in the evening. I chose correctly this time, having blue cod, which was very simply and nicely cooked, in a kind of lemon/butter sauce. I did not have a very good night's sleep, though, probably from eating too much potato.

The talks at the conference were entertaining this morning – John Finamore's to start (which I'd actually heard before in Orono) on Apuleius and the Soul, then dear old Eric Osborne on Clement of Alexandria and Middle Platonism (which he called 'Muddle Platonism!), and then, after a tea break, me, on the Middle Platonic commentary tradition, 'Pedantry and Pedestrianism?'

DAY 8, THURSDAY, JULY 18TH

Last night I managed to finish off Tim Buckley's thesis, and then he delivered an excellent talk this morning, which seemed a kind of thesis defence, so that I am convinced that I was right to approve it. This was followed by a totally chaotic talk by Sarah Rappe, who really seems to live on her nerves.

---

285 A major wine valley in California, not far from where we lived in Berkeley.

She very rarely completes a whole grammatical sentence. But she had an interesting text to discuss, on the interpretation of the Third Hypothesis of the Parmenides *by Damascius.*

After coffee, there was a talk by John Phillips of the University of Tennessee, Chattanooga – a confident, but not very substantial young man – on the origins of evil according to the Neoplatonists, where he seemed to me to misinterpret Enn. III 9. 3, *and criticise Denis O'Brien for interpreting it correctly.*

Then another pleasant lunch on the verandah of the hotel, and after lunch talks by a good Byzantinist, Ken Parry ('Proclus in Byzantium'), and the final talk by Harold Tarrant himself, on Cicero's De Legibus, *which was very good.*

I went for a walk about 12.00 – over, first, to the Rothbury Winery and down by the back of their vineyard, beautifully maintained, and then up to the end of our road to a T-junction, where I found a cheese factory. I bought a selection of cheeses and a large sourdough loaf. When I came back at about 2.30 pm, I had a picnic lunch on our verandah, while I caught up a little on this diary. John and Breda Cleary had decided to leave at about 2 pm, so I did not see them again. I met again the very pleasant Japanese couple called Saori and Akitsugu Taki,[286] and their eight-year-old bouncy daughter Sumio, who were great friends of Damien and Jocelyn Nelis[287] when they were in Durham.

At about 5.00, when John was taking his walk (the conference ended about 4.30), I noticed a Canadian lady called Twylah Gibson wandering around outside waiting for her husband's return from Newcastle. As it was rather cold outside, I asked her would she like to sit in our room. By this time, most of the conference members had transferred to another hotel in a town called Maitland, which was only half the price of this one, and this lady had already checked out of her room. She accepted gladly, and we opened the bottle of red wine that John

---

286 We remained in contact for many years afterwards by way of Christmas cards.

287 Damien had come to us in Trinity from Durham in 1999, to take up the Professorship of Latin, before passing on the University of Geneva in 2006.

had bought at Lindeman's. John came back, and a little later the Takis were passing, and we invited them in too. So we had quite a jolly party. Later, we and the Takis drove in Taki's car to a restaurant called Blaxlands, right beside this hotel. We had a very delicious meal and retired about 10.30. I didn't get much sleep, because of noisy neighbours, and neither did Saori, as they were on the other side.

DAY 9, FRIDAY, JULY 19TH

Once again, woke rather late (around 8.30 am), but in time to make a cup of coffee in the microwave, before catching the bus to take us on our expedition to Barrington Tops Rainforest – calling first into Maitland, to collect the others. The Maitland Hotel actually looked very pleasant, and Maitland a pleasant old town, so I wish that we had been given a clearer choice – but on the other hand, we are a bit tired of hauling bags around. We have signed on in Pokolbin for another night as well, after we collect the car. I'll charge it up!

The drive to Barrington Tops was really beautiful – rolling hills with clusters of eucalyptus, mainly, and a wide variety of bird life, expounded to us by Harold Tarrant, who is an expert ornithologist. Here is a list of some of the birds he pointed out to us:

>Kookaburra – most common bird (like a kingfisher, but less colourful)
>Wedge-tailed eagle
>Larrakeet
>Superb blue wren
>White-plumed honey-eater
>Pied butcher-bird (magpie-like, with hooked beak)
>Straw-necked ibis
>Gellaa (pink and grey)
>Brush turkey
>Pied currawong
>Lyre-bird (like turkey, with curved tail)
>Yellow robin

Scrub wren (yellow-throated)
Crimson rosella (very colourful – red and purple; cheekily friendly!)
Eastern rosella (have more green)
Wide-necked (faced?) heron
Yellow-tailed black cockatoo
Ibis
Cattle egrets.

We arrived at Barrington Tops, which is a small resort, very like a ski resort – just a main wooden building with a restaurant, and wooden lodges dotted around. As soon as we alighted from the bus there was a clamour of the most glorious bird-song (very reminiscent, to me at least, of the birds in the Yucatan).[288] We took a walk down to a river in the company of knowledgeable Harold, and then (about three-quarters of an hour later) had lunch at the lodge, which was a sort of buffet, but very good. We fed the crimson rosellas on the verandah and, with the help of some sunflower seeds, I had two of them feeding out of, and indeed standing on, my hand.

After the drive back down to Maitland, we said goodbye to the new friends we had made – particularly, I got to know, and liked, the Taki family, Sarah Rappe, John Finamore, and Conrad and Twyla Gibson. Unfortunately, we had not said goodbye to Hayden Ausland, as we hadn't realised that he was departing for Adelaide that morning. He in fact lived in Australia for several years as a child, when his father was on a diplomatic mission, and went to school in Adelaide. He decided to go and seek out his old school, etc.

John and I, and another man called Dirk Baltzly, an American teaching in Melbourne, were then driven to Williamstown Airport by Harold. We drove back to Pokolbin for the night. It was *very* cold, and I wished I had more suitable clothes. A noisy family was in the room next door, whooping and hollering, but they settled down by 10.30 or 11.00 pm.

---

288 Cf. our journey to the Yucatan recorded in *Being There I*.

DAY 10, SATURDAY, JULY 20TH

We rose at about 8.15 and made ourselves café-au-lait with some milk we had bought at the store, and some packages of instant coffee. We ate some *Marie*-type biscuits with it. We then set off in the direction of Port Macquarie. Drove a good deal of the way on the motorway before turning off at Bulahdelah to take the coastal route, passing through some very pleasant small resorts on lagoons and some rather dreadful towns, e.g. Forster and Taree. We stopped at the koala breeding reserve at Billabong. It was really no more than a zoo, but was run by a very pleasant man and woman. He really loved his koalas, who were in an internal enclosure. We arrived in time for their feeding time, so they were quite lively and interested. Two of them had the most adorable babies, and the owner was able to hold them while we patted them.

Having driven through Port Macquarie, we backtracked to North Haven, but in fact found what was really a holiday apartment in Kathy's Cove, a little settlement on an estuary, with lots and lots of penguins, and anglers obviously competing for the fish. The apartment was fairly grim, but it sufficed. It was run by a very pleasant, friendly man and his wife. He had just driven back from a camping holiday in Cairns with his wife and three girls – a distance of about 3000 miles!

On our way to Kathy's Cove, I should mention, we stopped at a tavern hoping to find coffee, but we found it was an enormous and amusing place with a monster TV screen, showing a rugby match. In another section, there was another TV, showing a horse race, and another section had slot machines. It was a jolly place, with all ages involved. No coffee, but we had a beer.

DAY 11, SUNDAY, JULY 21ST

We set out about 9.15, as we wanted to get as close to Brisbane as we could. We stopped in a nice little town called Grafton, and found a very good cup of coffee. We kept driving as fast as we could through the towns leading up to Brisbane, and round

Brisbane itself, until we came out the other side, and found ourselves in Queensland, stopping in a place called Redcliffe. We actually took a wrong turn, and found ourselves here – on a kind of peninsula.

We checked into a modest motel in a place called Kippa-Ring ($72 a night – a bit more than the budget, but still OK), and found a little Malaysian restaurant round the corner for dinner. Once again, the proprietors of the hotel are very agreeable – everyone we have met so far has been unaffectedly pleasant and chatty, we note. It is just a friendly sort of place. We phoned forward to Bundaberg, to enquire about voyages to the Reef, and were told they were on, but the wind was forecast to be bad for the next few days, and they mightn't go out till Thursday. The wind is a bit troublesome, so we decided to give up on that. It would have cost $139 a head, in fact, for a two-and-a half hour trip, plus four hours on an island, but if one couldn't snorkel, then there is not much point, really.

Our other project was to phone Mouse for Mummy's birthday, and we were in great confusion as to whether we were fourteen hours back or forward. So we left that till tomorrow morning.

DAY 12, MONDAY, JULY 22ND (BIRTHDAY!)

I started out by trying to phone Mouse. No reply from the house, but we then decided that it was probably 2.00 in the morning. So I asked the motel owner if there was an Internet café around, and she sent us to one in a shopping centre round the corner from the motel. After some trouble with the 'mouse', I sent a message to the other Mouse. The owner of the outlet was an Englishman, who had to tell me what to do several times. The trouble was that the 'mouse' they had had three sections to press, instead of just one, as we have. No message was waiting for us from Mouse (disappointingly – but let's hope it is a good sign that she is happy in Hyannis).[289] We then flubbed around the shopping centre, and I bought a wool scarf for when we get back to Sydney (which was *cold* in the evenings).

We left Kippa Ring at about 11.00 am and drove north to the Glasshouse Mountains – a group of small volcanic cones,

---

289 She was in New England for the summer, working.

revered by the Aborigines. Their legend has it that the largest of the 'gods' (volcanic hills) was looking away from his smallest son (the smallest hill) and out to sea, because his son was a coward. We climbed to a lookout point, which said it was 700 metres up, to view the volcanoes and the surrounding countryside, but it was more than we bargained for. It was extremely steep, and seemed much higher than 700 metres. We climbed in the company of a very nice couple from Victoria who were about our own age, which was consoling. So we encouraged one another all the way. We had a panoramic view from the top, on a kind of platform.

We drove then to the township of Glasshouse Mountain, which is a pleasant little settlement on the edge of the state forest, where we had a fairly awful sausage roll and a fairly good cup of coffee – but when I asked for a second cup, it was rather weak! We kept heading north, and ended up in Caloundra, on the Sunshine Coast, having passed through some fairly horrendous resorts, which reminded us of the Costa Brava or Fuengirola – high-rise apartments and tasteless shop-fronts. Caloundra is quite a nice little resort when you get off the main road. The houses along the sea-coast are pretty and exclusive-looking! We found a motel a block from the beach, owned by an Englishwoman and man (he an ex-GP). We explored the beach, which was full of surfers, but the sun was already going down (about 4.15), so the air was cooling.

We got back to the motel, and then drove downtown, looking for a place to eat. Found the main street, Bulcock Street, which turned out to be very pleasant, with a number of restaurants, finely tree-lined, and with a number of pedestrian malls. We found an Italian and a Greek restaurant, and J chose Italian for her birthday dinner. So back to the motel for a rest and aperitif (beer), and then down about 7.00 (didn't want it to be too late!). We are now happily stuffed, after an excellent dinner in Jerome's Italian Restaurant. We brought our own wine (BYO is quite common here!) – a Mount Pleasant Shiraz.

Then back to a rather disturbed night – my own fault for ordering garlic bread. We both woke up frequently, and both had nightmares – one of mine was that I had arrived for a conference without a paper, having taken the folder with papers out just before leaving!

DAY 13, TUESDAY, JULY 23RD

Rose rather late (around 9.00 am), glad not to be going anywhere much. Slightly cloudy today – possibly something moving up from the south – but not that much wind. We decided to head first for the Australia Zoo, which we had passed yesterday too late, since it seemed attractive. We stopped off to buy a new camera and some medicine.

This is a zoo specialising in crocodiles and snakes. It is run by a crocodile hunter, Steve Irwin. He and his father were crocodile hunters who collected rogue crocodiles or wounded ones from the wild. They do not try to tame them or teach them tricks, and the zoo is educationally oriented, with demonstrations and good instructional material in a lovely tropical setting. This Steve Irwin has become such a celebrity that he now makes a special TV programme, and has also made a couple of films. We were at the zoo for about three-and-a-half hours, and then drove back to the Glasshouse Mountain homestead to find a meat pie for lunch at the Bakery. This we duly did – the pies not spectacular.

Then back to the motel, and a walk on the beach before sunset (which is about 5.30 pm here), after which we sat on our beds and watched the international news. The odour from the drains, about which we complained to the management yesterday, seems to have been resolved, thank God!

We are now sitting in a Greek restaurant, The Mediterranean, in the town, having just eaten a plate of Mediterranean *mezedes* (spinakopita, moussaka, Greek salad, souvlaki, cannelloni, sausages, hummus, tsatsiki and pitta bread). We are their only customers, and as we are eating their dinner, we begin to see why. It is really not very good. As we walked back to our car, we noticed that our Italian restaurant was fairly busy, and even busier was the café in front, which has three musicians playing Eric Clapton kind of music. We did not sit down to listen, as we would have been obliged to eat or drink something further.

DAY 14, WEDNESDAY, JULY 14TH

We set off at about 10.00 am, to drive south again on the Bruce Highway, heading for Lamington National Park. We stopped for a cup of coffee on the way, at a small town, Nerang. Then a long and winding uphill country road to the mountains, past Conungra. We had another stop for a sandwich at an alpaca farm with a beautiful view of the surrounding hills.

We eventually arrived at O'Reilly's Rainforest Guesthouse, and it is truly lovely. We managed to book a room (at a much higher price than we anticipated – $230). Every possible facility is available here. It is a very attractive wooden building with guest rooms extending outwards, most of them with verandahs. A programme of instructional tours on the wildlife and vegetation, ping-pong, billiards, a lovely bar on an upper storey where one can watch the sun go down, a large dining-room, a library with a log fire, sauna, plunge pool, hot massage facilities, and a separate bistro/café with large verandah – all in a wonderful setting.

After checking in to our room, which, although the most modest class in the complex, is still fine, we watched the sun go down in the bar, over a cocktail. There was a splendid view of the valley and mountains, including volcanic Mount Warning! We decided to sign on for another night and to hell with it. We just got squeezed in! At dinner, which was excellent, we were seated with, and introduced to, two other perfectly pleasant elderly couples, one a retired maths professor called Bruce, and his wife. Afterwards, we joined a night expedition with a pleasant lad called Tim to try and locate gliders – a form of small possum which glides from tree tops – but no luck.

DAY 15, THURSDAY, JULY 25TH

Up early, to join a Bird Walk at 6.45 am, which was a most hilarious as well as instructive experience, led by Tim O'Reilly. We started with a pair of comical magpies, and their son who wouldn't leave home, who caught scraps expertly. Then the satin bower birds, male and female, also very agile, and sundry wrens and robins, and a honey-eater or two. Lastly, we visited the bower of Jock, an old-timer bower-bird. They are ridiculous animals; they construct elaborate 'bowers' for impressing the females, and they particularly like things of blue, so they profit greatly from the plastic junk of modern civilisation – spoons, bottle tops and so on. What they did before that, indeed, one is moved to wonder!

Then a copious breakfast, and after that we embarked on a half-day walking expedition to Elabana Falls. It was a very pleasant 7 km round-trip walk, nicely graded, leading down to a waterfall. It was quite spectacular, as one minute one was walking through moderate rain-forest, and looking down over the tops of sub-tropical rain-forest (the sub-tropical much more fern-like and luscious), and then we found ourselves at the sub-tropical level. We were told to watch out for the Albert's lyre-bird, which is a threatened species – they estimate there are only 1000 left *in the world*, and most of them located within a 70 km range of here. As it happened, we saw four of them on our way to the Falls, and on our way back John and I found one only ten feet away from us beside the path. He seemed totally unconcerned by our presence, and continued trying to overturn a log to get at insects.

Gradually the rest of the party joined us, warned by me to be quiet, and provided by J with binoculars, and yer man continued, quite unmoved, overturning his log. Finally, a film crew arrived, quite excited, and began to film him, so he is now immortalised.

We got back in no mood for a regular lunch, but took a snack in Gran's (which managed to be quite expensive, at $19, but good), and then decided to rest for a while. I was feeling quite stiff, so decided to try the hot tub. This was quite a success, and then I reclined on the terrace for a while, reading Jacobson's Oz[290], *and admiring the view.*

After John's dip in the tub, we decided to drive the 26km. down the hill to the winery (owned by O'Reilly's, of course), where there is a river and a platypus-viewing platform. We tasted a few wines, which were very good, and John bought one called 'Shane O'Reilly', after the grandson of the original O'Reilly. We then went down to the viewing platform, where we were lucky enough to see one platypus swimming around with his nose above water.

---

290 That is to say, *In the Land of Oz*, by Howard Jacobson – most entertaining and informative.

We got back in time for a cocktail in the bar, where we chatted with our German friends, Volker Lindner and his daughter Sara, who is in her last year in school and planning to spend a year in Brisbane. Then down to a good dinner, for a pleasant chat with our other friends, Professor Bruce Morton and his wife Alison (he retired from the Maths Dept. of Monash University).

After dinner, we were treated to a documentary on owls, which was certainly most interesting, and giving evidence of great effort in the filming, but which got a little repetitive in the end. And so to bed.

DAY 16, FRIDAY, JULY 26TH

We did not get up for the birds again, but we should have, as it was apparently quite different. Lots of birds at breakfast, though.

We said goodbye to the nice Mortons at breakfast, as well as to Volker and Sara, before packing our bags and putting them in the car. We had decided to go on one more outing with O'Reilly's, which was a trip in a 4WD bus to a look-out point called after one of the early surveyors, by the name of Belson. We saw the original homestead of one of the first O'Reillys, and travelled on an unpaved rocky road which was the first logging trail up the mountain. We stopped many times to look at spectacular views, and to view the incredible trails which the first visitors to the mountain had to negotiate. We climbed out of the bus, and walked the last 2 kms to the look-out point, where Warren, our guide, produced a billycan of tea (very good *without* milk) and damper, a sort of soda bread with some raisins in it. The binoculars that J bought me for my birthday have been a great boon, and we have enjoyed viewing the birds and mammals at close quarters.

We arrived back at O'Reilly's at about 12.30, and immediately set out on our journey in the direction of Bellingen. We stopped briefly on our way down the mountain to try to get another glimpse of a platypus at the winery, but were unsuccessful. We continued on until we decided to look at Byron Bay, and found it much pleasanter than we thought it would be. It was rather like a mixture between Berkeley and Carmel – half hippy, half chic, with lots of good cafés and restaurants, which were really buzzing with people, young and old, including lots of aged hippies! We found a very nice motel called the Wollomba, after a shipwreck on the beach. The motel had immediate access to the most gorgeous beach. We took a stroll on the beach just as the sun was going down, and it was very pretty. We wandered back up through the parking lot at the beach, which had a group of aborigine musicians playing, and where there was a very strong smell of pot! We strolled through the main streets, and went to one of those typical bars with TV screens and tables inside and outside.

We each had a glass of beer, and watched the surfers on the TV screens, and the customers at the bar, who were an eclectic group – from hippies to rugger types: the young were a mixture of smart and trendy, and hippy. From being a lovely warm day (about 22°), it was now beginning to cool. We went back to our motel and watched some of the Commonwealth Games from Manchester. We then drove back down to the town and had a delicious dinner in the fish restaurant closest to the beach, called 'Fish Heads'. We had very good crab-cakes to start. Then, John had *barramundi*, which was grilled and set on delicious roast veggies, and I had a triple 'something or other', which was a steak of tuna, steak of swordfish, and steak of *mahi-mahi*, with a tasty crab-leg included – also served on delicious baked veggies. A young couple from Ireland sat beside us, and we borrowed their salt and pepper! We were seated on an outside patio, and even though they had heaters on, we got rather cold. But we survived long enough to eat our dinner.

DAY 17, SATURDAY, JULY 27TH

We wandered down the town after checking out of our motel, to find an Internet café to contact Mouse. We found a pleasant one at the back of a music shop. This time we had only to ask for assistance once! They always say, 'I don't know why it did that.' No message for us, but we sent another to Mouse. We found a café which served me a short black coffee with a helping of vanilla ice-cream, which tasted very good. A strange couple sat beside us – an elderly woman lost in her own world, waving her hand about and mumbling to herself, and a very handsome and distracted-looking young man, who could have been her son. The weather was still lovely, and we left Byron Bay, rather regretfully, to head south towards Bellingen and the Waterfall Way.

 We turned off Highway 1 just before Urunga, and headed up the valley, arriving in the quaint town of Bellingen around 4.00 pm, but we were quite unable to find a motel. There was only a place for backpackers. Then we drove across the river, and found a nice man with a bad stutter, who ran a set of holiday cottages, a bit above our budget. He told us, though, that there was a Motor Hotel just beyond the town, and kindly phoned ahead to them, to secure a room for us (at $75).

 So we drove out to the very pleasant Bellinger Valley Motor Inn, and checked in. It is on a hill, with a fine view of the valley, and an opportunity to sit out and view the sunset. We took a walk up the hill behind it, hoping to see some wildlife, but only saw good views. Then we drove into town, to the local tavern, and had an excellent hamburger, while watching the first half of a rugby match between Australia and South Africa in Brisbane. Australia dominated the first half. We went back to our room for the second, when the South Africans came right back, but the Wallabies held on to win. An excellent match!

DAY 18, SUNDAY, JULY 28TH

We drove to Dorrigo National Park and took a walk on the skywalk. It is a very different rainforest to that at Lamington. The trees that we thought were Booyongs seemed to be identified as 'stinging trees', so we are little confused as to which is which. We did see another lyre-bird, much larger than the Albert's variety we had seen at O'Reilly's and a more common one, and many more pademelons.[291] We headed on up the Waterfall Way, and went to see the Wollomombi Waterfall, which was an impressive sight, apart from the fact that, because of the drought, there was very little water. It was at the meeting of two rivers, which were

---

291 This is a smaller version of a kangaroo.

really just puddles, but the gorge itself was quite spectacular. We viewed it from one side, and then took a walk round to the other side, passing through an area where poison had been put down to limit the number of dingos. A large area was fenced off, presumably to allow some of them to roam free from the poisoned area.

We then headed up to Armidale, which was a remarkably spread-out and spacious town, which we drove round in confusion, trying to find a motel which was mentioned in the Budget Hotel Guide. Having failed to find it, we checked into one which was opposite the Wicklow Hotel (!). It *looked* very nice, and had a bath (a rarity here), but we found the cups and glasses unwashed, and the bathroom bin unemptied. We drove about the town to locate the university, where it was suggested to John that he look up a friend of Harold Tarrant's called Greg Horsley.[292] We located the university, and decided to call on him next morning.

We returned to the Motel, and then went to the Wicklow Hotel for a beer, and found that they had a fairly decent restaurant, so we stayed and had our dinner there. John had an excellent steak, and I had a chicken thing which was OK.

DAY 19, MONDAY, JULY 29TH

This morning we started by phoning, first the University Classics Department, to try to make contact with Greg Horsley – unsuccessful – and then a Budget Hotel in Coonabarabran – successful – and then Hertz, to extend the car rental by one day – successful. We first drove down to find an Aboriginal Centre that has been founded in the town, but it really wasn't open to visitors, though they were most friendly. So, after talking to a nice German girl working in an ecological centre, we drove up to the University, on spec.

In fact, I was received most hospitably, first by the Chair, David Kent, and then by Greg Horsley, who was just between

---

292 Horsley was an authority on New Testament Studies and Early Christianity as well as Classics.

classes. He was very sorry to hear that I wasn't available for a lecture. I learned of their strategies for saving Classics at UNE, and they gave me some good ideas – distance learning, for example.

We drove out of town in the direction of Tamworth, the country music capital of Australia. We drove through parched farming country for some time, and then began a descent. At this point, there was a fine look-out at Moombi, where we stopped to take a photo and stretch. At Tamworth, we found an excellent coffee shop and refreshed ourselves, before heading up to Coonabarabran, where we had booked a Budget Motel. This turned out to be OK. It was slightly back in the woods, and one could take a short walk in the bush before twilight. We are still entertaining ourselves watching the Commonwealth Games – at which Australia is doing unprecedentedly well!

For dinner, we found in town a really excellent pizza house – Pizza Panash – which did us fine pizzas – half of which we kept for lunch tomorrow. After dinner, we went out for the 8.00 show at the Observatory, which was good fun, despite the fact that the clouds which had been following us all day – little rain gods from Ireland, not doing any good to the Australian countryside – kept obscuring the heavens. They are spectacular in these parts, and the Southern Cross shone out very well. We were given a great impression of the immensity and diversity of the universe: 'What ish the shtars?'[293]

As we drove through the countryside, we were struck with just how bad the drought has been. The fields are grey-brown, and the eucalyptus look as if they are dying or already dead. The farmers are in despair, and are having to feed their cattle supplements, which they would normally not have to do at this time of year. It costs them $1.45 a week per head to do so. I can't imagine, if you're a large rancher, with, say, 1000 cattle, how long they can keep it up.

Big rigs are a huge feature on the inner highway, and it seems at times that there are more of them than domestic traffic.

---

293 A quotation from Sean O'Casey, *Juno and the Paycock*.

Many dead kangaroos are to be seen along the Oxley Highway. We are almost in bush country here, with the land flattening out, and more wild grasses of a bluish hue. As yet we have not seen a koala in the wild!

DAY 20, TUESDAY, JULY 30TH

This morning we headed off first for the Warrumbungle National Park, 33 km up the road to the west. It is indeed a spectacular scene – jagged cones of rock, originally volcanic, rising up from the bush. We selected a walk of about an hour each way, and sat on a rock at the end of the walk, admiring the 'Breadknife' opposite.

It was not quite such an interesting walk as some of the other ones we have done, as some of it is actually *paved*, an indication of the popularity of the park. I imagine that at the weekends it would be fairly busy. We drove on from there to view a little more 'outback', and found that if we carried on, we would actually be going in the direction we wished to go – to Dubbo. The road became a (fairly smooth) dirt road for about 10 km, and then linked up again with the highway.

We found a funny little township called Gilgundra, just before the main road to Dubbo, which was plainly trying to improve itself, and we bought some drinks at a local store. We stopped then at a halting place on the main road, and had the rest of last night's pizza (which was still excellent), before driving on to Dubbo.

The intensity of the big rigs increased, as well as the frequency of dead 'roos. Dubbo itself is quite large and interesting. It is home to a large zoo, as well as to the Old Dubbo Gaol. It was the latter that we decided to visit, as the zoo, though apparently excellent, is not of indigenous animals, and we didn't come here to see the 'tions and the ligers'[294] *Anyhow, it was already 3.30, and almost too late for the zoo. The gaol was very entertaining, with various animations available – including an Irish bum called Moore, who*

---

[294] A reference to a Montgomery family joke, celebrating the confusion of an inebriated friend, who, on hearing that the children had visited the Dublin Zoo, asked if they had seen the 'tions and the ligers'.

was hanged. We were the only visitors. The gaoler was very pleased to see us, and had visited Ireland some time ago.

We then went to find our motel, and it proved to be rather worse than the gaol. It was called 'The Cross-Country Motel', one of the Budget chain, and after experiencing it, we decided we would abandon Budget. The carpet was filthy, not only with stains, but with crumbs, the shower was grotty, and the sheets on the little bed were stained and unwashed. The whole room smelled of stale cigarette smoke. I was loath even to put my head on the pillow!

Jules' Crêpe and Steak House was recommended by the Lonely Planet for dinner, and it was indeed excellent. I had a Seafood Mornay pancake and John had a Chicken and Tarragon one. There was unfortunately only one other couple dining – it amazes us how empty most of these restaurants are, and how they manage to keep going!

DAY 21, WEDNESDAY, JULY 31ST

We had the awful breakfast in the hotel, which included Nescafé! Then we drove down the road to the nice old town of Orange. It has the wide streets typical of all towns in Australia. We decided to visit the Modern Art Gallery, but before doing so called into the very pleasant Visitor Centre-cum-shop-cum-café in front of the Gallery. The very nice lady there made us some excellent coffee. The Gallery was a beautiful modern building, with some moderately good art.

Next we drove to a really charming old town called Bathurst, supposed to be the first town to be built across the Great Divide, and was at one time a candidate for the capital of Australia.[295]

---

[295] The Great Dividing Range, also known as the East Australian Cordillera or the Eastern Highlands, is a cordillera system in eastern Australia consisting of an expansive collection of mountain ranges, hills and plateaus. It runs parallel to the east coast of Australia, and forms the fifth-longest land-based mountain range in the world, and the longest entirely within a single country. It is mainland Australia's most substantial topographic feature, and serves as the definitive watershed for the river systems in eastern Australia, hence the name.

We bought some lunch and picnicked in the town park. The buildings around have been very tastefully restored, and there is a sense of old-style grandeur about the place.

We headed on then for Katoomba in the Blue Mountains, where we checked into the Cecil Hotel, a quaint, old-style, slightly decrepit guest house recommended by Lonely Planet. It was just off the main street. Katoomba is both prosperous and hippy, with good cafés, lots of bookshops, rug stores, and a general atmosphere of Berkeley in the 1960s.

We drove to Echo Point, and viewed the Three Sisters [296] – together with innumerable Japanese visitors – and the fantastic vista of the canyon at sunset. But they are rebuilding the whole viewing area, which slightly spoiled the effect. Back in town, we looked into a few second-hand bookstores, and a rug shop, before settling on a jolly Italian restaurant for pasta.

DAY 22, THURSDAY, AUGUST 1ST

Mild chaos about the starting time of breakfast this morning, but it all got underway by about 8.30 am. It had been left in charge of the daughter of the house, it would seem, who overslept a bit!

First we walked up to a cinema called The Edge, for an excellent nature film on their big screen, which centred round the discovery of a previously unsuspected ancient tree, the Wollomi Pine, which is indeed an odd-looking object. Then back to the main street, where J bought two small kilims, which seemed genuine enough, for a mere $70. Then we drove off to travel on the Scenic Railway down over the cliff into the gorge. There was also a sky train, but that was too exciting for J. The railway got us down half-way, and then we walked along to a little waterfall – much littler than it should have been, because of the drought!

Then we drove off in the direction of Sydney. The modern road makes it hard to see what all the fuss about getting across the Blue Mountains was in the first place! We got as far as Parramatta, now a mere suburb of Sydney, but found a rather nice park in which to have lunch. I was just finishing the bottle

---

296 A cluster of three rock peaks.

of Tyrrell's Shiraz bought for last night (BYO), watched by the intolerant eyes of various magpies who had assembled, when I reflected that this was probably seriously illegal. So we poured out the remains of the Shiraz, and dumped the bottle.

Then on to Sydney, where we found the Corus Hotel on York Street without too much trouble, parked the car in their garage, and checked in. It is actually a very pleasant hotel, centrally situated, and not really much inferior to the Sheraton. Our concierge, Johnny, took charge of the car and phoned Hertz, so we hope that's in order. They apparently decided not to collect the car that evening, but that shouldn't be our problem.

Once we were settled, we called down to the Sheraton to see if John and Breda had by chance got back in, or had left a message. In fact, John had bluffed his way back in, at $185 a night, and Breda was there to greet us. A daughter of friends of theirs was meeting her, and in the event we all went off to a pleasant fish restaurant up town, near the Corus Hotel.

And so to bed, in considerable luxury. Slightly worrying, though, to hear that the car had not yet been collected.

DAY 23, FRIDAY, AUGUST 2ND

We had an excellent breakfast in the hotel, from a most princely spread, and then set off to walk up to Circular Quay and the Opera House, before taking a ferry to Manly. The Opera House is indeed most impressive. We went in and enquired about shows for tonight, but Richard Strauss's **Ariadne auf Naxos** *was not very tempting, though some seats were available. A Mozart recital was more so, but we have agreed to go back to Phillip's Foote with John and Breda, so it is unrealistic to plan concerts for the evening.*

Circular Quay is nicely laid out, with memorials to writers inset in the pavement. We were attracted by Barry Humphries' (of Dame Edna Everidge fame) Salute to the Australian Pie:

> "I think that I shall never spy
> A poem lovely as a pie –
> A banquet in a single course
> Blushing with rich tomato sauce."

Then we got on the ferry across the Harbour to Manly. Unfortunately, the three Right Whales that had been seen in the harbour for the previous few days had now gone.

Over to Manly, then, walked around, and had a pleasant lunch. It is a bit tacky, but not a bad place on the whole. Then back to the city, and took an interesting walk through a park and Botanic Gardens – a large colony of fruit bats manifested themselves at one point – and then to an Art Gallery, where there was a most interesting exhibition of Aboriginal Art.

Then back to the hotel, and phoned John and Breda at the Sheraton. We agreed to meet around 5.00 pm, and go back to our steak house in The Rocks. We walked all the way up this time, and had another excellent steak – but who should walk in but Katharine Scott[297] and her husband, with friends! And she had actually never been there before! She seems to be having an excellent time. We took photographs. Then back to the hotel, promising to see John and Breda tomorrow evening in Singapore.

DAY 24, SATURDAY, AUGUST 3RD

We got to the airport very efficiently, and onto the plane. No great queues or fuss. Splendid views of the centre of Australia, and then of islands offshore, all the way to Indonesia, as the weather was quite clear.

And there, sadly, the diary ends. However, my ordinary diary relates simply that we reached Singapore slightly after 7.00 pm that evening, and arrived back in Dublin at 10.25 pm the following evening – all in all, a most memorable adventure.

---

297 The daughter of our old friends Adam and Celia Scott in Howth, who had emigrated to Australia.

John, Corsica

Jean, under an ancient archway, Euboea, Greece

Barrington Tops National Park, Australia

One of Jean's favourite Australian birds, The Crimson Rosella

Charles Bridge (Kavluv Most), Prague, Czech Republic

The Church of St John The Russian, Prokopi, Evia

Entoto Maryam, a traditional Church in Addis Ababa, Ethiopia

The changing face of Addis Ababa, Ethiopia, in 2008

15. Directorial Visit to Athens:

April 12th – 16th 2003

I had just agreed to take over the directorship of the Irish Institute of Hellenic Studies in Athens, which was still established in modest quarters in a street just on the north slope of the Acropolis, lent to us by an amiable American millionaire, Robert McCabe, and this trip has the purpose of orienting myself, and sorting out our new premises on Odos Notara, in the district of Exarchia, which we occupied for the next twenty years.

Day 1, Saturday, April 12th

An uneventful trip – thankfully! – to Athens, *via* Amsterdam, by Aer Lingus and KLM. Everything was on time and efficient. I arrived in Athens just on midnight. The baggage emerged pretty promptly, and I got a taxi by about 12.25 am. There is a fine new road from the airport, but it is still a long drive – the best part of an hour, and cost €30 – post-midnight supplement, presumably, as the normal charge seemed to be €21 or so. The Olympia Palace was all set to receive me, and I hit the sack about 1.30 am – not too bad!

The hotel is very pleasant and convenient, but the cost was rather a shock – €176 a night, plus €23 for breakfast! Athens is not what it used to be. Makes Dublin look good! Admittedly, we are just by Syntagma Square (Philellênôn 16), and very handy to everything, but still, a modest hotel!

DAY 2, SUNDAY, APRIL 13TH

I am now enjoying a copious breakfast, at 9.00 am. I had thought of going out, but it was too much trouble. I might look about for a little coffee shop for subsequent mornings, though.

After breakfast, I went out for a wander through the Plaka. First, I found myself up near Prytaneiou, so went past the Institute – which is looking extremely grotty, I am sorry to say. Then down to the Roman Agora, which was almost deserted, and very pleasant. I brooded there for a while, and called home. It is a lovely time of year to be going about – all is green and full of wild flowers, and not too hot. The Roman Forum is inhabited by *dogs*, rather than cats. There is a nice little old mosque in a corner of it, very neglected. One can get a good idea of the layout of the forum, though.

I went down past Hadrian's Library and the Agora, which was closed for refurbishing, and on to the Kerameikos,[298] where I had never been. It was quite a job to find the entrance, which was round on the north side, but very pleasant to stroll through – out the Dipylon Gate, up the beginning of the Sacred Way, lined with fine tombs. Again, lots of wild flowers. Heavens, but Athens is grotty, though! Ermou, beyond the Agora, is a total kip – and of course there is constant rebuilding and repairs – which, however, never seems to achieve anything. Much is being done for the Olympics, though.[299]

Back then to Monasteraki, and found a taverna for a beer and snack, and so to the hotel for a snooze and some reading. I found *Crocodile Dundee* on the TV, and watched a bit of that. Later I took a stroll through the National Gardens and had a coffee. On

---

298 Kerameikos, also known by its Latinized form Ceramicus, is an area of Athens, located to the northwest of the Acropolis, which includes an extensive area both within and outside the ancient city walls, on both sides of the Dipylon Gate and by the banks of the Eridanos river. It was the potters' quarter of the city, from which the English word "ceramic" is derived, and was also the site of an important cemetery and numerous funerary sculptures erected along the Sacred Way, a road from Athens to Eleusis.

299 The Olympic Games were due to take place in Athens the next year, 2004.

the way, I called in to the metro station at Syntagma, which is a splendid effort – marble halls, a fine archaeological exhibition, worthy of the Moscow underground![300] The gardens are very pleasant – children chasing ducks. Almost had a thunderstorm, but it blew over. The weather is changeable, though pleasant – around 15 to 17 degrees, I should say.

I got through to the McCabes on the mobile, and walked up there at 6.30 pm to have a drink. They really are a very pleasant pair. Their daughter Ann was also there, a Byzantinist, and their son, whose name I forget. Bob pledged to pay the fees of any fund-raiser, which is most helpful, and Dina was most keen on the purchase of the Church house – by somebody![301]

Wendy came and collected me at 8.05, and we set off to walk to the restaurant in Pangrati, which was not too bad – about 20 minutes. There we found Steve Tracy,[302] Stefanie Kennell (Director of the Canadian School), and Rebecca [303]– Jorgen Meyer arrived a bit later. It was a very pleasant, if unpretentious, dinner – it served to introduce me to the community! Meyer knows my work, but – embarrassingly – I don't know his. I must check him out.[304] He seems interested in Aristotle.

Wendy assured me that she negotiated a price of €90 a night for the hotel, which is a relief (it was actually €110, as I discovered later!). I forgot to bring the smoked salmon to the McCabes, so perhaps I can persuade her to deliver it to them tomorrow.

---

300 This had made good use of the archaeological remains that had been uncovered in its creation, and was indeed a fine effort.

301 That is to say, the Athens town house of Sir Richard Church (1784-1873), an Irishman who played a significant part in the establishment of the modern Greek state, which was just down one block from the McCabes' house, in the Plaka. Dina is Bob's wife.

302 Steven V. Tracy, professor of Greek and Latin at Ohio State University, and the Director of the American School (2002-7).

303 My cousin, Rebecca Sweetman, a distinguished authority on the archaeology of Roman Greece, and professor at the University of St. Andrew's, who was at this time Assistant Director of the British School.

304 He was actually a professor of History and Archaeology in the University of Bergen, Norway – and currently head of the Norwegian School.

DAY 3, MONDAY, APRIL 14TH

I went down to breakfast in the hotel again, abandoning my notion to go out on the town – I like the yoghurt, and so on, too much, I'm afraid, and it's simple. After breakfast, Wendy rang (I had forgotten to turn off the phone!) to say that Mrs Korka wished to postpone me till tomorrow, so I decided to go up to the Institute instead, and take a look at certain properties.

Up to Prytaneiou, then, which is grottier than ever (of course), and went over details of the lease (which Wendy and our lawyer have well sorted out, I think), and then down to look, first, at the Church house, which is in fact just below the Institute, but a thorough ruin by now – much of the roof has fallen in over the last winter, it seems, and there are large cracks in the walls from a recent earthquake; a very sorry sight! Someone should save it, but we may forget about it. Down then, and round to the south of the Acropolis, to view a much more promising house, just beside the Dutch Institute, on Makri Street, off Dionysiou Areopagita. We were shown round the Dutch Institute, which is beautifully done up, and the next door house is identical, but currently gutted. The owners want to sell, but it is rumoured that they are threatened with bankruptcy. This could be a good or a bad thing. What we need is about two-and-a-half million euro, and only someone like O'Reilly could come up with that.

After a cup of coffee, I returned and discussed the situation with Wendy. Wendy has just finished her thesis, and is about to defend it back in Dublin. That should strengthen her position. She seems very competent, though, and is in command of things. The bould Eleni, though, does not seem so satisfactory. She has no secretarial competence, and seems to think that *she* should be Assistant Director. I wonder if Andrew had promised her something?

Back at the hotel, I can't help sneaking looks at CNN, but it is all very depressing – everything in Baghdad sacked, and now Bush and the Bushies are threatening Syria![305] I went up in

---

[305] The American assault on Saddam Hussein's Iraq had begun on March 19th, and continued for about a month. Baghdad was captured on April 9th.

the afternoon to the Benaki Museum, where I had never been, and which is really most impressive, though I only looked at the ancient stuff, and then a special exhibition on The Bull in Mediterranean Culture, which was excellent. Finally, I bought a Cycladic bowl – a piece of foolishness, but I liked the look of it.

In the evening, after doing a bit of work, I set out to walk round the Acropolis, by way of working up an appetite for dinner. It was a pleasant evening, though chilly, with a full moon already established, and everything looking well in the evening light. Dionysios Areopagita Avenue is beautifully laid out. I paid respect to Proclus' House and the Theatre, then strolled up past the Areopagus, and round to above the Agora. Just as I was coming down, though, I came upon a fine building all lit up, and it turned out to be the original home of Athens University, now the University Museum, and there was a musical event about to take place. I hung about, unsure what to do, since everyone who arrived seemed to know each other, and there was no desk at which to buy a ticket. I asked someone, and was told that I was most welcome to stay if I liked. Only later did I learn that it was a musical evening staged by the Law and Economics Departments! It featured a very fine musical quintet, called *Septeria*.

Then back down to the Plaka, where I found a pleasant restaurant for dinner, and was serenaded by a harpist. I phoned home, and got Mouse – Mummy was out at something.

DAY 4, THURSDAY, APRIL 15TH

The weather is still cold – but sunny this morning. This is the big day, really – though I may actually have done more important things on Sunday and yesterday; who knows? The sight of the Cleanthes House (the University Museum) – of the same age as the Church House, and finely restored – leads me now to hope that the latter might have its chance. It also gave me an idea for a music and poetry evening for the faculty.

Wendy collected me at 10.00 am and we proceeded up by Metro to the Ministry, where we were well received by Mrs Korka and Mrs Fakarou – both young(ish) and charming ladies. There is really no great fuss about my credentials, and in other respects the Institute is in good odour. They were pleased to hear that we were to be their neighbours. Mrs Korka is interested in old illustrations of Greek antiquities, and in that connection is anxious to pursue a clue that she has heard of, that drawings of Charles Dodwell are present in an Irish collection. I must check up on this.[306]

We went round, then, to view our proposed residence in Odos Notara, not thinking we could get in, but we found the place open, and being worked on. In fact, both the architect and the designer were there, and it proved most useful, as regards specifying where telephone terminals might go, and what colours things might be painted. It probably should be available in mid-June or so.

And so back on the Metro for a short recuperation, before heading out to lunch with Mrs Hennessy, the Irish Ambassador, in the Grande Bretagne. It was very splendid, and she is a delightful lady. She has a daughter in College,[307] doing Mediaeval History, who was at Alex![308] She is keen to have a celebration of the 100th anniversary of Bloomsday in Athens in June 2004, but I can foresee difficulties! We spent almost two hours over lunch, though she had to head off to the airport to shepherd Irish delegates to a big EU gathering here tomorrow – first Dick Roche, and then later Bertie himself. It sounds as if a massive security operation will be mounted tomorrow. It is not quite clear how that will affect travel to the airport!

---

306 I am no longer sure what this was all about. There was a Charles Reginald Dodwell (1922-1994) who was a distinguished art historian, but he had no connection with Ireland that I can see. It could in fact be Edward Dodwell (1767-1832) that is at issue, since he travelled extensively in Greece, and produced many drawings of its antiquities. He was of Anglo-Irish ancestry, and was born in Dublin.

307 Sc. Trinity College.

308 Alexandra College, which our daughter Ruth also attended.

After lunch, back to the hotel for a siesta. Then, around 6.00 pm, I set out for a short walk down to the Temple of Olympian Zeus, but found already roadblocks and police and army – and a dreadful loudspeaker in Syntagma, blaring songs and slogans; no people, just a set of loudspeakers! Who these idiots think they are impressing I can't imagine. It should annoy *everyone,* and I can't see why the authorities allow it.

Anyhow, back to the hotel, and then, at around 7.10, off to give my lecture in the Danish School – only a few minutes' walk, really, to Chairephon Square, beside the Lysicrates Monument. I found quite an impressive crowd there – around 40 souls – despite the difficulties of travel at the moment – and Polymnia Athanassiadi, Pavlos Kalligas, and Evangelos Moutsopoulos[309] all turned up, each reprimanding me for not letting them know where I was; but they all wanted to entertain me, and that would have been impossible. The talk went off OK, I think. I even ventured to read 'Waiting for the Barbarians' in Greek![310] There was a drink afterwards, and then Wendy, Eleni, Polymnia, and another lady came out to dinner at a nice old restaurant, called Psarra.

And so back to the hotel. Polymnia accompanied me back, thinking that John[311] could pick her up from there, but it was too complicated with the roadblocks, so she took a taxi.

DAY 5, WEDNESDAY, APRIL 16TH

The day began with a call from Evangelos, proposing to come round to breakfast, which he did at 8.30, despite road blocks sealing off the whole street! The awful loud-speakers are still blaring away. It looked as if the whole city was closed down. We had a bit of breakfast, and he presented me with yet more of his books!

---

309 All distinguished Classical philosophers in their own modes, and old friends. Evangelos (1930-2021) was a rather prolific author, and tended to present me with his books.

310 That is, the famous poem of Cavafy's.

311 John was her second husband, succeeding Garth Fowden. I cannot recall his last name.

Evangelos then went off to the hospital, for treatment on his wrist, which he had broken some months ago. Jean phoned about 9.30 am, complaining that my phone was on the blink, so some difficulty may be foreseen this evening. Then Wendy phoned, stuck at the beginning of Philhellenôn, blocked by police, but I came out and rescued her, since they were really quite friendly. She helped me pay the bill, which really did only come to €88 a night, *with* breakfast! Remarkable, since it was €272 on the door, *excluding* breakfast!

We set out, then, with the bags, to call in on Rebecca in the British School. It was a bit of a slog up the hill from the Evangelismos Metro, but we had a. very pleasant coffee on Rebecca's verandah, and met her cat Calypso.

And there the diary ends, but we may assume a reasonably smooth journey to the airport, and so back to Dublin.

17. Expedition to Münster (Germany)

September 26 – 30, 2003

The occasion for this trip was a meeting of the Academia Platonica Septima, founded some years previously by my old friend Matthias Baltes, Professor of Ancient Philosophy in the University of Münster (so called reckoning the Platonic Academy of Marsilio Ficino in Florence to have been the sixth!) to bring together the Platonists of Europe in regular yearly meetings, where we would focus on a particular text, and for this meeting he had chosen a treatise of the second-century A.D. Platonist philosopher and rhetorician, Apuleius of Madaura (also author of The Golden Ass), of which we were commissioned by the Wissenschaftliche Buchgesellschaft to produce an edition (comprising text, translation, notes and interpretative essays) for their SAPERE series. Sadly, however, Matthias himself, who had been in failing health for some time, had actually died back in January, so the project was brought to completion by his former assistant Marie-Luise Lakmann, aided by a committee. The meeting was in fact originally planned to take place in Dublin, but Matthias' state of health made it impossible for him to travel, so it had been re-scheduled for Münster. I persuaded Jean to accompany me on this trip, to convey our sympathies to his wife, Renate, and his daughter, Sabine, who had stayed with us on a number of occasions during her teenage years, to improve her English. Her contributions are in italics on this occasion.

DAY 1, FRIDAY, SEPTEMBER 26TH

Now sitting, at about 2.30 pm, in a café in the little town of Haltern, off the A43, north of Bochum, on the way to Münster.

We have had quite a struggle to get here, over the German autobahn system. We rose early, at about 4.30 am, having woken up early, to get to the long-term car-park at the airport for a 7.10 flight to Düsseldorf.

In fact, we ended up with plenty of time to spare. The plane sat on the runway for nearly forty minutes before take-off, but managed to arrive in Düsseldorf only about fifteen minutes late. The service on board was rather minimal, as was the snack they (not too generously) served: a cold muffin – which I refused – and a tea or coffee.

On arrival at the desk in Düsseldorf, where we were to pick up our hired car, they had never heard of us! I had no voucher from Holiday Autos, for reasons rather complicated (I had tried to hire a car from HA-UK, while being in Ireland). But the girl was very gallant, phoned up, and found (a) that I had the number of my booking wrong, and (b) that Budget Travel was handling it. So all ended well, and we found ourselves driving out of the car-park onto the German freeway system in a little Nissan Micro, which J decides is a cute little car – and indeed it bowls along fine, although the radio keeps wanting to turn on.

The signs worked fine, until we turned off the A52 to Essen onto the A3, and found that it was blocked. At that point we lost the plot – no provisions made for lost foreigners. We almost ended up in Holland, at Venlo – crossed the Rhine, but turned back just in time, and stayed on the A40, through Essen, to Bochum, where we joined the A43 to Münster. But there were periodic traffic jams all the way, mainly due to road works.

15.40: we are sitting in the courtyard of the magnificent Burg Vischering, a mediaeval castle adjacent to the town of Lüdinghausen, just 30 km south of Münster. The sun is shining, it is still quite warm, and the pigeons are burbling in the eaves. We had a coffee, and then toured the small museum. It is most interesting. The Burg was built originally by the Prince-Bishop of Münster in 1271, to keep the rebellious lords of Lüdinghausen in check, and he put his steward, Droste, into it to manage it. The family of Droste in Vischering is still there in the 21st century!

We drove up from there to Münster, and coasted into town without trouble, on a street that led straight to our little hotel, the Kolping Tagungshotel on Aigidii Strasse. The hotel is most comfortable, though there is a curious religious cast to everything: crucifix and bible in room, photos of clergy on the wall of the dining-room. Dinner took place at 6.00, where we met everyone. Marie-Luise Lakmann[312] is organising everything. We dined with Carlos Steel, Luc Brisson, and Alessandro Linguiti.[313]

After dinner, we went up to the university, where a fine memorial service was held for Matthias – music, then speeches from the Pro-Rector, Christian Pietsch (Matthias' successor), Marie-Luise, and Horst-Dieter Blüme (a colleague, who shared his office for many years); then more music (the choir of the Classics Department was excellent!), and an address by Michael Erler, on 'Das Kind in Man'. Then a wine reception.

I was thoroughly exhausted by this time, but yet, about 10.30 or even later, I had to attend a meeting in Christian Pietsch's office to talk with Herr Holzboog[314] (a very pleasant fellow, in fact), Cristina D'Ancona Costa and Luc Brisson, on the possibility of an *editio minor* of the Platonismus project, which went on till midnight, by which time I wasn't making much sense.

I went back to the hotel, accompanied by Andrew Smith, who suggested a nightcap in the bar. I didn't like to say no, as he obviously wanted company, so I had a Bailey's, while he had some schnapps. Then he decided we should have another, so I had a fizzy water instead. We chatted for an hour or so, and then I excused myself. I slept very well, in a comfortable bed.

---

312 She had been an assistant to Matthias, and is still a distinguished member of the faculty, and specialist in the history of Platonism.

313 All distinguished Platonists, and the first two old friends. They are, respectively, professors of ancient philosophy at the University of Leuven, the CNRS in Paris, and the University of Siena.

314 The publisher of *Der Platonismus im Antike*, a vast project which Matthias had been engaged upon, and which Christian Pietsch had now inherited (and on which he was roping us in!).

DAY 2, SATURDAY, SEPTEMBER 27ᵀᴴ

John went to breakfast at about 8.40 am – after most of the others had finished. I got up about 9.10, and had a roll and coffee in the restaurant. I was deciding what to explore when I met Christoph Helmig,[315] who brought me to the tourist office to get a brochure on Münster, as I had mislaid the one that Sabine[316] had given me. We came across a Scottish regiment performing in the marketplace (where the market was in full swing) – they had a band, including bagpipes, and two men performing a dance. After bringing me to the tourist office, Christoph left and went to meet some friends. I went first to see St. Lambert's Church, which still has hanging on one of the sides of its steeple three cages which exhibited the dead bodies of three 'heretic' Baptists killed in the mid-1500's.[317] It has impressive Romanesque decoration on the outside, which luckily did not suffer in the bombing of the last war. Next, I visited the Rathaus, which was the setting for the signing of the treaty ending the Thirty Years' War between the Netherlands and Spain in 1648. It has rather magnificent high gables, which had to be restored after the bombing.

I, meanwhile, after my late breakfast, first set off to the University, under the impression that we were meeting there, only to find it completely closed. In fact, we were meeting in the hotel, and I got there about half an hour late. We were due to

---

315 Christoph, a former student of mine (and previously of Matthias'). He later became professor of classics at the University of Köln.

316 That is to say, Matthias Baltes' daughter.

317 In 1534, an apocalyptic Anabaptist sect, led by John of Leiden, took power in the Münster rebellion and founded a democratic proto-socialistic state. They claimed all property, burned all books except the Bible, and called it the "New Jerusalem". John of Leiden believed he would lead the elect from Münster to capture the entire world and purify it of evil with the sword in preparation for the Second Coming of Christ and the beginning of the Millennium. They went so far as to require all citizens to be naked as preparation for the Second Coming. However, the town was recaptured in 1535; the Anabaptists were tortured to death and their corpses were exhibited in metal baskets, which can still be seen hanging from the tower of St. Lambert's Church.

devote the morning to discussing the future of the Academy[318], but in fact we settled all our business by the coffee break, and so we all went off to the cemetery to view Matthias' grave. It was a pleasant walk in delightful weather, and the grave was most effective – a simple, natural stone, with 'Matthias Baltes, Platoniker' on it – a slightly ambiguous title, perhaps! Then we walked round the Aasee, and settled in a beer garden for a beer before lunch.

After the Rathaus, I visited the Dom (Cathedral) of St. Paul, and timed my visit to coincide with the 12 o'clock chiming of their famous astronomic clock, from the Middle Ages. The grave chapel beside it, of Cardinal Clemens August Graf von Galen, has impressive modern stained glass, made by Georg Meistermann of Cologne, 1985-1990. As I was about to depart the Cathedral, suddenly, it seemed, a beautiful male voice choir started to sing in the back. They sang about four pieces, and then, just as suddenly, left. So far, I have been very lucky with impromptu concerts!

At this point I decided to stop and have a coffee and a sausage roll at the café just down the road from our hotel. At 2.30, Sabine came to meet me, and we drove to her apartment, where her mother, Renate, had prepared a most delicious tea, of home-made bread and a lovely marzipan tart (marzipan with one yolk of egg added, some vanilla sugar and butter, and a liqueur (I can't remember which!). After tea, we walked to Matthias' grave, in a beautiful graveyard, with each grave beautifully planted, and not a single plastic flower or glass dome to be seen. The inscription on his stone: 'Matthias Baltes, Platoniker'.

We then took the loop in the opposite direction back to their house, passing the Schloss on the way back, through the lovely gardens and lakes around it. The Schloss is quite bare and uninteresting inside, and is just used as university offices, but is beautiful on the outside. This was also restored after the War. Sabine insisted on guiding me back to the hotel, and she got as bus back, which made me feel rather bad.

We had dinner at the hotel, and then a large group of us went to a beer house, and drank a special 'Pinkur' beer or two. Andrew Smith in flying form, as usual.

---

318 That is, the Academia Platonica Septima, founded by Matthias Baltes to form a basis for regular meetings of the Platonists of Europe. It still continues, I am glad to say.

The afternoon was taken up with two sessions on the first part of the De Deo Socratis,[319] a rather literary analysis by Christian Pietsch (ss. 1-5), and then a rather philosophical one of Alessandro Linguiti (6-11). In neither case did we come to very close grips with the text – but then Matthias had rather preempted us by providing a translation and fairly full notes. This is not as satisfactory a relation to the text as in previous meetings, but then we are generating an edition, and that is good.[320]

As usual, I'm afraid, there is rather too much to eat and drink – a big lunch in the middle of the day, and then a full dinner, is not a good idea. I will skip the former tomorrow, I think!

In the pub after dinner, we were regaled at one point by two travelling apprentice carpenters, in ceremonial dress, who were collecting for their subsistence during their travels. They are 'journeymen' in the full mediaeval sense – the German term is 'fahrende Zimmerman'. We came home around 11.00 – the general party *claimed* to have broken up around 12.00, but we wonder. A subsidiary group, of Bert, Christoph, Riccardo Chiaradonna, and Jan Opsomer, were in flying form also.

DAY 3, SUNDAY, SEPTEMBER 28TH

I collected Sabine at her home, and we drove to Cologne. It took two hours, because there was a terrible traffic jam about 20 km out of Cologne. We left the motorway, hoping we could get there faster, but it wasn't much better. We finally managed to get there, but missed the entrance to parking under the Cathedral. We found parking close by, however, and walked to the Cathedral. It has huge high Romanesque steeples and very elaborate decorations – styles spanning the hundreds of years it took to complete! Miraculously, though all around it was bombed in the last war, the Cathedral was not hit.

We noted that there was a Mass at 12.00, and since we had half an

---

319 On this, see introductory note.

320 This was in fact published in the following year, edited by Hans-Georg Nesselrath. I contributed a section on 'Dämonologie im frühen Platonismus'.

hour to spare, we went to a large, elaborate café opposite, and had an apple strudel and a coffee – very kindly provided by Sabine. Then to the Mass. I was disappointed that it was not a High Mass, and the only organ music we heard was the accompaniment to the congregation singing. Many beggars clustered in the doorway of the church. The proportions of the Cathedral are beautiful – very high naves and pretty Gothic stained glass windows.

We were very pressed for time, so we went to the Ludwig Museum[321] directly, where there was a very good exhibition – an 'Introspective' by Richard Hamilton, the 'father' of pop-art.[322] It was huge, and we didn't get to see all of it. We were deciding that it was difficult to recognise his own particular 'style', as he experimented with so many different materials and techniques, when I noticed four paintings very much in the style of Francis Bacon. I was explaining to Sabine about him, and describing to her his work (blues and orangey reds), when she read the notes. It turned out that the four portraits were by Bacon, of the artist!

We then had to rush, as Sabine was to leave for a holiday in Crete the next day, and she had to re-pack her bags. We made better time coming back, and arrived at the hotel around 3.45. I rested and read till dinnertime. John also, from about 5 pm.

We spent the morning on the rest of the *DDS*, led by Frans de Haas (12-16) and Carlos Steel (17-23), and that went fine. We got a good feel for the rhetorical flow of the *DDS*. At 12.30, instead of lunch, I carried out my intention to take a walk, and chose the Promenade round the old walls, which is pleasant, and of which I did a segment, until 1.30, when I had a meeting with the rest of the Vorstand[323] as to how to proceed – Frans de Haas, Christian Pietsch, Luc Brisson and myself. I tended to stress keeping it small and informal – and to try to find a rich sponsor!

---

321 The Museum Ludwig houses a collection of modern art. It includes works from Pop Art, Abstract and Surrealism, and has one of the largest Picasso collections in Europe. It holds many works by Andy Warhol and Roy Lichtenstein.

322 Richard William Hamilton CH (1922 – 2011) was an English painter and collage artist, and indeed widely regarded as the 'father' of pop art.

323 That is to say, 'Board of Directors' of the Academia Platonica.

After that, around 2.15, Marie-Luise led us on a tour, first to a Bible Museum, housed on the ground floor of the building where her office is, and then to the Rathaus. I survived these two, but then my back gave way, and I sneaked off home to lie down, where I found J already returned from her adventure, at around 4.30.

We rested for a while, and then went down to a pleasant dinner – the buffet again. We had a bottle of Pinot Grigio this time, which was perfectly good, for €15 or so. I talked to two of the Hungarian delegates, Laszlo Béne and another fellow who has been translating Apuleius into Hungarian – perhaps Tomás Baroczi? Then out again on the town, this time to a Weinstübe beside the Rathaus, which served good wine – advised by young Ralph Hafner of Berlin, who is something of an expert. Smith was again in flying form, and Thomas Leinkauf was good fun.

DAY 4, MONDAY, SEPTEMBER 29TH

Up at 7.30, since I had to be ready for my talk at 9.00, and have a read of Pier-Luigi Donini's contribution as well (which follows on mine). I talked to Dominic at breakfast. Today is devoted to the various introductory chapters to the SAPERE volume. I was first off, with 'Demonology in the Earlier Platonist Tradition'; then Donini, on Plutarch and Maximus (read by Franco Ferrari)[324]. Then lunch – had a salad, after which I headed off on a Rundfahrt – completed the circuit of the Old Town, along the Promenade (the Old Walls), in about an hour. Very pleasant – rain had been threatening, but it passed away.

After breakfast, I wrote some diary, and set off to shop at about 10.00 am. – the museums are all closed on Mondays. After searching a bit, I found a corduroy jacket for John in a large department store, but waited to buy it till John could come to try it on. I found in another department store, slightly more down-market, a pair of slip-on everyday shoes (€45) and a

---

[324] This paper actually concerned 'Socrates and his Daemon in the Platonist Tradition', a topic on which both Plutarch and Maximus had quite a bit to say.

watch (€24). Afterwards I dropped in to the café on our street and had a slice of plum tart and a cappuchino.

Then back to the hotel, and sat and read my book – 'Grace Notes', by Bernard McLaverty, which is a good read. When John came up for a while before his next session to rest, I took a walk around the lake and its periphery. Found a little shop with handmade leather goods – very nice, and 'keen' prices; but it was closed! Also found a little shop with handmade marzipans, and bought some as gifts.

In the evening, we had a 'festliches Abendessen', in honour of Renate, who came, and even made a little speech, which was replied to, in very friendly terms, by Dominic. A pretty good dinner was served this time, and then there was a move to go once again to a Weinstübe – which we resisted, going for a walk round the town instead. A very pleasant evening in the Old Town – which was quite deserted, in a strange way.

DAY 5, TUESDAY, SEPTEMBER 30TH

This morning we rose fairly promptly, hoping to do a bit of shopping, and visit the Picasso Museum, before meeting up with Christoph at 11.15 am, and driving down to his house in the country for lunch. We said goodbye to lots of people, and then went up the town to see if we could buy a corduroy coat for me. In fact, we found a pretty good fit, for €99.95! Then we bought a few other items, such as a diary and pens. We found that the museum did not open till 11.00, so we left it, and went instead to a little leather shop at the end of Aigidii Strasse, where we bought some booties for young Colin. A very jolly young lady ran it.

Back to the hotel, then, and settled up – only charged €20 a day for J. Very reasonable! Kolping is a sort of movement or sect, but pretty benign, it would seem. Very Catholic, though! There seems to have been a Cardinal Kolping.[325]

---

[325] Adolph Kolping (1813-1865) was a German Catholic priest, and the founder of the Kolping Association. He led the movement for providing and promoting social support for workers in industrialized cities, while also working to promote the dignities of workers in accordance with the social

Christoph Helmig and his sister Ricarda invited us to lunch at their lovely house in the country, about half an hour's drive from Münster, in the district Tetekum. It was a picturesque bungalow, surrounded by the original farmhouse and outhouses. Their mother takes great care of the garden, which was a mass of begonias and geraniums. We did not meet the parents, who were away on holidays, but we met Ricarda's horse and cute little pony. Also their Alsatian, who greeted us warmly.

We then drove in convoy about five minutes to the most lovely little inn, 'Zur Linde', in Seppenrade, which served a very good lunch. I had a schnitzel covered with the most delicious spinach. They seemingly specialise in schnitzels with various accompaniments. The inn itself dates from the mid-18th century, and has been beautifully maintained. The lovely rose garden at the back used to be a rubbish dump, it seems! After lunch, we visited the local Schloss, a very fine Renaissance palace, which had belonged to the Prince-Bishop of Westfalen.

And here the diary ends. We must presume a safe return to Düsseldorf, and so home.

magisterium of the faith. He was called Gesellenvater (the Journeymen's Father). He was never a Cardinal, in fact, but Pope Pius IX made him a Monsignor. The process for his beatification commenced on 21 March 1934, and he was later titled as Venerable in 1989. His beatification was celebrated under Pope John Paul II on 27 October 1991.

17. EXPEDITION TO PRAGUE:

OCTOBER 8 – 13, 2003

This was an expedition to attend the 4th Symposium Platonicum Pragense, devoted to a study of Plato's Parmenides, and organised by Alex Havlicek and Filip Karfik, as a spin-off of the International Plato Society, of which I was a member.

DAY 1, WEDNESDAY, OCTOBER 8TH

This time I am on my own again, feeling a bit foolish and exhausted, but J had had enough wandering, and anyhow Ratso[326] came back lame from Loretta's, with a dislocated patella, and so has to be nursed. She left me to the airport at 1.15 pm or so, for a 2.25 flight to Prague. Aer Lingus was slightly late once again – "owing to the lateness of the incoming flight" – but actually managed to get us to Prague early, at 5.40 (for 5.55). I had changed €50 into koruna in Dublin (which proved fortunate later), at 30 k to the €.

I was met at the airport by two students – Denis O'Brien, Kenneth Sayre,[327] and Beatriz Bossi[328] also came in at the same

---

326 A nickname for our dog, Benson, an opinionated Yorkie. Loretta was his minder.

327 Kenneth M. Sayre (1928 – 2022) was an American philosopher who spent most of his career at the University of Notre Dame. His early career was devoted mainly to philosophic applications of artificial intelligence, cybernetics, and information theory. Later on his main interests shifted to Plato, philosophy of mind, and environmental philosophy.

328 Beatriz Bossi was professor in the Philosophy Department of the University of Madrid, and an active member of the International Plato Society.

time – and they drove us in a van straight to the Villa Lana, a fine old house belonging to the Czech Academy, in the northern suburbs of Prague – a posh district, full of embassies! We were let in by the housekeeper, after a little delay, but she indicated, after registering us, that the Villa was actually closed till the morning, so, if we wanted dinner, we would have to forage. However, she recommended a restaurant in the neighbourhood, so, after checking into our rooms, which are perfectly fine – clean, warm and modern, in new buildings in the garden – we set off in a bunch to find the restaurant.

The restaurant was actually excellent (Na Razhrani, on Srbska, 7), and very cheap – a slap-up meal, with beer or wine, for less than €10 a head. Monique Dixsaut joined us from town, summoned by her student Dimitri El Murr,[329] a very lively and articulate young Lebanese, bilingual in French and English. Vassilis Karasmanis,[330] and his wife Maria, also turned up. In good form.

And so home to bed, with a light rain falling.

DAY 2, THURSDAY, OCTOBER 9TH

Rose somewhat after 8.00, after a not very good night – too much to eat, and bed a bit hard, while pillow was a bit soft – but got enough sleep. Had a good breakfast – chatted with Denis, and with *Julius Tomin*, who is still surviving, in the Bristol area, with a new wife and some children (remarkable!), and Christopher Rowe[331] and his wife. Luc Brisson and Catherine arrived, despite

---

329 Dimitri El Murr is now Professor of Ancient Philosophy at the Ecole Normale Supérieure (Université Paris Sciences et Lettres) and a member of Centre Jean Pépin, UMR 8230, and a considerable authority on Plato in particular.

330 Vassilis Karasmanis was Professor of Ancient Philosophy in the Department of Humanities, Social Sciences and Law of the National Technical University of Athens.

331 Christopher James Rowe OBE (born 1944) is a British classical scholar, and distinguished authority on ancient philosophy. He is Professor Emeritus in the Department of Classics and Ancient History of Durham University,

trouble with his passport, which had to be renewed because less than 90 days to expiry!

Proceedings began around 9.00 am, with speeches of greeting from Alex Havlicek and Luc. Various people have failed to turn up, for various reasons: Andreas Graeser, Francisco Lisi, Franco Ferrari, and Francesco Fronterotta – which is probably just as well, since all talks and discussions are running over time! Constance Meinwald also failed to turn up, but her paper was read by Chris Rowe. Then we had FP Hägler, who was rather unconvincing on the relation between the two halves of the dialogue. Then a coffee break, and then Beatriz Bossi on Conceptualism in *Parmenides* 132b3-c11.

A copious lunch, then, in the beautiful dining hall, with frescoes and moulded ceiling, after which I went off for a short walk, managing to find the park nearby – a fine big one! Then two more long papers, by Dimitri El-Murr and Karel Thein, after which Monique and I had a chance to sit down and plan Denis's *Festschrift*.[332] I'm hoping to get an essay out of him reflecting on his intellectual development – it would be an interesting innovation!

Then followed a copious reception, in which I chatted mainly to Vassilis Karasmanis and Beatriz, and then discussed theology with Sam Scolnicov,[333] before we were all chased out by the staff.

DAY 3, FRIDAY, OCTOBER 10TH

Up a bit late, but grabbed some breakfast before 9.00 am. All talks are running over time. Monique started off instead of

---

England, where he was Head of Department 2004–2008. He is a former President of the Classical Association, and was appointed OBE in 2009 for "services to scholarship".

332 Monique Dixsaut had invited me to join her in editing a Festschrift, or memorial volume of essays, in honour of our mutual friend Denis O'Brien. This was duly published, as *Agonistes: Essays in Honour of Denis O'Brien*, (Ashgate, 2005). And he did compose an Apologia for himself!

333 For Sam Scolnicov, see my two visits to Israel in the previous volume. He was an excellent Platonic scholar, based in the University of Jerusalem, and a most hospitable and entertaining host.

Denis (who is in the afternoon), and spoke about the hypotheses as representing 'possible worlds' – quite a plausible idea! Then Luc Brisson, on the last four deductions – also good. I see more clearly now what Luc is up to in declaring that the hypotheses are about 'the world'. Then a rather foolish young American fellow called Ambuel, on nothing much at all.

Instead of lunch, I set off for a walk in the Bubenec Park – very pleasant weather and ambience, but I managed to get lost, and asked my way back *in Czech!*

The afternoon session featured Ken Sayre being rather silly,[334] with a cube representing the various relations of the deductions; Denis, attacking Luc (very characteristically) for attributing the concept of *to pan*[335] as a world to Parmenides; and Filip Karfik, being a little obvious on the question of the relations *kath' hauto* and *pros alla*.[336] I can't say that I am learning an awful lot at this conference, pleasant though it is. I am always astonished at the capacity of many scholars (mainly Southern or Eastern European, but not exclusively!) to solemnly relate once more what is already there in the text, and think that they are saying something.

Anyhow, after that, there was initially a move to go downtown, but in fact a group of us decided to go back to Na Rozhrani, and had another excellent and inexpensive meal. After that, Denis, Ken Sayre, and Dimitri El-Murr assembled in my room for a nightcap of Jameson, since I had brought along a little bottle of it, and we tried to persuade Denis to compose an intellectual autobiography for the Festschrift.

DAY 4, SATURDAY, OCTOBER 11TH

This morning there were just three papers, beginning with a pleasant fellow from Prague, Spinke, speaking in German on

---

334 I am probably not being quite fair to Kenneth Sayre here (see note 298 above).

335 Sc. 'the all', or the totality of things.

336 Sc. 'to oneself' and 'in relation to others'. Filip was at this stage in the University of Prague, and one of our hosts, but later moved to the University of Fribourg, Switzerland.

'Relation, Sein und Zeit', but, once again, I'm darned if I can see what he was contributing. Then Sam Scolnicov, giving a good analysis of the conditions of knowledge as set out in the dialogue (one can't have knowledge of a simple object, *kath' hauto*). And then me, bringing up the rear, giving the troops the lowdown on what the real subject of the *Parmenides* is – or at least what Speusippus[337] thought it was! This seemed to go down reasonably well.

Then lunch – Radek[338] had come up at last, for my paper, and after lunch he undertook to take Christoph and me for a walk in the city. To this group Ken Sayre attached himself, but mixed in very well. It was a splendid walk, if rather tiring. Radek disdained any form of public transport, and marched us off at a brisk pace all the way down to the Castle – entering by the Castle gardens, and then across the moat into the Castle proper. The Castle is really a little town on its own, built originally in the 9th century, and not just the presidential palace, but lots of little streets of houses, including one very quaint little street where Kafka was alleged to have lived for a while. Then we looked in on the prison – an oubliette, where you were just dumped – and finally the Loreta Church, which is an impressive piece of baroque built by one Kilian Dientzenhofer, with the alleged House of the Virgin in the middle of the courtyard.

Then he headed down into Mala Strana, where we stopped for a beer, and then called into the Waldstein Gardens, with a bizarre stalactite wall – sort of something like Antoni Gaudí [339] would have constructed, but much older!

And so across the Charles Bridge, and back home.

DAY 5, SUNDAY, OCTOBER 12TH

Today I set out with Sam and Hannah Scolnicov to visit the old Jewish Quarter – not a ghetto, just a quarter! The Jews actually

---

337 Plato's nephew, and successor as head of the Academy.

338 Radek Chlup, scholar of ancient philosophy, who had spent some time the previous year at the Trinity Plato Centre.

339 That is to say, architect of La Sagrada Familia cathedral in Barcelona.

enjoyed quite good conditions in Prague, it seems, until the Nazis arrived. Hannah herself had lost many family members to the Nazis – and in the cemetery she met an old lady, now Israeli, formerly French, who had lost fully *fourteen*.

Going round the cemetery was actually a sad business. At one point, though, just outside it, Sam and I were accosted by an enthusiastic young orthodox Jew, who invited us into a tent for a glass of wine and a *prayer*, so we went in. As we passed inside, Sam muttered to me: "Don't worry, he's not trying to convert you. He's trying to convert *me*!"

And here, sadly, the diary ends. I will have flown home safely the next day.

18. Trip to Southern Italy:

MAY 11 – 23, 2006

The occasion for this trip was the wedding of my nephew, Nicholas Gore-Grimes, which was scheduled to take place in Ravello, above Amalfi, on Saturday, May 20th. We took the opportunity to come over a week early, and enjoy a brief tour of Puglia in advance of this – a plan that could easily have gone seriously wrong, but happily did not. It gave us a chance to see parts of Italy that we had not previously visited. Jean's contributions are in italics, as being (slightly) less than mine.

DAY 1, THURSDAY, MAY 11TH

The day began at around 4.14 am, when our alarm went off. I only got to bed around midnight last night, as I was messing with Syrianus[340] and a book review – of which I finished the latter, at least! Frank[341] rose to the occasion, and drove us to the airport. No trouble checking in. We had a coffee at Butler's. The plane was very prompt, a bit turbulent, but we arrived at Naples almost half-an-hour early – to find ourselves in a rainstorm! Vesuvius was barely visible through the clouds.

Hertz was a bit slow with the car, but produced a pleasant Mazda (instead of the promised Ford Fiesta), and we steamed out of the airport at about 12.30 pm, and hit the Autostrada in the direction of Bari. We bowled along happily for about an

---

340 One of my Neoplatonic philosophers, a work of whose I was translating.
341 Jean's brother, Frank Montgomery, who was minding the house for us.

hour, in driving rain, which seemed to be following us from west to east, stopped for lunch at a snack bar on the Autostrada, and then decided to head off in the direction of Foggia, with the idea of staying the night in Bovino, and exploring its neighbourhood.

That turned out to be a mistake. We had ignored an earlier sign which said the road to Foggia was blocked (we think they must have had serious mud-slides this winter, as we seemed to see evidence of it along the way; the roads are in very poor condition). Having driven by a suggested diverted route, we reached, after about half-an-hour's driving, another sign, saying that the road to Bovino was blocked. We had noticed (about ten minutes prior to this) a sign for the motorway, so we doubled back and forgot about our plans for Bovino and the Gargano peninsula. We suspect that the peninsula will have similar problems.

The upside of the journey was that we travelled through rolling, beautiful, lush countryside, with wonderful panoramas, including little hills, with towns perched on top. The wild flowers were abundant. All very green – rather ominously!

Back on the freeway, we decided to head for the Adriatic seaside town of Trani, which sounded attractive. And so indeed it proved. The rain finally passed over as we reached the town, but it was slow to clear, and there had plainly been a deluge. We drove down to the seafront, first up to an interesting monastery on a promontory, and then found a nice little hotel, the *Riviera*, just off the front (€70 a night for two – we think!), and then set off down the town to see the sights. It is in fact a fine old town, with narrow, old streets round the harbour, a fine cathedral, and a park which we took a walk in (some Roman milestones on display, from the Via Traiana), and we are now sitting in a café on the front,[342] having a beer, and about to go an find a pizza for dinner.

In typical Italian style, the old town has many attractive little courtyards and walkways, mainly of lovely square marble stones, and a lovely harbour area. We are now sitting in a pizzeria just off the harbour, about to eat the most incredibly inexpensive pizzas. I have chosen the most luxurious (called 'Marcus'), for €7 (considering that Mouse pays €12 for

---

342 Note from J: This was called the Bar Jaxo! The young man who greeted us first said he couldn't serve us for a few minutes because he was 'lonely'!

a medium Margherita). We had so much left over that we asked for a bag, and bundled it up for a picnic tomorrow.

We retired back to our hotel around 10.30 pm. I've been wondering what they will charge us for our breakfasts, remembering Mouse's and my visit to Rome last summer, when they charged us something outrageous!

DAY 2, FRIDAY, MAY 12TH

We had a very good sleep, in spite of a rather hard bed. Our bedroom looks out on the Adriatic, but a few unfinished buildings in the foreground rather spoil the view.

Breakfast was fine – good rolls, excellent coffee – but what the extra cost is we have no idea! Anyhow, we decided to stay on another night, and spend the day exploring the area. Our first destination was Castel del Monte, Frederick II's remarkable folly – a hunting lodge arranged entirely in octagons, perched on a hill overlooking the Murge. It has been well restored, and is indeed a wonderful sight. It is comprised of a central octagon, flanked by octagonal towers, and has eight rooms on each floor. Much Moorish influence, as Fred was very much into Arabic culture!

After exploring that, we moved on to Minervino, a town billed as the 'balcony of Apulia', and indeed it has fine views. We came upon pleasant people in a little shop, who pointed us to the cathedral and the view. The cathedral was in fact tight shut – and indeed we did not have much luck with cathedrals in general on this day!

The cathedral was up steep, winding roads, to a position overlooking the plains of Apulia. We failed to get into the cathedral itself, but the buildings around, including a science school and a primary school, were impressive. We found a man selling fruit from his cart, and bought some pears and some quinces (which we had thought were apricots). He put in an extra pear for free. We are having fun practising our Italian (quite successfully), as very few people around speak English. They are very friendly and helpful, if we ask for directions, which we frequently have to do, due to very poor road signs that constantly let us down, usually when we are almost at our desired destination.

Next we went to Canosa, where the cathedral was also closed (every day things shut down between 1.00 pm and 5.00 pm, as of old). The countryside around was dotted with fascinating little ancient houses called 'trulli', which were cone-shaped, of stone. A little like beehive huts – slightly different in shape, but also using stones to form the roofs.

We then decided to drive to Barletta, which is quite a large city, really, and found a large Castello on the seafront. Ruth phoned from London when we were in the grounds of the castle. She has Reiko visiting from Japan, and they had visited Kew Gardens, Madame Tussaud's, and rowed on the Thames.

We had the rest of last night's pizza on the seafront opposite the Castello, with some Fanta bought in Minervino, and very good it was! Then we drove up the town to see if we could find the Cathedral. We found it duly, and also the front of the Castello. The Cathedral was closed, but the castle open, so we went round that. It was originally Hohenstaufen, but re-done by Charles V – a massive fortress, very nicely restored. We never got to the colossal bronze statue (of Theodosius II?),[343] as it is up the town, at a busy intersection.

We drove back then by the coast road to Trani – very built-up, very industrial – and rested in the hotel for a few hours. We sallied out again at 6.00 pm or so, to find a cathedral. We finally did that, but it was closed – this time for repairs (even the bronze door was covered over!). We then parked in a square slightly inland from the port and made our way back to our 'lonely waiter' on the seafront, where we once again had a beer,

---

343 Barletta is home to the Colossus of Barletta, a bronze statue, representing a Roman Emperor (perhaps Theodosius II). This statue, called "Eraclio" by the inhabitants of Barletta, is about 4 metres (13 feet) tall, and remains the biggest statue that survives from the late Roman Empire (i.e. the Roman Empire after Constantine). According to a local folk story, Eraclio saved the city from a Saracen attack. Seeing the Saracen ships approaching Barletta's coast, Eraclio waited for them on the sea shore. Here Eraclio acted as if he was crying so the Saracens asked him why he was sad and Eraclio answered that he was sad because he was the smallest among Barletta's inhabitants and so everybody made fun of him. The Saracens thought that Barletta's inhabitants were all giants, so left the coast, fearing to face them.

and watched the sun go down, and then worked our way back a bit to a nice family restaurant a block back from the front, where we are now seated, eating far too much. Really, we will have to find a way to take *one* primo piatto, and *one* secondo, and live with that!

We found our way back to the car without trouble, and so back to bed. The weather continues clear, but we got a bit damp as we were sitting out. A fuzzy moon!

DAY 3, SATURDAY, MAY 13TH

We had a rather disturbed night, unfortunately. A man was snoring next door, and then I woke up with a bad leg, from the bed. So we did not get much sleep. We checked out after another good breakfast, to find that bed *and breakfast* cost only €65 a night for the two of us, so that was fine!

We headed off in the direction of Bari, through rather dismal coastal towns, and then headed up to the coastal highway, with the idea of trying Bitonto, which is said to have a fine cathedral. So much for that idea (*Magari!*) – there was a festival and procession in progress, and the centre of town was sealed off. Then we headed down into Bari, but got more and more depressed by our surroundings – dismal commercial and residential suburbs, lots of traffic, and no signs to the *Centro Storico,* or anything relevant, so we just headed out again – this time deciding not to settle again till we got to Egnazia, a promising Roman site on the Via Traiana. First of all, though, we called into a fishing village called Savelletri, and found a possible hotel on the water, at €80 a night.

Then we drove up the road to Egnazia. It is a excellent site, comprising a necropolis, a section of the Via Traiana and downtown Gnathia, with a forum, basilica, and a sanctuary of oriental gods – not to mention a fine museum. We spent a while there, being phoned in the middle by a miserable Mouse, who has been vomiting, and then drove back to Savelletri and checked into the hotel, which is pretty functional, but perfectly nice.

After settling in to the hotel, we went off to scout for a place for lunch and a possible swim. We found both a little way north of the village – a little cove with some sand, occupied by an elderly playboy and his twenty-year-old mot, who were not entirely pleased to see us. I swam a bit – not very warm, but OK – and then we had our roll with cheese and sausage (from last night).

Then we decided to journey up into the hills to see what we might find. First stop Fasano. We parked in the main square, which was very nicely paved with marble, as are most of the towns in these parts. We needed to get a parking ticket, and found that one could get one free by buying a cup of coffee at a bar. They also had delicious ice-cream, so we bought a chocolate one and shared it – poor John! The coffee is universally good. Always you get what is virtually an 'espresso', and then you can add some hot milk.

We strolled round the block, and then drove further inland towards Locorotondo, the centre of which we failed to find. We might try again tomorrow. Then to a really charming town called Martina Franca, with a lovely Ducal Palace and a fascinating sort of double square. The Caracciolos[344] were the strong influence here, and their palace was highly decorated by local artists – sometimes one might think a little amateurishly!

We actually ended up with a personal guide, quite by accident. We were wandering about, looking for the basilica (mainly baroque – not too elaborate), and I stopped a girl coming towards us and asked for directions. I didn't notice at the time that she had an ID tag as a guide! She spoke at great speed, and was delighted with the €5 John gave her at the end. (She obviously thought that because we spoke in Italian we would understand everything even at speed!) Very few people in these parts speak English, which is great for our Italian.

I think that, on the whole, our visit to Martina Franca has been one of the highlights of our trip so far. It is a truly pretty – and obviously chic and wealthy – town. We then drove through winding, beautiful countryside, full of ancient olive trees with enormously thick trunks, to a little town called Alberobello, which is almost completely built of these little 'trulli'. You could perhaps say that it first seemed a little 'twee', but then

---

[344] This is the family with whom Jean had stayed in Rome as an au-pair, back in 1962-3, while she was studying at the Accademia delle Arte.

remember that it hasn't been built like that for tourists (unlike, say, Solvang in California), but has been there for hundreds of years. We wandered up and down their steep little roads, and ended up on the main square, drinking a prosecco. By the time we left, it was already about 7.00 pm, and at the last minute, by trying to avoid going through Fasano, we took a wrong turn. After driving for what seemed ages, we arrived back at our hotel about 8.30. A party of Germans had arrived, and were tucking into their dinners, so we decided to eat in, as we were exhausted from the day's travels. The weather is lovely now – mostly low 20's.

DAY 4, SUNDAY, MAY 14TH

A little warmer again today – very pleasant, with a slight breeze. We are now sitting out on the terrace of the hotel after breakfast, deliberating what to do next. The Germans have all departed in their bus – the Weltenbümmler – and we are left alone, it seems.

The first thing we did was to walk round the town, down by the harbour, and back by the main street. It is an unpretentious fishing village, not much concerned with tourists – though there are quite a number of fish restaurants (looking rather closed!). Then we decided to set off again, to make another attempt on Locorotondo. This time we took the right turns, and found a delightful little town – more or less circular, round its central square (the Vittorio Emmanuele), though not quite. We wandered quite a while through tiny, winding streets, found the citizens coming out of 10.30 am Mass, then joined them in a *passagiato* in the park.

Encouraged by that, we decided to go south a bit, to visit Ostuni, also highly praised by the guidebook. This proved *not* such a good idea, as we never found the *centro storico*, and got stuck in rather tedious surroundings and lots of traffic.

On the way back to Fasano, feeling rather peckish, we saw a sign for one of the 'fortified' farmhouses which are common round here. It was called 'Lo Spagnolo' and was more like a castle, really, built of stone, with lovely orchards and outhouses, with some bits of old Roman columns and friezes. There was a large party of Japanese there already, being entertained for lunch, but we found to our disappointment that we couldn't be served because we hadn't booked! We heard horses neighing, and they had a tennis court, and outbuildings where one could stay.

We drove on towards Fasano, and the next thing that caught my eye was a sign to a restaurant (near a dolmen!), called 'Forchetta d'Oro'. We drove towards it, but on the way we met another 'Masseria' (fortified farm). We followed their signs, but first came upon a family restaurant called 'The Dolmen'. We were served a delicious lunch of 'Gnocchi di Patate della Casa' and 'Frittura Mista' (little fish deep-fried).

After lunch, we went to find the dolmen, which was a few hundred yards up the road. Earlier, we had stopped and taken a photo of one of those marvellous ancient olive trees; their trunks are so large that they must produce very little in the way of fruit. In fact, the branches on top seemed very few and far between. We think that, as of old, they are regarded as sacred, and won't be cut down. This countryside is truly lush and beautiful at this time of year. The wildflowers are abundant and I wish I could identify them! The bright red poppies are everywhere.

We settled down for a bit of a rest when we got back, and only revived at 6.30 pm or so. Considering where to go for dinner, we decided to take a little cruise, to see if the restaurant on the other side of town was open. The hotel looks very forlorn and deserted! What we found we did not expect! First of all, the sky had clouded over, and a spectacular thunderstorm began. Then we found that, in the village, a market was in full swing, and obviously another one in Torre Canne, as the roads suddenly filled up with an infinite line of cars going in all directions. We drove out of town in the direction of Torre Canne, and reached a pleasant waterside restaurant called *El Moro*, where the waiter explained that it was the *mercato* that was causing the traffic – all the people from the hills come down to the coast on Sundays for shopping! They would be gone in a little while. And meanwhile, the thunderstorm provided a spectacular show – sheet and forked lightning, and great rumbles.

We had two excellent pizzas – *diavolo* and *boscaioli* – of which we saved some, and a bottle of prosecco (€10), and rolled home to the accompaniment of the end of the storm.

DAY 5, MONDAY, MAY 15TH

After breakfast, we paid €190 (for 2 nights and dinner), and headed off over the peninsula in the direction of Taranto – determined, however, not to get involved with it. We drove back, past Locorotondo and Martina Franca, to Massafra, where there are rock dwellings in a ravine – but not accessible; a grotty little town otherwise. Then we tried to get to Matera, but no signs, so we ended up on the road to Taranto. We got off just before it, amid shipyards, oil refineries, and every sort of ghastliness.

We headed down the coast towards Reggio di Calabria, until we reached Metaponto. We actually saw the Temple of Hera there from the road as we coasted along, and managed to stop in time. Two hordes of schoolchildren were just leaving, and we had the place to ourselves, except for a little dog. There were fifteen columns still standing – some look re-erected – and it presents a fine sight.

However, that was all of Metapontum that we found. We headed down to the Lido di Metaponto, a dismally tacky and very dead resort, found the Museo, but it was closed till 2.00 pm, so had a coffee (this was around 12.00), and headed down the coast to Heraclea. Here we were more successful, after initial disappointment at Lido di Policoro. We found the museum, and the site of ancient Heraclea (earlier Siris) inland from the town of Policoro, on a bluff over the river, and that was very fine. There was a good, well-stocked, and informative museum.

We then set off back up the road, and turned off for Matera. As usual, when we had followed various signs, they let us down, and as we were hesitating at a fork in the road, we were approached by a man in a yellow jacket with 'Sassi Tourismo' written on it, who informed us that, either because they were making a film or premiering one, with Brad Pitt, it would be difficult to find accommodation. We said we were looking for Hotel del Campo (recommended by our guide book), but he said that it was very far out, and would cost us €130 a night. He had a better idea, and bullied us into following him (on his motor-bike) to a peculiar house – which also had 'casino' in its name. I stayed in the car, and John went in to inspect it. It was a poky little room, which the owner at first said would cost €95, but John bargained with her, and she came down to €80. But we had a nasty feeling of being 'had', and told our friend we would decide later. And so we set off for the 'Hotel del Campo', which we found by asking a man at a gas station.

It is indeed somewhat far out, but really only ten minutes or so in a car from the centre, and it did officially charge €130 – but offered a reduced price of €104, B & B. It is a most grand place, a converted 18th century country house, with a nice formal garden. After a short rest, we headed into the centre, to view the Sassi. The hotel gave us a guide to the place, which was just as well, and we managed to find a park just outside the Piazza Victor Emmanuele, on the edge of the Sassi. This is an area, divided into two sections, where the cliff beside a ravine has been cut away over the centuries to allow the building of a grand complex of houses and churches, some carved out of the rock, others built on top of it. We walked half-way round the periphery, almost totally deserted, deciding not to go down very far, in order not to have to come up again, but getting a pretty good idea of what there is. Some nice little churches – one open, S. Biagio – and a Museum of Torture, which we passed up.

We decided to stay another night in our luxury hotel, and explore the older side of the town tomorrow.

DAY 6, TUESDAY, MAY 16TH

A comfortable night in luxurious surroundings. J watched Roger Federer and Rafael Nadal slugging it out on Sky Sports till quite late – Nadal just won. After a good breakfast, we headed down to the old town again, to do the other Sasso, the Caveoso. First, however, we visited the Palazzo Lanfranchi, which houses an art museum, partly various rather minor mediaeval to 17th century Italian painters, but also a nice collection by Carlo Levi,[345] who was really quite a good painter, on top of everything else.

---

345 This actually makes sense, as Carlo Levi (1902-1975) had been exiled to Lucania for political activism during the Fascist period, an experience commemorated in his novel, *Christ Stopped at Eboli* (1945), and thus helped to bring the problems of the South of Italy to national notice.

We walked down a ways into the Sasso Caveoso, which in a way is more impressive than the other, since it is more palpably carved out of the rock, and less restored, so you can see how they lived in the old days, which was pretty grim. One gets also a good view of the whole environment.

Again, rather than go down too far, we decided to go off in search of rock churches to Laterza, which was reported to have up to 180! When we got there, however, the inhabitants denied all knowledge of any rock churches,[346] so we drove out again, in the direction of Ginosa – where, again, no rock-churches, though a very nice old palazzo.

Then, driving out of Ginosa back to Matera, we came upon a national park of rock churches. Joy! But in fact we found a young man there, guarding a barrier, who said that it was closed till June, and that now a film was being shot there, called *Nativita*, 'The Birth of Christ'. I asked if Brad Pitt starred in it, and he laughed, and said 'No'. But there was then a grain of truth in our friend's tall tale of yesterday. And indeed there was much coming and going, as we sat there and had our lunch.

We nevertheless took a short walk down towards the site, and it seemed to be miles away. At this stage it was getting very hot, so we came back to the car, which was parked near the entrance, and ate the lunch we had bought in a Patinaria in Laterza – having discovered that no cave churches existed there, in spite of Insight Guide's recommendation to go and see them in the centre of the town.

We then drove towards Altamura, which was situated to the north of Matera. We drove past Matera, and stopped along the way in a shaded parking lot for a short nap. Altamura was beautiful. It is a completely walled town, which has lovely narrow streets, beautifully maintained, and an elaborate cathedral in the Romanesque style – founded by Frederick II in the 13th century, and restored or added to up to the 18th century.

We came back to our hotel, and decided to eat in their restaurant. We had our best dinner so far on this trip. John had a very fine steak, and I had a selection of grilled fish.

We made the acquaintance of a jolly fellow-diner, who was

---

346 In fact, it seems, there are prehistoric tombs in the vicinity, but no rock churches.

an Australian businessman, making furniture in partnership with a firm in Matera, which he asserted was one of the biggest furniture manufacturers in Italy! There is much more industry going on in Matera than we thought. He ended up bequeathing us a large book on the Australian campaign against the Japs. I started it, and it reads very well. Very heavy, though. He didn't want to carry it home!

DAY 6, WEDNESDAY, MAY 17TH

We paid our bill (€258 – not bad, for the two days and a dinner), and decided to head off for the Pollino National Park, before reaching the Tyrrhenian coast. We decided against returning to the park of rock-churches, despite our friend's urging to come back tomorrow when it would be quiet – it was too complicated. We got down to the coast, but took a slightly wrong turning after Policoro, and messed about in the vicinity of Rotondella, before finding a fine new motorway, which got us up to the park very briskly.

We had a very pleasant walk on a forest trail, hoping to see a panda (which was pictured on their signs for the forest!). The only wildlife we saw, in fact, was the usual green lizard, and heard lots of lovely birdsong along the way. We met two large dogs, which could have been half wolf, but did not encounter any skunks, wolves, badgers, deer or wild cats – all of which are said to be there, but which were lying very low!

After we came back out of the park, we headed for the coast at Sapri, at the base of the Cilento peninsula. It seemed a pleasant seaside town, but we decided to strike north for Palinuro, which would give a better base for Velia and Paestum.[347] We found a fine motorway through the mountains,[348] but that let us down badly when it came to an exit for Palinuro. We were left wandering hopelessly round the hills till we got back on the motorway, and this time headed for Paestum.[349]

---

347 Two notable Classical sites on the west coast, Velia (Elea) being the home town of the philosopher Parmenides.

348 This could have been the SS18.

349 Paestum was established around 600 BC by settlers from Sybaris, a Greek colony in southern Italy, under the name of Poseidonia. The city

We got off the motorway at the Paestum exit, and immediately found both the ruins – most impressive town walls – a host of hotels and loads of cars driving about. It looked bad, but we noticed a very pleasant hotel, just beside the ruins, set back from the road, the *Villa Rita,* and it proved delightful – just €78 a night, with swimming-pool and nice cabins in the garden, one of which we took. We had a swim and a beer round the pool, and then took a stroll before dinner over to the ruins. We are now enjoying a pleasant dinner in the dining-room.

It took, in fact, a day to make this journey, which we thought would take a few hours. A combination of minor winding roads to start with, and then getting lost did not help. It would have been about 6.00 pm by the time we reached Paestum.

DAY 8, THURSDAY, MAY 18TH

We rose moderately early, had a good breakfast, and first headed off to visit the site. The temples are certainly splendid – both, it seems, dedicated to Hera, in the Doric style. We had them to ourselves for a while, but then a series of busloads arrived, with schoolchildren, and Germans and French. We got round the rest of the site in short order, and then back to the hotel.

We had a pleasant chat with our immediate neighbours, who are from British Columbia, Brian Mitchell and Louise Iccario, he an artist, she a teacher (he did Classics and English at UBC – he remembers Malcolm McGregor – graduated in 1968). They have been here a couple of months, Louise learning a bit of Italian, and rediscovering her roots.

This hotel is a really delightful place – one of the staff is a young Indian man, Jimmy, who is most amusing: very keen,

---

thrived as a Greek settlement for about two centuries, witnessing the development of democracy. In 400 BC, the Lucanians seized the city. The Romans took over in 273 BC, renaming it Paestum and establishing a Latin colony. Later, its decline ensued from shifts in trade routes and the onset of flooding and marsh formation. As Pesto or Paestum, the town became a bishopric, but it was abandoned in the Early Middle Ages, and left undisturbed and largely forgotten until the eighteenth century.

wants to know already if we are planning to be in to dinner. We drove off around 11.00 am in the direction of Velia (the Elea of Parmenides and Zeno)[350], via the coast road. A most scenic drive, but tiring for the driver, and we arrived around 12.30. It is actually a very fine site, though there are no standing temples – a larger circuit of walls than Paestum, and a fine acropolis (now crowned by one of Frederick II's castles), and some good gates. We walked up as far as the Porta Rosa, and then back, leaving the acropolis aside. The site was wasn't rediscovered until the late 19th century, excavations only began in 1927, and are still going on.

We went and found a local restaurant for a plate of excellent pasta, and drove home by the motorway, with took only three-quarters of an hour. We were determined not to eat the hotel dinner, and made clear our decision to Francis.[351] We rested a while, then I took a swim and short sunbathe, and then we headed off to the Museum, assuming the crowds to have dispersed. This proved to be the case, and we viewed in comfort a fine collection of pots, and in particular a remarkable collection of wall paintings from Lucanian tombs. The Lucanians took over the Greek colony of Poseidonia in the 4th century, before the Romans arrived in the 2nd. Very fine paintings, whoever did them!

Back then to have a glass of wine with Brian and Louise, who wanted me to describe Zeno's Paradoxes, which I endeavoured to do.[352] They then went off obediently to dinner, while we went up the road to a pizzeria called *Simposium,* and had excellent pizzas, which we have kept half of for dinner tomorrow.

We never did find the Hotel Ariston, recommended by the Insight Guide, but it can't have been better than the Villa Rita – an unusual recommendation for Baedeker, which generally mentions only top hotels. The only problem has been – but that is common to the area – a certain degree of *dampness* – but Paestum

---

350 Two distinguished early Greek philosophers.

351 Presumably the Indian mentioned above.

352 There were originally forty paradoxes of Zeno, but we have knowledge of only four of them, which I refrain from discussing now.

was a mosquito-ridden swamp for most of the Middle Ages and early modern era. And the rooms are not very well insulated, at least in the cabins.

My hair as a result is knotted with curls! We are assured by Brian that the flies buzzing around out window are not in fact mosquitos. He says he should know, because he is so used to them in their part of Canada.

DAY 9, FRIDAY, MAY 19TH

My sinus is rather bad this morning – swimming is probably responsible, but also dust. We set off after breakfast – bill €198, and I left a tip of €10 each for Jimmy and Katerina, the Russian girl, which they greatly appreciated – and hit the coast road for Salerno. We decided not to go up to the A3, which was a mistake, as there is no good way to get past Salerno along the coast – the *lungomare* actually is one-way the other direction, south. So we got badly tangled in Salerno and its suburbs – truly a dismal place – and only emerged on the road to the *Costiera Amalfitana* after fully an hour of floundering around.

But that was by no means the end of the trouble.

The coastal route to Amalfi was hair-raising. The road was narrow, steep, and constantly curving, and the Italians drive as if they are on any ordinary road. We had one extremely near miss, as a 'person' (I can think of other ways to describe him – always a 'him'!) overtook another car coming towards us – on a bend! He was absolutely in our lane, fully facing us. I managed to brake suddenly, and luckily the people behind us were far enough from us to screech to a halt without hitting us. He managed (at speed) to dodge around, and we all let him have it with car horns – not that he cared in the slightest. I have never been so close to a head-on collision.

We arrived eventually at the turn up to Ravello, and then toiled up the hill to the town. There we found – predictably, but we had not been warned of it – that it is relatively impossible to drive into, or park in, the town itself. There is only some parking in a few of the top hotels, if one can get into them, and one must park down below the piazza. This was actually not too bad, especially as our hotel, the Toro, is just off the piazza – some others, such as Katharine and

Anthony's,[353] the Villa Maria, or Hilda's,[354] the Villa Amore, are way up long alleys.

Anyhow, we hauled up the hand-luggage, and then found most of the wedding party ensconced in the square, having lunch. We chatted for a bit, and then checked in – a very nice little hotel, even with a little garden, just down a side street. We then went back to have an ice-cream with Peter[355] and Anthony. Then we rescued the pizza, ordered a beer from the hotel, and had our lunch in the garden.

Next we found Celia and John GG[356] coming down the street, where they and Adam and Kate[357] had been swindled in a restaurant. A and K had gone back to remonstrate, and actually got €50 back – they had spent €225, though, for lunch! A different world.

Then we decided to take a turn up the town to see where everyone was staying – found the *Giordano* and then the *Villa Maria*, where, in turn, we found Celia and Adam, and had a beer on the patio in a restaurant there – magnificent views everywhere!

After, we ambled down the hill, and into the Villa Rufalo at the corner of the Piazza, a fine old palazzo with a nice garden, where we noted that a concert would take place that evening at 9.30 pm. But parallel parties were planned for the ladies and the men for the evening, starting at 7.00. The men had a succession of beers in the Piazza, and then moved to a pizza restaurant nearby, where we were progressively joined by the ladies. I ordered a plate of *fritto misto*, which J nibbled at, and then decided, along with Peter, that we could make a run for the concert.

---

353 Sc. Gore-Grimes, my sister and brother-in-law, parents of the bridegroom, Nicholas. I will refrain from identifying all the guests mentioned!

354 Our friend and neighbour in Howth, Hilda Tierney.

355 My brother Peter (Dom Christopher Dillon, OSB), who was performing the ceremony.

356 Sc. Gore-Grimes, aunt and uncle of the bridegroom.

357 Spouses, respectively, of Celia and John.

We got to it just in time – a duet of piano and cello, playing Beethoven and Brahms (admission €20 a head). We found John and Olive O'Neill there. The concert actually took place indoors, in an upper room of the palazzo, and was really *not very good* – though they got four encores! It must have been packed with their friends.

DAY 10, SATURDAY, MAY 20TH

And so the day of the wedding dawns, bright and sunny. After breakfast, I retired to the little garden, which is strangely peaceful, seeing as it is in the middle of town, while J washed her hair. Then we took a little stroll about, to get the feel of the geography. It is quite a small, compact town, when one sorts it out. Very up and down, though.

We walked up first to see if Hilda was in residence at her hotel, which is very far up (the Villa Amore) – and she with an injured knee! But she was out, so we went to visit the Villa Cimbrone, an astonishing achievement by an English milord, Lord Grimthorpe, at the beginning of the last century, involving a reconstituted bogus mediaeval palazzo and a very fine series of gardens, culminating in a stunning view down to Amalfi. We stopped for coffee and ice-cream in the grounds.

Then we met Peter out wandering as we came back to the piazza, and were prevailed upon to come to lunch in the Rufalo, on the grounds that it would be a long time till dinner. It was good, but rather filling. I had a curious concoction involving grilled buffalo mozzarella wrapped in lemon leaves – which are *not* eatable, unlike vine leaves! And then back to change for the wedding, at 4.00 in the Duomo.

The wedding was simply lovely. The Meaghers,[358] *and all of our young men and women, were a credit to Ireland. They were so elegant and good-looking. Simon*[359] *and Judy, of course, came from America. We are all staying at various hotels, some way way up the cobbled streets. We*

---

358 The family of Nicholas' bride, Elizabeth (Lizzie).
359 Simon Gore-Grimes, elder brother of the groom.

luckily were beside the main square. Peter and the parish priest conducted the ceremony in the cathedral in the main square. The music was lovely – provided by the church, I think. The reception was way up at the top of the hill, which we all staggered to on stilettoes (though some of us brought hip-hops in our bags!). Katharine even paraded down the church in her gorgeous elegant dress – clutching her hip-hops!

We set out, then, more or less in procession, up the hill to the Villa Eva, where splendid drinks were laid out. There was rather too much standing around for me – we were out in a garden – so I sat, and various people gathered round me. There was a wait of about two hours, during which some clever people went back to get more clothes, since it showed signs of becoming quite chilly (as it eventually did), before the speeches, which preceded the dinner. All very good – one by the bride's brother David, since her father, John Meagher, is dead (he was high up in Independent Newspapers), another by best man Jeremy Whelehan, and finally one from the father of groom[360] – who gave a most amusing speech, in fact.

Then back to the tables for dinner, which was a copious one, with *two* primi piatti! Christine De Ruyk turned up with a new boyfriend, rumoured to be Giorgio Armani, but in fact just a Sicilian prince from Palermo – very jolly; I never did get his real name. We sat with the O'Neills and Scotts. The cake was cut sometime before midnight, and then we survived for a bit of dancing inside. We left about 12.30, but the young persons carried on till around 5.00 in the morning – latterly in the piazza, drinking limoncello, and were fairly mouldy the next day.

DAY 11, SUNDAY, MAY 21ST

Up this morning pretty slowly, but not as slowly as our fellow-guests. The young Coyles struggled in to breakfast about 10.00 am, wondering where they were. I sat in the garden for a while, reading *OSAP*[361] for a review – articles not at all bad, in fact!

---

360 Sc. Anthony Gore-Grimes.
361 Sc. Oxford Studies in Ancient Philosophy.

Today is the feast-day of St. Pantaleone, and celebrations went on all day – there was a band in the piazza from mid-morning. The middle of the day was reserved for a splendid lunch given by Anthony in a very pleasant restaurant over in Scala, the next village across the valley. Excellent hors d'oeuvres and a choice of main course, and great fun had by all.

Then, in the late afternoon, back to Ravello, and St. Pantaleone was carried out of the Duomo (where he had been brought last night), and a procession formed to escort him back up the hill. We joined Adam and Celia and various others in escorting him some of the way – Adam said that of course, he was used to parades![362] – but we gave up after the second pause for a decade of the rosary.

In the evening, we joined Andrew,[363] Isabelle, and the children for dinner in a restaurant off the square, which proved to have an excellent view of a fine firework display, again in honour of the saint.

DAY 12, MONDAY, MAY 22ND

We checked out, and decided to spend the day journeying up to the airport via Pompeii and Herculaneum. We drove over the hills, and into the valley below Vesuvius. Called in first to Pompeii, but were appalled by the hordes of turkeys there to greet us, and drove on to Herculaneum. This proved a fine site, and not too crowded at all. We parked nearby, had a coffee, and then worked our way round the site. Lots of fine houses with mosaics and other decorations – the Ville dei Papiri was off by itself, though, and we didn't get to that.

Then we drove up Vesuvius, where we stopped for the usual picnic of pizza and orangeade, but decided not to go all the way to the top. We decided also against trying to drive into Naples, but did want to find a nice monastery that we had noticed on the way out from the airport. However, no way could we find the

---

362 As being a Northern Irish Protestant!
363 Sc. my younger brother Andrew, and his wife.

right turn, so we just came back to the airport hotel that we had noticed (beside the Hertz office) on our way out – something like the Splendid, or the Marvellous (I have already forgotten the name!) – found a room, and then had to explore the delights of the airport and its surroundings, which are *minimal*. In fact, it only takes a few hours to get to the airport from Ravello, so we needn't have fussed. We dined in the airport, adequately.

DAY 13, TUESDAY, MAY 23RD
We met up with most of the others next morning, and had an uneventful flight home.

19. RETURN TO KATOUNIA:

SEPTEMBER 17 – OCTOBER 1, 2008

[This was our first visit back to one of our favourite places on earth for fully seven years (see above, pp. 208), mainly due to the distractions of the Westminster Tours, and it was particularly pleasant to return there with our old friends Dinah and Michael Cunningham, with whom we had been there last, in 2001. I write slightly more of this diary, so Jean's contributions are in italics.]

DAY 1, WEDNESDAY, SEPTEMBER 17TH.

We were collected at 12.00 (approx.) by a very talkative taxi-man (Joe Dolan), for Coastal Cabs, and got to the airport in good time for a coffee in Butler's before catching the plane at 2.30. The weather not wet, but still pretty grim. There was no chance to mow the lawn before leaving – too wet.

The flight was efficient and uneventful – nice views of the Alps – and we arrived about ten minutes early, at 8.20 pm. As soon as we got to the baggage area, J phoned Dinah, and they were just there ahead of us. We met up at the Easycar (Hertz) desk, did the paper-work, had a little break (and M and D had got nothing on their Easyjet flight from Luton), went and found the car in the lot (a Hyundai Accord), learned the ropes, and set off into the night at 10.00 pm, with Jean driving.[364]

The car is very comfortable, and easily took our bags. It was easy driving up the freeway as far as the Khalkida turn-off, then

---

364 An oddity of flights from Dublin to Athens, until quite recently, was that they were scheduled to arrive quite late at night, which involved us, for many years, in exhausting late-night drives to Limni.

across the bridge, skirting Khalkida itself, but then, when we set off up the ridge of the island, it was much more of a slog. However, J soldiered on, helped by the automatic gears, and we got to Katounia just after 1.00 am, more or less as we had reckoned. We drove up the back of the house (J being very nervous at this stage, for good reason!), and found the house open and in good shape. We unpacked the bags, and so to bed. It is warm, but not too warm – and there were traces of rain on the way up!

DAY 2, THURSDAY, SEPTEMBER 18TH

We rose not very early, naturally, and set off in the car into town for breakfast, and a bit of shopping. The villa is indeed very fine, as we remembered it, but now adorned with electricity! Weather just right, really – low 20's – though a bit cloudy. We found our former café on the sea-front, just at the turn , beside the bank, and it served quite good coffee, but otherwise only biscuits and cake – no loukoumades! Still, we had a good breakfast, and then set off to shop. The town is not crowded – the holidays are plainly over. We went to the baker and the butcher, and even bought a pair of sandals for me, as we had forgotten to pack them. Then back to the sea-front, and visited the greengrocer, where we ran into Elizabeth Fowden, and invited Garth and herself to dinner next Thursday.[365] Then finally to Roussos' supermarket, where we got everything else. A large shopping spree – spent over €93.00 – but all good value!

They were very helpful in Roussos' – especially a young boy behind the cheese counter, who cut us some Evia feta, and grated some local cheese which was supposed to be Parmesan-like, but was more earthy. When we came back with the shopping, John wanted me to drive up the back driveway so that we could unload the groceries, but I refused, as it was just too tight a turn into the house, and not worth the hassle. So we parked below, in front of the garage, and lugged the groceries up the steps. It was a bit of a heave, but we managed it OK.

We had a nice lunch on the terrace, of bread, cheese, and tiropita (cheese

---

365   For the distinguished historian of Late Antiquity, Garth Fowden, see the record of our last visit.

pies), and only finished eating around 4.00 pm! We lay about reading and/ or sleeping for a couple of hours, and then took a walk up the mountain at the back of the house. We also paid a visit to Liadain, to report a bulb gone in the kitchen, and she gave us a replacement. She seems in good form, and the same as ever – worried about drought, though, and hoping for rain!

Dinah and Michael said they would cook dinner, and they made a tasty spaghetti Bolognese. We only started to eat at 10.00 pm (but 8.00 pm our time!), so we didn't finish until about 11.30. We stayed up until about 1.15 gossiping, and then retired.

DAY 3, FRIDAY, SEPTEMBER 19TH

Rose not very early again, and had a fine breakfast of Greek yoghurt and honey, and nectarines we had bought yesterday.

The day started rather cloudy, with storm-clouds seeming to build over Boeotia, and heading our way – and Liadain does maintain it is due to rain for the weekend – so we decided to take a drive, round the north of the island.

We set off up the coast road, past Rovies, to the spa of Aidepsos (very crowded with fat old ladies taking the waters), and then on round the coast road to Orei, to pay our respects to the Bull, and have some lunch. We found a supermarket to do some shopping, and then a pleasant taverna for lunch, of calamari (J and Dinah), sardellas (Michael), and saganaki with shrimps (me) – which last proved a mistake: just prawns in tomato sauce with melted cheese on top; not great.

Then we drove home, by the inland route from Histiaea to Rovies, via a grotty little village where Michael asked the way of a very voluble peasant.

We found our way back through the town, and so home. We went straight down to the beach, where John and Michael swam, and John built a new path into the sea. At about 6.30 pm we came back up to prepare dinner (J and I cooked pork chops). Denise had come round to check on us, with her dog, and have a glass of wine. When she stood up to go, we didn't notice where the dog had gone. She said not to worry, that he knew his way home. But he turned up, and wouldn't leave, all the time we were eating and long after. We finally told Denise at about 10.00 pm that he was still here, and she came to collect him. Apparently, the poor fellow thought Demise was still inside our house, and was waiting for her to appear. When he finally realised the shadowy person at the door was Denise, he was beside himself with joy, and bounded after her. We stayed at the table chatting until about 1.15 am.

DAY 4, SATURDAY, SEPTEMBER 20TH

Woke to rain, which had been going on all night. We went to town around 11.00, and had delicious hot chocolate in a café near the post office, though we got pretty soaked walking from the car. We did lots of shopping, buying bread in the bakery, fish in the fish shop, and finally general groceries in Roussos' – including some ouzo and some Samian muscatel to bring to Denise's tomorrow, as we are invited to lunch.

Back to a copious lunch, composed of Thursday's Bolognese, plus sausage and salad, and then a siesta. The rain is being rather Irish, but good for the ground. Liadain was almost despairing of her plants, after two years of virtual drought. This looks like a wet year – if only it would relent for a week or so yet! After the siesta, we were called upon by the young man who is staying in the little bungalow (Uncle Richard's), Marcus Plested, an Orthodox theologian from Cambridge,[366] whom we are to meet also tomorrow for lunch, and we gave him a cup of tea and chatted for a bit.

Then the others went off for a walk, while I entertained Marcus for a bit longer. When I followed them, they had vanished. I took a brisk walk down the road to Limni, up to the new 'luxury apartments', but no sign of them They turned up only at 8.00, having taken a different route. The rain had stopped for a bit, but it came back later.

We had an excellent dinner of *tsipoura*, or gilthead, cooked by J, with rice and green beans. The weather is now pretty grim.

DAY 5, SUNDAY, SEPTEMBER 21ST

---

366 Later Professor of Theology in Marquette University in Milwaukee, Wisconsin. The small bungalow was where we usually stayed

Woke to further rain, but it seemed brighter, and indeed it stopped after breakfast (which lasted about two hours!). I am getting some reading done, stories of Papadiamandis.[367] A book by Andrew Louth[368] on Maximus the Confessor, and Elizabeth Fowden's chapter on Neoplatonic views on children's education.

We decided before lunch to take a walk up to Philip's chapel, to view the frescoes which Denise said had been added. These were indeed very fine, and on the way back we met Denise herself, coming up from her garden with vegetables, who urged us to go also and visit the amphitheatre and a studio designed by an architect friend of hers, Alexandros. This was also very fine – a nice little odeon being built out of the remains of the funicular railway constructed by the mining company. His wife is a sculptor, and we saw some of her works. It all looks splendid.

At 2.30 we wandered up to Denise's for a very pleasant lunch, with Liadain and Selga, and young Marcus. A very good meal, featuring special meatballs (with mint), good graviera cheese, and local white wine. Denise also showed her new addition, an upper storey made of wood. This went on till well after 4.00 pm, and we tottered back down the hill. All we were able for later was scrambled egg on toast.

DAY 6, MONDAY, SEPTEMBER 22ND

Michael's birthday today, so we produced various presents, including the Novel,[369] and made a birthday cake out of a sweet bread, plus one candle in the shape of a question-mark. The weather has cheered up considerably, so we had breakfast out

---

367 Alexandros Papadiamantis (1851-1911) was a Greek novelist, short-story writer and poet, native of the island of Skiathos. I think this work of his must have been *The Boundless Garden*, a translation of which had just been published by Denise (who was a publisher).

368 Andrew Louth (b. 1944) is an English theologian (of the orthodox persuasion), who was Professor of Theology at the University of Durham, and whose works I have found repeatedly useful.

369 This must refer to the first edition of my own novel, *The Scent of Eucalyptus*.

on the outer buttress, and that went on for some time. Then the others went out shopping, and I went up, by invitation, to Denise, to check the e-mails. Very largely garbage, but one or two things that needed decisions.

Dinah, Michael and I went on into Limni to do some shopping. All the shop owners are very pleasant and patient with us when we try to describe what we want. The only people here who have some English are the restaurant owners or workers, and even some of those don't either. It is wonderful to be able to buy locally produced vegetables from the farmers themselves – beans, courgettes, aubergines, tomatoes, spinach, onions, potatoes, okra, leeks, cauliflowers, lettuce, celeriac and more. The farmer has his own little shop in the village – on the right side of the shop is all his home-grown produce, and on the left is bought-in veg and fruit.

We went back to the house for lunch, where John waited. We had decided to go out to dinner that evening, but the skies darkened, and it ultimately became a raging thunderstorm.

In fact, while swimming in the afternoon, we had invited young Marcus to join us, and he had accepted happily, so in the event we entertained him to dinner in the house, with an excellent roast chicken, put together by J and Dinah. The plants should love the thunderstorm!

DAY 7, TUESDAY, SEPTEMBER 23RD

The day in fact dawned very pleasant after the thunderstorm, and, after a leisurely breakfast, we went into Limni for more shopping. Then back, and headed down to the beach for a swim. The pebbles are troublesome, but I have found some swimming shoes, which make things easier.

Our lunches get later and later every day – admittedly, so do the times of our getting up and eating breakfast! Each morning I get up early-ish (7.15-7.30 am) and light the furnace for hot water. In other years, we have not needed to do this, as the sun alone was enough to keep the pipes warm. Our bedroom is at the back side of the house, with a door leading to the yard and boiler room, so it is easiest for me to do it.

Most days we go for a longish walk, either up Denise's valley to the chapel and beyond, or up the dusty road behind the house, or past the taverna. One positive thing about the weather is how good it is for walking.

Late dinner again (10.00 pm).

DAY 8, WEDNESDAY, SEPTEMBER 24TH

Woke again to mixed weather. Just about managed to have breakfast on the terrace, shifting ourselves out of the (coolish) breeze. The house has a wonderful choice of places to sit, depending on the weather. To the back, but still facing the sea, is a covered terrace, and we use it often when it is breezy on the front terrace. The front terrace is lovely, and has four tables, two near the house, one large marble one, which seats about ten, and the stone circle, overlooking the bay.

Marcus came over to say goodbye at 11.00 am. We all went swimming. An escaped goat appeared below the stone circle. We told Liadain, and she said it was the bane of her existence, eating her plants.

DAY 9, THURSDAY, SEPTEMBER 25TH

Dinah and I went shopping in Limni in the morning, and in the evening Garth and Elizabeth Fowden came to dinner, in the midst of another thunderstorm, leaving poor Denise to babysit their son. We served leg of lamb, which had been cut by the butcher, when we weren't looking, into chops! We roasted them in the oven anyway, with roast potatoes, rosemary and garlic, and made a Greek lentil/rice bake, green beans, and aubergine and tomato pie. The Fowdens brought a delicious box of sweets from the sweeterie in Limni. They left at about 11.00 pm.

Michael and I had taken a walk in the late morning along the road to the convent, newly tarmacked in a most disturbing manner. We found the reason a mile or so along, in the shape of a new development of villas – not too bad at the moment, but may be the start of something nasty. On the way back, we were met by the ladies in the car, and we drove up to the convent, via the beach, which was now deserted. We didn't bother the nuns, though, as they close up sharp at 1.00 pm. Not much change on the beach, at least.

DAY 10, FRIDAY, SEPTEMBER 26TH

Today started pleasant, and we decided to make an expedition to Cerinthos,[370] to see what we could find. We had some trouble finding the turn down to the sea and the archaeological site, and ended up in Mantoudi, where there was a fair going on – mainly low-quality carpets, being sold by local traders. We worked our way back, and found a way down. There is an impressive amount of agriculture inland, not least cotton, which surprised us, since it needs a lot of water, and is disapproved of by local ecologists.

The old headland looks much the same since we were here with Philip long ago, but Garth says that the Germans are due to start an excavation next year. I wish them luck – there is not much visible! We admired the industry of the ants, though, and trudged all over the site.

Still extremely mixed weather, though John and I managed to take a swim around midday. Quite a bit warmer down at the beach, and the water reasonably comfortable. Rain arrived later, however, and we ate lunch inside. We lit a large fire, and stayed in and read most of the afternoon. We are having a dreadful time trying to dry our clothes.

Liadain and her friend Jenny (who had visited us in Dublin with Liadain) came over for drinks at 6.00 pm, and we sat in the stone circle – or the turret, as they call it.

DAY 12, SUNDAY, SEPTEMBER 28TH

We were supposed to drive to the convent for services this morning, but we had such torrential rain overnight that rocks came spilling down at the back of the house – one very near to the kitchen window. I heard a huge thud at 5.25 am, and saw the rock later. So I decided to chicken out of driving there, thinking

---

370   The ruins of an ancient port city on the north-east side of the island.

the roads would be littered, or flooded, or both, but Denise told us later that she got through with no trouble.

During lunch (inside), we suddenly saw Liadain running round the garden. We asked her what was going on, and she said she was trying to corral the troublesome goat. After some manoeuvring, the goat got trapped by the fence near the gate. We tethered her to a tree with a rope and called Denise, who told Liadain the name of a goatherd who would help. The poor animal looked so miserable I felt really bad. After a walk, we came back to find that the poor thing had shortened its lead rope round and round the tree. We released it a little, but later checked and found it too tight around the neck. By now the goatherd and our local butcher had come, and said they didn't know who owned it, and just left. Checking later again, we found the poor animal prostrate on the ground, soaking wet and shaking. John went down to the taverna to find Liadain and Denise, who were at a party given by Bruce Clark (an Irishman and correspondent with the Economist). We had been invited, but weren't going to go.

In the meantime, I had untied the tether. The poor creature was so weak I thought it would die there and then, and felt so bad at our part in it. Luckily Denise (a rock of sense and an animal lover) immediately jumped into action. She drove over with Jenny in her jeep (Denise's). We gathered up the goat in a tarpaulin Dinah found in a shed, and brought her to Denise's shed. We made her a bed of straw and laid her down, covering her with a blanket. Having done that, Denise got in touch with the local vet, who will come tomorrow midday. We then all went down to the taverna to extend the party. We came back to the house for dinner – fish this time (not so good, but expensive). Worried about the goat all evening.

DAY 13, MONDAY, SEPTEMBER 29TH

We all went to Limni, to have breakfast of waffles and hot chocolate, at the fashionable café near the centre of town.

At first, the girl tried to maintain that it was not the time for waffles, but we insisted, and Dinah and I ordered ones with fresh fruit and strawberry sauce, while Michael and Jean had chocolate and caramel ones. The latter proved rather a mistake, as the waffles were enormous. Still, a pleasant excursion.

On the way, we had looked in on the goat, and found it still very poorly, but met Liadain and Jenny in town, and they said the vet was coming. Michael, Dinah and I chose to walk home, and dropped in on the goat, which we found standing up and much better.

The weather is steadily improving, at last, but still rather cool. We decided in the afternoon to go for a drive, to try and find a petrified forest, declared to be north of Haghia Anna. We drove through beautiful country, but the actual forest proved elusive. We found a fine herd of goats, though, and a nice little chapel, and then drove home via the monastery of St David and Rovies.

Gin and tonics on the verandah to watch the sun go down. The vet did come, and said that the goat was undernourished and had parasites and an infection in her stomach. He gave her a double shot of antibiotics – one which lasts five days, the other one month. By the time we saw her, later in the afternoon, she was on her feet! We heard later that she was starting to eat, So, very good news. I would never feel the same about Katounia if we had been responsible for her dying in misery. Jenny said the same.

[And there, I fear, the diary ends. We must assume a smooth return home in the next day or so!]

20: The Addis Ababa Expedition:

NOVEMBER 23-28, 2008

[This was something of a sentimental journey for me, as being a return to Addis after some 45 years, since my return home, in July 1963, from a two-year stint there, teaching English, in 1961-63 (an adventure depicted, in a rather heightened form, in my novel, The Scent of Eucalyptus). There was a serious purpose involved here, though, in the shape of a most worthy project, Connect Ethiopia, founded by a number of Irish businessmen, notably Philip Lee and Brody Sweeney (who roped me in), who had some interest in Ethiopian products, such as coffee, and wished to help Ethiopian entrepreneurs with advice and, to some extent, grants. My brief was to establish contacts between Trinity College and the University of Addis Ababa – an effort that did not really get very far, I fear. Connect Ethiopia, sadly, folded in the aftermath of the economic collapse of 2009.]

DAY 1, SUNDAY, NOVEMBER 23RD

We all met duly at the BMI desk in the airport at around 2.00 pm, for a 3.20 flight to London – Brody and Philip (Lee) presiding and introducing, but most names just flowed past me. We have a list of biographies in our instructions, but many aren't on it. The plane was actually delayed 40 minutes, but it was no problem as we had lots of time.

All went well in Heathrow. In Terminal 3, I checked in with Ethiopian Airlines, and then repaired to a fish bar (very posh!), where I consorted with Brody and another colleague. I had a plate of seafood, and shared some of Brody's champagne.

We boarded fairly promptly. It is a rather small plane, really (a Boeing 737-200), and quite full. Far too many bags being stuffed into inadequate storage racks! We foosthered around a bit on the runway, and got going almost an hour late. Harry Whelehan,[371] I should say, joined us in LHR, having been to Birmingham to hear a Leonard Cohen concert! He is heading up a group on the Rule of Law. I met two nice young ladies from that group on the plane from Dublin.

We landed in Rome to take on more people with too much hand luggage. Finally packed them in, after a delay of about one-and-a-half hours, and headed off for Addis – flight time 5.40 hours.

DAY 2, MONDAY, NOVEMBER 24TH.

I managed to snooze a bit, but it was not very comfortable. I travelled beside a lady from Zimbabwe, who was going back to visit – I don't envy her! She had a connecting flight to catch from Addis.

We arrived just before 10.00 am (instead of 8.30), at the splendid new airport at Bole. There was no great trouble getting through the formalities. The weather was fine, and really quite cool. There were buses on hand to take us to the Hilton.

It was an impressive drive into Addis up the Bole road – a great deal of building has obviously taken place since my day! It looks more like the outskirts of somewhere like Athens now – though that is hardly a compliment – than the Addis of old. I could see no tukuls or tej-bets,[372] just corrugated iron shacks, with little shops, apart from modern buildings.

The Hilton is very splendid, of course, and quite heavily guarded. It was not there in my day – originally built, it seems,

---

371   An old friend from Howth, Harry was a distinguished barrister, and had served as Attorney General in the Fianna Fáil- Labour government, from 1991-1994. He had been roped in to advise the Ethiopians on legal matters.

372   A tukul is a traditional Ethiopian house, with mud walls and conical straw roof; a tej-bet is, strictly speaking, a bar (a house for drinking tej), but also generally a brothel. The Addis of old abounded in these.

in 1969. It stands on Menelik II Avenue, south of Arat Kilo.[373] I have a fine room, with a balcony, on the second floor, looking back out on the avenue (through trees).

I snoozed for a few hours, and then strolled down to the pool, to see if there was any action. Initially there was none – hotel quite thinly populated at the moment – so I ordered a beer (St. George) and a bit of lunch, and was then joined by a nice young man who is in banking (didn't get his name), who had had a rather pointless meeting with a micro-banker there that morning, who didn't really know who he was. Obviously a certain degree of Ethiopic chaos pervades this end of the operation! I haven't met Eta yet, but will later.

I took a short stroll outside the hotel, down Menelik Avenue to Tito Road, but very quickly felt dehydrated and faint (could be the altitude!), and then was accosted by a young conman, who wanted to show me around – a coffee ceremony? Dancing? Mercato? – and I had to shake him off politely.

Then back to wait for our 'briefing' by Brody at 5.30 pm, which took place round the pool, assisted by copious beer, and really didn't add too much to our knowledge. Various people have been sent on virtual wild goose chases so far, and an atmosphere of mild confusion prevails, but everyone remains cheerful.

At 7.00 pm we piled into buses, and drove through the town to the Irish Embassy. Again, the town looks somewhat more developed, but there are still lots of shacks, and down side streets things look pretty basic. There were loads of people out in the streets, doing a sort of volta (presumably) – or perhaps they have nowhere else to go. The Embassy is situated just at the beginning of a very rough road, but itself is a very fine mansion, just newly acquired and furnished. The new lady ambassador, Síle Maguire, our first (there was previously a Chargé d'Affaires) is very young and enthusiastic (as I suppose ambassadors should be!), and served a great spread. There was a speech of welcome

---

373   This was a square and cross-roads four (arat) kilometers out from the centre of town, not far from my old school.

by herself, and then Trevor Sargent[374] said a few words – and later Steve Wall sang a few songs. There was a most interesting lady from the Sandford School,[375] Maeve Kelly, who will show me round on Wednesday morning. The party broke up around 10.00 pm, and we all bussed home to bed.

DAY 3, TUESDAY, NOVEMBER 25TH

I slept pretty well, and woke at 7.00 am – rather to my relief, as I thought I might sleep too late. Went down to a fine breakfast, but saw no one from the team. Then I went out and sat in the lobby, and Gina turned up with plans for me. I am booked in to see President Andreas of the University at 9.30 am, and a bus was on hand to take me up at 9.00. We drove up past the Palace (now the Prime Minister's residence, it seems) up to Arat Kilo (all quite new), and then up the fine Entotto Avenue, to Siddist Kilo,[376] and so into the University – a fine compound, originally the Gennete Leul Palace, only handed over to the University in December 1961, just after I arrived.

President Andreas received me in his office, which is in the central building of the old *ghibbi*,[377] beside the Institute of Ethiopian Studies of Richard Pankhurst, and the Ethnological Museum. He is rather shaky still, after his stroke, but in pretty good form. Phil O'Dwyer was to have come, but had an insurance seminar, and so couldn't, so Andreas and I just chatted rather generally. He invited me to come out longer and teach a seminar in the Philosophy Department, perhaps next spring for two weeks, and bring Jean, so we will plan for that. We

---

374   Trevor, who was leader of the Green party, was at this time Minister of State at the Department of Agriculture, Fisheries and Food in the Fianna Fáil-led government. I cannot recall whether he travelled out with us.

375   This was my old school, then known as The English School, but now called after its founders, Brigadier and Mrs. Dan Sandford. It had survived the bad times by being the school for the international community.

376   That is to say, a square six (siddist) kilos out from the centre.

377   A term for the compound surrounding a royal palace.

could live on campus, and go on a trip up north afterwards.[378]

After parting from Andreas, I took a tour of the ethnological museum, which is most interesting in its way, and then I was driven back to the Hilton. I had had ideas of pottering around for a while, but it was not really possible.

On return, I went down for a swim and a bit of a sunbathe, met Harry and chatted, and then had a hamburger for lunch by the pool. After this lunch, I took another short stroll out from the hotel, and this time came closer to the old Addis. I walked up the avenue to the top, where the Palace is, and gazed out over the city from the parapet at the side of the avenue, as it curls round towards Arat Kilo. Then I dodged down a lane into a wilderness of corrugated iron huts, this time with the strong smell of piss (and worse), but no burning eucalyptus leaves! These people have, to all appearances, nothing, not even any private space to speak of, and this is cheek by jowl with the pomp of Menelik Avenue. A large government office has just been built -- the Mapping Agency – by just biting into a segment of the slum, and doubtless razing the miserable huts of the inhabitants to the ground, without compensation. Where is Tekla Mariam in all this, I wonder?[379]

At 4.00 pm, a number of us set off in the charge of a nice young woman to Adana (Nazaret), about a hundred kilometres to the south-east, to view a project called Camara, which recycles computers from Ireland for use in schools in the neighbourhood. It was a two-hour drive along a (generally) good tarmac road, with lots of traffic – mainly commercial – through a countryside that is rapidly being developed in all sorts of commercial directions. Subsistence agriculture continues as well, with people still cutting crops by hand – not a tractor or other machine to be seen! Addis has expanded enormously, as has Bishoftu, and Adana is a very large town, now the capital of the Oromo – formerly the Galla Nation. Hardly any old-style tukuls to be seen. Harry joked that those we saw must be

---

378   Unfortunately, nothing came of this.

379   My former servant. I pursue this question further tomorrow.

Club Med! I couldn't identify any *tej-bets* either – they must have abolished the red lights! I had driven this way, down to the Awash River, with Cousin Charles[380] in 1961, and that was definitely another era.

We were taken for dinner to a hotel, rather unfortunately named the 'Dire International Hotel'[381], but actually we had a very good buffet meal, half Ethiopian and half ferenj, and then drove back around 9.00 pm, arriving a little before 11.00. Had a nightcap in the bar, with Harry and other (lady) lawyers, one of whom works with Maurice Manning[382] in the Human Rights Commission. I had a Cuba Libre, which needed ice, and that bothered me slightly, but I seem to be surviving.

DAY 4, WEDNESDAY, NOVEMBER 26TH.

Felt a bit unwell in the night, and took some Imodium, which seems to have headed off anything serious. Had a continental breakfast but still substantial, and then, at 9.30 am, was taken up by minibus to the Sandford School (nice elderly driver, Geradu).

Returning to the school after 45 years was a mind-blowing experience. At first it was a bit daunting, since there is a different entrance – very well guarded by a group of zabanyas,[383] I was met by Maeve Kelly, who had undertaken to show me round when we met at the Embassy party. My school magazines[384] were

---

380 My cousin, Sir Charles Mathew, who was at that time acting as Legal Advisor to Haile Selassie, and who had got me the job in the English School (there is a description of this expedition near the beginning of *The Scent of Eucalyptus*).

381 Actually, 'Dire' (pronounced dirreh) is an Ethiopian proper name.

382 Maurice was President of the Irish Human Rights Commission from 2006 to 2010.

383 Zabanya is a term for someone who guards the gates to a compound.

384 I had actually initiated the idea of a school magazine when I was serving in the school, and published two editions of this, with the help of my students. I had brought them along for reference.

a great success, that oriented everyone. One elderly zabanya almost wept when he saw the picture of the senior class, with my old headmaster, Leslie Casbon – he kissed the photograph! I ventured to ask him about my former servant, Tekla Mariam Wolde, and he told me that he remembered him, and that he had continued to live in the neighbourhood, but that he had died some years ago.

We looked around the newer part of the school – all added since my day – and met an older teacher, Ato Makonnen, who is a delightful old boy, and remembered a good deal of the past. In particular, he recognised Kiya Ayele from one of the pictures, as Kiya was an administrator in the school in later years. I was introduced then to Anna Fernyhough, who seems to be one of the bosses of the operation – very pleasant and informative, including about the family. Crichton Casbon,[385] it seems, is still to the good, though now back in England, as is Philippa Stanford.[386] I was much photographed for the Millenium volume that is being put together.[387]

Then my faithful driver brought me back to the hotel, and I proceeded to a lunch by the pool. I decided not to swim today, as I had a suggestion of a sore throat and a bit of congestion, and, sadly, swimming is often a bad idea in such circumstances.

At 1.30 pm, a group of us got together to take a tour of the Mercato, the Piazza, and the National Museum. The drive to the Mercato took us through the older part of town, which is somewhat more coherent than our area, but I can't say that I recognised anything in particular. The Mercato itself is a paradigm of chaos, a sort of hell, but undeniably fascinating. Everything conceivable is for sale, almost none of it relevant to us, though. Vast crowds of people milled about, but virtually nobody seemed to be buying anything, though there were enormous amounts of vegetables, spices, and pieces of household equipment on sale – even scrap metal and old shoes! I bought

---

385   Son of my former headmaster, Leslie Casbon.
386   Grand-daughter (presumably) of the Stanfords.
387   I have no idea what this was.

an Ethiopian cross, our Jordanian-Irish colleague Tamsin some spices, but not much else. Then up to what our young guide, Yared, billed as the Piazza, but which must in fact have been just a street in its vicinity, as it bore no relation to my memories of that part of town, where we were introduced to a fine jewellery shop, where I bought a little pendant of silver (I looked at a large one of gold, but it cost $300). We took so long here that we decided that the Museum would be too much, so came back to the hotel around 4.30.

At 6.00 pm we set out in buses to a restaurant on the Bole Road, the Hiber, hosted by the Addis Chamber of Commerce (but certainly helped by our own Philip Lynch), which turned out to be a lot of fun. We had a largely Ethiopian meal, accompanied by a native band, and then followed by some splendid singing and dancing. They could do a Riverdance-style tour! I talked with Joe Mulhall, interested in bread and biscuits, Eta (who used to be in the Foreign Ministry), and Elena Negussie, an interesting girl (Swedish-Ethiopian), who lectures in UCD and knows Martin Kelly.[388]

I was beginning to feel a bit queasy, and glad to go home, but some of the more lively sparks, such as Harry W., Fran Stewart, Brody, and some of the young women colleagues, went off to a further club.

DAY 5, THURSDAY, NOVEMBER 27TH

I took further pills, but am still feeling not quite right. Probably lucky not to be worse. I took things quietly for most of the morning, but then decided, around 12.00, to take a taxi up to the National Museum, where the driver waited an hour for me, for 100 birr. The Lucy exhibit[389] was very good, and most thought-provoking. Many possible ancestors of Jackie Healy-Rae have turned up in various parts of the Rift Valley, particularly in the

---

388   That is, my nephew, being my sister Elizabeth Kelly's eldest son.
389   'Lucy' (Australopithecus Afarensis) is arguably a remote ancestor of the human race, found in Hadar, in the northern part of the Rift Valley, the Danakil Depression of Northern Ethiopia.

Danakil Depression. The rest of the museum, though, is pretty disappointing. They plainly have a lot of interesting stuff from the Axumite period, and much older (5th-4th centuries BC), but not much is on display, and that little is largely unlabelled. An interesting South Arabian inscription was not translated, and so on. And there is a lot of junk upstairs. Back then to the hotel, and found a gang having lunch on the pool patio. I sat with Brody and Gina, then joined by Dara O'Mahony and others.

I had to miss the Soddo[390] expedition because of my scheduled talk to the Philosophy Department at 4.00 pm. I went up rather apprehensively to the University, expecting to find total chaos, but in fact I was received cordially by the head of the department, Dr. Bekele Gutema. He guided me to a classroom that was occupied, in fact, by a class, which we had to displace! Eventually, about fifty undergraduates, graduates and faculty (including one American) gathered to hear me hold forth on the topic of 'Platonism and the World Crisis' – with apologies for the unsuitability of some of the subject-matter to the case of Ethiopia. We had a good discussion afterwards, though, the main topics being: 1) Can capitalism change its spots, to the extent of embracing 'steady-state' economics? Answer: probably not! 2) Can Barack Obama turn America around? Again, sadly, probably not!

On leaving the Department, I met a faculty member, Dagnatchew Desta, who had both studied at the Sandford School, and had been taught in Boston College by John Cleary! I had to tell him the troubling news of John.[391] Also, while seeing me off, Ato Bekele proposed next autumn as a good time for a return visit, ideally to teach part of a seminar on Metaphysics![392]

I returned at 5.30 pm to the hotel, where I found a formal

---

390 Soddo is a city in Southern Ethiopia, the political and administrative centre of the Wolaita Zone and South Ethiopia Regional State.

391 John (then Professor of Philosophy in Maynooth University), was suffering from liver cancer, which was to kill him the following April.

392 Alas, nothing came of that!

de-briefing in progress round the pool, with the help of a piña colada. At 7.50 pm, we set off for an evening at Tony Hickey's restaurant DD (= Dining Delights). Hickey is a larger-than-life character right out of Graham Greene, who has been here for many years – actually fought with the rebels against Mengistu,[393] and is a friend of the Prime Minister Meles Zenawi.[394] He deals in 'import-export', and runs this restaurant. Very good nosh, I must say – more Lebanese than Ethiopian – with good red wine, and great dancing afterwards!

Then the bolder spirits went on to another, Rasta, nightclub chosen by Steve Wall, where he played with Rasta musicians. I chickened out of that, I'm afraid, but now rather regret it. I got back about midnight, the others between 1.30 and 3.00 am.

DAY 6, FRIDAY, NOVEMBER 28TH

Woke up in good time, finished packing, and went down to breakfast, where I found Harry, who is actually not leaving till midnight, since the lawyers have another meeting this morning. The weather is actually getting warmer day by day. I took a walk round the estate after breakfast, taking in the miniature golf course and other exotic corners.

I have the curious experience over the last few days of re-reading pieces of the novel[395] which describe the city, and finding an odd mixture of accuracy and confusion – e.g. it is from Arat Kilo rather than Siddist Kilo that one gets to the English (or Sandford) School; and then there is the question of the Piazza. I didn't manage to get to the real Piazza – now

---

393   Mengistu Haile Mariam is an Ethiopian former politician and former army officer who was the head of state of Ethiopia from 1977 to 1991 and General Secretary of the Workers' Party of Ethiopia from 1984 to 1991, as leader of the infamous Derg. After his deposition, he retired to live in Zimbabwe, where he still resides.

394   Meles Zenawi Asres was an Ethiopian soldier and politician who served as President of Ethiopia from 1991 to 1995 and then Prime Minister of Ethiopia from 1995 until his death in 2012.

395   Sc. *The Scent of Eucalyptus.*

Tewodros Square – to see if I had imagined that, but I heard that they have completely rebuilt it, so no doubt there is no trace any more of Giannopoulos' Bookstore, or the Ras Makonnen Bar.

We bussed off to the airport shortly after 10.00 am, and checked in with not too much trouble, though with not enough time for much browsing in the Duty Free. But anyhow, better for Jean to choose her own clothes and scarves, and so on! We left about half-an-hour late, and then foosthered in Rome for about two hours – one runway was closed! Half the plane disembarked in Rome, and no one seems to have got on, so the plane is now more or less us! Let's hope that it can get us to London in time to catch our connecting flight.

[They did, just about, and I got home safely; bags came along later.]

www.ingramcontent.com/pod-product-compliance
Lightning Source LLC
Chambersburg PA
CBHW011126070526
44584CB00028B/3798